Pictures from the Water Trade

JOHN DAVID MORLEY

Pictures from the Water Trade

ADVENTURES OF A WESTERNER IN JAPAN

PERENNIAL LIBRARY

Harper & Row, Publishers
New York, Cambridge, Philadelphia, San Francisco
London, Mexico City, São Paulo, Singapore, Sydney

A portion of this book appeared in *Vanity Fair*, in slightly different form.

A hardcover edition of this book is published by Atlantic Monthly Press. It is here reprinted by arrangement with Atlantic Monthly Press.

PICTURES FROM THE WATER TRADE. Copyright © 1985 by John David Morley. All rights reserved. Printed in the United States of America. No part of this book may be used or reproduced in any manner whatsoever without written permission except in the case of brief quotations embodied in critical articles and reviews. For information address Atlantic Monthly Press, 351 West 19th Street, New York, N.Y. 10011.

First PERENNIAL LIBRARY edition published 1986.

Library of Congress Cataloging-in-Publication Data

Morley, John David, 1948–
    Pictures from the water trade.

    "Perennial Library."
    Reprint. Originally published: Boston : Atlantic Monthly Press, © 1985.
    1. Japan—Social life and customs—1945–   . 2. Japan—Description and travel—
1945–   . I. Title.
[DS822.5.M67   1986]   952.04   85-45770
ISBN 0-06-097041-3 (pbk.)

86 87 88 89 90 MPC 10 9 8 7 6 5 4 3 2 1

mizu-shobai, water trade

The vulgar term for any precarious form of trade yielding an income entirely dependent on the patronage of its customers; for example, entertainment provided by geisha, bars, cabarets and so on.

The Kojien

Contents

Acknowledgement

For their help with this book I would like to thank:

Diana Athill, Myrna Blumberg, Upton Brady,
André Deutsch, Harold Evans, T. Hagiwara,
Anthony Holden, Alfred Luyken, H. Mizuma,
J. A. E. Morley, Hilary Rubinstein, Shoichiro Sasaki,
Hiroko Shimizu, Armgard & Wedigo de Vivanco,
K. Yasue

Pictures from the Water Trade

Mr One-Gate-Temple. At about five o'clock one afternoon in mid-December Boon stepped out of a shop where he had purchased a sheaf of rice-paper and set off down the darkening wintry street in the direction of Shinbashi station. The air was bright and sharp. Because he was cold rather than anything else he turned in at the first suitable restaurant he came to without giving it a second thought, glancing only casually at the sign overhead before going in. It identified beer and pizza. That'll do nicely, he thought, and started to make his way downstairs.

Sunk in thought, he went past the little door on the landing halfway down without even noticing it, and he arrived at the bottom of the stairs unaware that he had in fact come down a very long way indeed. The thought that he might have made an expensive mistake occurred to Boon the moment he opened a pink leather door and stepped into the premises, where two large, blunt-nosed men with ties whose knots resembled cauliflowers came forward smiling and relieved him of his coat before he had time to protest. They performed the operation expertly but rather alarmingly, as if skinning an animal, and he was not at all reassured to see his coat disappear with them behind a curtain down to the end of a long corridor. Clutching his wad of rice-paper he sat down at the nearest table, propped up the menu and discreetly examined the contents of his wallet: clearly it would not be enough.

Just as he was reaching the conclusion that, no damage having yet been done, he was still at liberty to get up and go, one of the men who had relieved him of his coat reappeared from behind the curtain, came up to his table, bowed, presented him with a slip of paper and retired to his post at the door.

It was the ticket for his coat. Boon idly turned the ticket over and then stared at it in disbelief. Printed on the reverse side was a staggering cloakroom charge of two thousand yen, exactly three hundred more than he had just counted in his wallet. He was horrified. That was more than the coat itself was worth.

Would anybody want to buy his coat? Boon had once stopped a man in the street and persuaded him to sell him the shoes he was standing in, but one glance at the sleek doormen in their cauliflower ties and dark suits was enough to rule out the possibility of coat-bartering. Feeling angry and rather foolish he got up and went over to the doormen to present his case. He was a foreigner; there had been a mistake.

The doormen could perfectly well understand what Boon explained to them in halting Japanese, but because they didn't much like what he was telling them they looked at him with their smooth, helpful faces and pretended to be at a total loss. Sympathy yes, their faces said, leaning forward as if this would ease the troubled passage of information, default of payment no. Boon had already sunk quite deep into this quagmire of wilful misinterpretation, in fact was about to go under completely, still followed by the anxious-unassisting eyes of the doormen who had manoeuvred him there, when the band struck up and a fierce soprano launched unexpectedly into a thunderous aria, bringing negotiations to an immediate halt.

In the wake of this sudden vocal cataclysm even Boon's own predicament began to look trivial, and apparently it set a number of other things in motion too, a general flinching and shrinking from the blast, notably among the waiters, who fled from their customers in front of the stage and took refuge along the walls. One of these waiters went into conclave with the doormen; Boon gathered that he was the subject. Quite how or why was not at first clear, but it began to look as if there would be a stay of execution. The waiter asked him if he spoke Japanese. Yes, said Boon. Then come this way, the waiter replied, and allow me to present my sincere apologies for this unfortunate misunderstanding. I did not know that you were the guest of Ichimonji-*sensei*. Neither did I, said Boon, and he obediently followed the waiter to a table in the corner of the room.

He found a powerful man in his early forties sitting in his shirtsleeves, chin in hand, ruminating over the shell of a lobster which he had just finished eating. Among the wreckage of half a dozen kinds of lesser shell-fish a row of limp excoriated prawns, neatly arranged beside their jackets, lay gleaming and still untouched on a dish in the centre of the table, apparently having escaped either his attention or his appetite. It was clear that he was a man of very capacious eating habits, and Boon took the precaution of apologising for the intrusion before introducing himself.

"What's that?" said the man with a start. "Mr Bun, is it? Pleased to make your acquaintance. My name's Ichimonji. Do make yourself comfortable."

He rose a fraction out of his chair, waved airily at the seat in front of him and relapsed into silence. Boon sat down on the opposite side of the table, lit a cigarette and waited for his enigmatic host to say something more. But he said nothing, continuing to gaze mournfully at the dismembered lobster. Boon was becoming increasingly puzzled by this unexpected silence when suddenly the aria came to an end as abruptly as it had opened, the soprano smiled and bowed and Ichimonji burst into frenetic applause. Then he turned to Boon and said, "Mozart – marvellous, isn't it? You know, it's over a year since I last heard her sing and so – well, this is rather a sentimental occasion for me. I'm afraid I forgot myself, and having put you to the trouble of joining me here there can be absolutely no excuse for my behaviour. But you of all people, my dear fellow," winking mischievously at Boon, "are not the man to hold that against me, if you will pardon me for saying so, young and vigorous as doubtless you are. The moment you came through the door I said to myself: here is a man whose opinion will be worth listening to. Perhaps I am speaking to you in a very direct fashion; but, as no doubt you already know since you speak such fluent Japanese and are therefore quite familiar with our customs, that's one of the worst Japanese habits – vague, meandering talk, neither one thing nor the other, neither yes nor no, full of sounding phrases worth absolutely nothing. But let me assure you of one thing. The native sons of Tokyo, the true *edokko*, are different. No beating around the bush, straight to the point and not afraid of rubbing the salt in – "

This astonishing flow of words was interrupted by another burst of applause, to which Ichimonji contributed as enthusiastically as before. Having completed her second aria the singer appealed very prettily to her honoured customers to come up on stage and sing a song, handed the microphone to a man who had been forcibly volunteered by his friends, and stepped down onto the floor. Ichimonji signalled to her to come over.

"Friends from the old days, you see, twenty years or so," he said to Boon, leaning conspiratorially over the table. "Wonderful singer, and a splendid girl altogether, I can tell you." He chuckled gustily.

The singer was a tallish, handsome woman who looked about thirty-four or -five but was in fact nearer forty. Later in the evening, when she asked Boon what he thought her age was, as Ichimonji had warned him she would, he told her she looked about thirty, likewise following Ichimonji's prior instructions (younger than she looks, but not too young, he advised, or else she will know it is just flattery). She was both entertainer and manageress, so she was always either circulating discreetly among her customers or performing, rather less discreetly, as the volume on the stage really could not be ignored.

"Quite wonderful," said Ichimonji; and he squeezed her hand as she sat down beside him.

"Remarkable," said Boon, and the singer turned to look at him, as if noticing him for the first time.

She had the most beautiful head, superbly coiffeured, and a very striking face. The slant to her large, oval eyes was barely perceptible, with the curious effect that one was kept guessing, in Boon's particular case as to whether he was looking at a Japanese or a European face, but also more generally, as to quite what one should make of her: the chief characteristic of the face was its ambiguity, which was why Boon found it increasingly difficult to keep his eyes off her.

The woman turned to Ichimonji and said coquettishly,

"*Sensei*, aren't you going to introduce us then?"

Ichimonji had forgotten Boon's name and then had a lot of trouble distinguishing the long English vowel from the similar but shorter Japanese *u*, a difficulty which was exacerbated by the fact that *bun* was a common Japanese word which could be written with at least five different characters and had over a dozen meanings. Like other Japanese, Ichimonji eventually managed to get the sound right, but as time passed the vowel would gradually get narrower and by the end of the evening it was always unmistakably *Bun-san*, ostensibly the honourable Boon, but with the alternative and, unfortunately, often more appropriate meaning of Collapse and Bankruptcy.

"So the name is *Bun*, isn't it," said Ichimonji at last, who had turned this minor point into an exhaustive discussion, not satisfied until it had been well and truly talked into the ground. Hardly pausing for breath and obviously taking a dim view of the usual practice when introducing people of merely teaching them each other's names, Ichimonji settled down to a long and at times preposterous encomium of the woman beside him which omitted nothing except just that – her name.

"D'you know, Bun-*san*, that I once ran a cabaret? Well then, there aren't any tricks in the water trade you can teach me." (It was the first time Boon had heard the term *mizu-shobai*, and he parted company from Ichimonji under the impression that he had once worked for the municipality as an engineer.) "I've known hundreds of girls, literally hundreds. Some of them were plain bad and they all had their faults, which of course is only human. I have my faults and you have yours. This one here, however, she's the only one – the only one among hundreds! – who is as straight as a die. When I say that all the others had faults I don't mean the usual human weaknesses, or not just that. I mean their character as professional girls. The habits they acquire in their professional lives, and inevitably these are not good habits, get carried over into their personal lives. Business and pleasure, professional and private, it all becomes one. But this one's different. Is she beautiful? You yourself say so, and I can only agree: she is. She's a very beautiful woman. Not only that. She sings marvellously; she's a successful business woman. And that's the astonishing thing. Despite all this she's as straight as a die. You take my word for it."

This was the gist of what Ichimonji said. It went on much longer and was full of tantalising phrases, which Boon could not remember and whose meaning he could only guess, but the richness of the language made his skin prickle. He also felt a bit guilty about not having taken Ichimonji's word for it, as he still hadn't made up his mind about the singer-manageress and her ambiguous face.

Naturally she smiled at the extravagance of her customer's

largesse, but she smiled encouragingly and was in no danger of blushing.

"How do you do. My name is Shimizu," she said to Boon, bowing gracefully. He now knew her name, and felt honoured by her graceful bow, but regretted that Japanese introductions gave no indication of a person's marital status.

At this stage Ichimonji excused himself and mysteriously disappeared, not returning for almost an hour. Ms Shimizu turned and watched him leave the room, offering Boon an opportunity to study at his leisure one of her most delicious parts: the nape of her neck. Until his arrival in Japan this was not a part of a woman's body to which he had paid much attention; through no fault of his own, as women in modern Europe unfortunately kept the back of their neck hidden. In Japan, however, necks really came into their own. Boon was introduced to an entirely new dimension of aesthetic experience and sensual pleasure, best symbolised by the *geisha*'s daring décolleté, which allowed the neckline of her *kimono* to drop revealingly not at the front but the back.

Ms Shimizu was dressed in Western-style clothes. Her luxuriant black hair was brushed upwards and fixed with a wide-toothed comb at the crown of her head; the exposed nape of her neck, naturally white and subtly powdered to make it appear even more so, somehow seemed very vulnerable. The sight of this exposed neck aroused in Boon a deep animal instinct, and he wondered if it was the draw of this instinct that made the sight so irresistible.

The inspection completed, Ms Shimizu turned back to Boon and began to ask him all the usual questions, where he came from, what he was doing in Japan, how long he had been in the country and how long he intended to stay, subjects on which his Japanese was deceptively fluent as a result of having covered the same ground a great many times already. Eventually she got round to asking him the leading question of how old he was and Boon, duty-bound, threw her back the ball she was waiting for. She clapped her hands, eyes sparkling.

"How old do I look?"

He looked at her carefully and said, "I should think about thirty or so."

"That's just flattery . . ."

But the smile of real pleasure, ingenuous and even naive, which accompanied this protest, showed that she believed him.

Feeling that it was now his turn, Boon embarked on a devious strategy to find out if Ms Shimizu was married, but on the way he changed his mind; it added piquancy to the duel to leave certain questions open. A minute later she had to get up and sing again in any case. Whether intentionally or not, she left on the table the small pink handkerchief she had been winding and unwinding round her fingers throughout their conversation with an intensity it was impossible to ignore, as if the smoothing out of creases was a subject which she generally had very much on her mind. Boon had just folded up the handkerchief and put it in his pocket when Ichimonji reappeared, accompanied by another man.

The other man must have been a good ten years older than Ichimonji, but although he was accorded the deference to which his seniority entitled him there was no doubt that Ichimonji was the one in charge. He plied his guest with a combination of watered bourbon and his own brand of exuberant talk to such good effect that the quiet-mannered man who had at first refused anything but orange juice was soon in the best of spirits, calling loudly for a bottle of whisky and a bowl of mussels.

Within an hour three-quarters of this bottle had been emptied. A business proposition which Ichimonji had broached unsuccessfully earlier in the evening was now taken up voluntarily by his companion, who had drunk the lion's share of the bottle, only to find that Ichimonji had meanwhile lost interest. The positions were now exactly reversed. The more ebullient his companion became, the more sober and statesmanlike Ichimonji's manner. At last he allowed himself to be bullied into some kind of agreement, conceded with a show of the greatest reluctance and only because of his "obligation as an old friend". Boon was surprised by this uncharacteristic docility, but the incident was put into another perspective when the time came to settle the bill. Without waiting to be contradicted Ichimonji pressed two notes of ten thousand yen into the waiter's hand and insisted that he be allowed to do the honours. There followed one of those risible scenes with which an evening's drinking in Japan so frequently ends: two rivals baying at a hapless waiter who stands between them with arms raised, transferring the sum of money he has been given from one hand to the other according to the merits of the argument it is his job to referee. Ichimonji finally backed down, leaving to his friend the satisfaction of paying for refreshments he had not himself consumed, for the most part not even seen, and a coat belonging to a foreigner he would never meet again.

The gracious Ms Shimizu accompanied her customers to the door and bowed them out. Somehow she's not here at all, thought Boon, as he pressed the warm dry hand she held out to him. He was halfway up the stairs when unexpectedly he heard her call.

"Here, you forgot this . . ."

She handed him the envelope with the rice-paper, adding an afterthought in English: "I hope you'll come again."

"So do I," said Boon, remembering the handkerchief that lay safely in his pocket.

By the time he surfaced to the pavement he found that Ichimonji's companion had already disappeared. Ichimonji himself stood waiting with his hands in his pockets, looking very much more cheerful than he had five minutes earlier. Boon thought that the time had now come to go home, but this feeble idea had not even crossed Ichimonji's mind.

"It's only eight o'clock, you know," he said reproachfully, "*mada yoi no kuchi da zo!*"

"What does that mean?"

Ichimonji was taken aback by this question. He seldom had dealings with foreigners, and being asked to account for his use of language was something quite new to him. He tried half-heartedly and gave up in disgust, so Boon noted the phrase down on his envelope for future reference. (It meant "The mouth of the evening", i.e. the night is yet young.)

Where did Bun-*san* want to go now? Did he care for Japanese music (even if there was nothing to hold a candle to Mozart)? And did he like "colour" with his drink? Before Boon was able to answer any of these questions Ichimonji had made up his mind for him and was pushing him backwards into a taxi.

"Ikebukuro," he said to the driver, and then, turning to Boon, "Where do you live by the way?"

"Oji."

8

"Oh really? That's just round the corner from me in Higashi-jujo, and no distance from where we're going now – you know your way around Ikebukuro, of course?"

"I'm afraid not."

"Well where on earth do you go drinking then? Surely not in Oji? Only good thing there is that place by the sewer under the bridge, doesn't open till three in the morning, which is useful in our part of town, but it really is a bit of a hovel and you've got to have a strong liver to accept anything that doesn't come straight out of a bottle from that really filthy woman who runs the place."

"As a matter of fact, until this evening I haven't been out drinking on my own – "

"And the glasses, absolutely disgraceful. I doubt she washes them once a month. – What was that you said?"

Ichimonji broke off abruptly and looked at Boon in astonishment. He had the habit of speaking so fast that he needed a couple of sentences to take in what somebody else had said.

"It's the first time I've been out drinking on my own," repeated Boon. "I've hardly been in the country three months, you know."

"Good," said Ichimonji, at once getting back into his stride, "so you have a lot of time to make up for, and we now have something to celebrate. Not that we *didn't* have something to celebrate, I hasten to say. A meeting as propitious as this – "

At this point Ichimonji disappeared into a particularly dense thicket of language where Boon was unable to follow him, not reappearing, except for a brief instruction to the driver, until they were already within sight of Ikebukuro station. He realised that Ichimonji was a lot more drunk than he appeared to be, held together by his sheer animal vitality and his compulsive talk, which he needed to keep himself afloat and his faculties more or less in focus.

"This place here – *hai, kore de ii* – this place here specialises in traditional Japanese song and dance, not the best place of its kind – the best are in Asakusa, of course – but still pretty good, perhaps one of the best ten in Tokyo. I thought I'd bring you along here because I'd like you to meet my nephew, who joined the house six months ago – I arranged the introduction myself, actually, as I've been a regular customer for the past fifteen years and could put in a good word for him with the owner of the place. You don't happen to have a thousand-yen note on you, do you? Driver says he can't change this . . ."

When Boon had paid the driver and got out of the taxi Ichimonji had vanished. He stood on the corner of the main street opposite Ikebukuro station wondering where on earth he could have gone. It was not inconceivable that Ichimonji had left him in the lurch, but Boon didn't think he was the type of man to do that; and sure enough, when he wandered off down a sidestreet he discovered Ichimonji urinating against a wall, still talking volubly, not to himself, it seemed, but to Boon, whom he obviously assumed to have been standing behind him all the time. Boon unbuttoned and followed suit, wondering what Ichimonji had been saying to him since getting out of the taxi, for the conversation had now taken, appropriately enough, a very much more personal turn.

"You're a good sort of fellow, Bun-*san*. I've not had much experience of foreigners, of course, since there was never any occasion, but . . ."

He paused and began to shake himself with the exaggerated thoroughness of a man who has drunk enough to know he must take special care with such actions, groped for his zip, sighed contentedly and pulled it up at the same moment he reached the parallel conclusion.

"We're all the same human beings, after all."

Boon whole-heartedly concurred with this sentiment, adding how curious it was that the things most obviously true were often those most neglected in practice; he, Boon, had himself been the object of discrimination in a bar in Shinjuku only last week. As he and his friend Sugama were leaving the bar a stranger had come up to Sugama, seized him by the lapels and threatened him with violence if he ever accompanied a foreigner there again. He reminded Ichimonji how frequently the Japanese would preface some critical remark about foreigners with the words *onaji ningen na no ni* (human beings are the same and yet . . .), and asked him whether it was not true of his countrymen that they tended to use unimpeachable sentiments about the community of man as a stalking-horse for covert prejudices against the remaining members of that community whose misfortune it was not to have been born Japanese; discrimination was bad but hypocrisy was surely worse, and what pleased him most about Ichimonji's invitation was that it had been spontaneous and genuinely felt, which he took to be a true reflection of Ichimonji's character. Boon arrived at this earnest profession of friendship by a route which must have looked as if it were leading him firmly in the opposite direction, but perhaps this was what made it sound plausible to Ichimonji, for he suddenly grasped Boon's hand and shook it firmly. With this gesture a lasting pact was sealed.

About fifty yards along the street they turned down an unlit flight of steps that led into a cellar lined with racks for customers' shoes. On the little *tatami* ledge level with the sliding door that separated the cellar from the inner room was a long row of slippers from which, if he were lucky, the customer could choose a pair that fitted him. None of them fitted Boon, but it didn't matter, because the slippers were only worn to cross a few yards of wooden floor when arriving and departing or when one went to the lavatory, where yet another set of slippers lay ready. Shoes off and slippers on: Ichimonji slid back the panel and ushered Boon into a bustling, brilliantly lit room.

At two long tables on a raised *tatami* floor, stretching the length of the room from the stage at one end to where Boon was standing at the other, about a hundred people were sitting cross-legged, clapping rhythmically to the weird, harsh voice of a woman who had just begun to sing. Behind her a group of instrumentalists in formal skirt-like trousers, a *shakuhachi* (bamboo clarinet) player standing and two *shamisen* (three-stringed guitar) players seated on low stools, their instruments resting in their laps, waited motionless; two other young men, apparently singers, wearing gaudy broad-patterned *yukata*, stood at the back of the stage swaying and clapping in time to the music, while four women dancers in *tabi* and white *kimono* with red sashes turned and wheeled, stooped and stretched in a perfect opposing symmetry of motion on either side of the stage.

Obako nanbo ni na-a-ru
ju na-a-na – tsu
yuri-i o . . .

The woman's piercing voice suddenly dropped and sank into a

rising wave of applause, and the audience stumbled raggedly into the first discordant syllables of the refrain.

"Ha! Sensei!"

A couple of men sitting at one of the tables facing the door had recognised Ichimonji the moment he came in and at once started calling and waving boisterously to him. He shed his slippers and padded over to them, ducking his head for some reason, rather as if he were trying not to obstruct someone's view. Boon had often seen the Japanese do this before taking their place somewhere, even when there was no view to obstruct. He also noticed for the first time that Ichimonji was now wearing a tie, which he had presumably put on while Boon was paying the taxi-driver. He began to wonder if many apparently casual details about Ichimonji's dress and manner were not in fact carefully studied to produce a deliberate effect. Perhaps it was just coincidence, but in the sophisticated bar in Shinbashi Ichimonji had been distinguished from the rest of the well-groomed clientele by his rolled-up shirt-sleeves and open collar, whereas in the altogether more homely atmosphere of the Ikebukuro establishment his appearance was conspicuously formal and likewise set him apart.

Curiouser and curiouser: altogether an improbable man. He had appeared in the mouth of the evening and his name meant One-Gate-Temple.

His suspicions once alerted, Boon thought that along with the new appearance he could also detect a change in Ichimonji's manner. Space was made for him beside *sensei*'s friends, and as he replied to their questions about where he came from, how long he had been in Japan and what he was doing there, his eyes followed Ichimonji's triumphant progress around the room; a smile here, a wave there, a hand resting momentarily on a shoulder, in fact very much like everybody's local politician looking in after business hours.

The song having ended the dance began, to the dissonant gutty squall of a solo *shamisen*; the strings, Boon knew, were made of cat-gut, and the sounds that were plucked out of them reminded him of an animal in pain. The cat-gut buzzed and twanged, faltered, faded and subsided onto a sequence of five low notes which it repeated over and over again, at first barely audible but becoming perceptibly louder, like the buzz of a hornet circling in gradually tighter loops. Imperious and repetitive, the sound at last awoke a figure kneeling motionless in the centre of the stage. A woman, head bowed and face hidden by a corn-coloured cone-shaped hat, the form of her body unapparent in the splash of a white *kimono*, corn colour on white, white and gold like a flower, slowly, flower-like, began to rise and unfold.

Boon watched spellbound. The *shamisen* jarred on the last of the five notes of its theme, repeating it querulously until Corn Flower raised her head and revealed the lower half of her face, her bright red lips and white cheeks. The last note shuddered into silence, the dancer was obediently still. The *shamisen* attacked at a high pitch; her body jerked with a spasm, as if she had been stung, and with sharp, stiff movements of her hands and arms, warding off the jangle of chromatic sounds, the dancer began to retreat. She moved backwards to the left side of the stage, her face blind in the shadow of the wide-tilted hat, her body in profile to the audience displaying a classic *kimono* figure, one straight line from the head to the small of the back, bent knees pulling the material taut under the curve of her buttocks, both suppliant and erotic. Her white *tabi* never left the ground. She raised each heel slowly, the instep arched, sliding the sole of her foot noiselessly over the polished floor, lowered the heel. The rhythm of the *shamisen* became faster and more aggressive, breaking the dancer's controlled sequence of movements and forcing her into confusion; the straight neck suddenly buckled and slumped, no more than a few degrees, Boon saw, but exaggerated by the corresponding tilt of her hat. She stopped, flounced, pitching her head back and her buttocks out, straightened, shuffled forward a few paces and stopped again, turned from side to side as if searching for an escape and fluttered submissively to her knees. The strident, masterful music of the *shamisen* beat her still further down, she drew her arms into her sleeves and gently sank, nothing but white and gold, back into exhausted repose.

This performance was greeted with tremendous applause. Boon was entranced; it was the most ravishing, sensual dance he had ever seen. Players and dancers assembled on stage to take their bow, an interval was announced, and they came down into the audience for refreshments with guests and friends.

"Wonderful! Superb!" he burbled enthusiastically to Ichimonji, who had detached himself from a group on the other side of the room and had just returned to their table.

"*Hai hai*," he said obligingly, "I'll just see if I can . . ."

Boon watched him intercept the performers as they came down from the stage; the masterly *shamisen* player, the young man in the colourful *yukata*, whom Ichimonji had already pointed out as his nephew, and several dancers, among them Boon's exquisite Corn Flower. In a flurry of red sashes and rustling white silks they settled around him like a bevy of doves, presenting so many shapely necks at once that for a moment Boon lost all powers of speech and sat dumbfounded, turning from side to side under a gentle shower of questions.

The Local Politician (Ichimonji) came adroitly to his rescue, presenting to the company his Foreign Adviser (Boon), a young man, he said, already shrewd for his years but of outstanding moral character (but?), whom he had not yet known for any great length of time (three hours) and whom he much hoped to get to know better in the future, as he had an unmistakable human smell (human smell? what was this?), which was surely the best recommendation one could give him. Boon was not sure if he had understood all the innuendoes of this curious introduction right, but reassured by a dazzling montage of smiles and eyes he decided he must speak now or perish, and he replied to Ichimonji's speech with a series of deft compliments that delighted everyone and astonished himself.

"Is the name Bun?"

"Boon."

"Ah, it's Mr *Boon*, is it?"

Corn Flower on his left side, folding the long *kimono* sleeve daintily over her arm, reached over the table and picked up the little white porcelain flask between thumb and forefinger, holding it at a slight tilt, the base resting on the tips of the outstretched fingers of the other hand.

"Would you care for some *sake*?"

"Yes indeed," murmured Boon, and he raised the tiny cup, not much bigger than a thimble, a few inches from the table. Corn

Flower poured just short of the brim and then allowed Boon to take the flask from her hand.

"What about you?"

"Thank you, just a little . . ."

"A little is all you'll get," said Boon. "These are the tiniest cups I've ever seen."

Corn Flower offered him her cup with the same formal modesty with which she had held out the flask. Boon, informal, poured for Corn Flower, exactly to the brim.

"One all."

She laughed, drank, replaced the sacred cup and patted her lips with her fingers.

The *shamisen* player called something across the table to her which must have been rather rude, because Corn Flower wasn't at all amused. None of your business, she told him crossly, eliciting a cacophonous laugh very like the sound of his instrument. Keeping their hands in, thought Boon, and: what business? *Their* business, perhaps, mutual? He turned and looked at the musician with curiosity.

He was a man of about forty; sitting there in his formal robes, spectacles on nose, with his sharp, quizzical face, he looked more like a professor or a judge than a three-stringed guitar player.

"Did you know," said Ichimonji, who had his eyes and ears everywhere, "that *sensei* is one of the best players in the country?"

"As a matter of fact I didn't . . ."

"He ranks fourteenth – and that's at the national level, you know."

Boon was much intrigued by this remark. Fourteenth: better than fifteenth, not as good as thirteenth. And playing in the tenth best place of its kind: was this a recommendation? He wondered by what standards the contestants in this musical league could be so accurately judged; the aggregate number of notes played in one season, perhaps, or something along those lines. He decided Ichimonji must be pulling his leg.

"I was very impressed," said Boon, "although, I must admit, I'm still not quite used to the sound, the tone."

"What sort of a tone is it then?" number fourteen asked good-humouredly.

"Well, at least to my ears, it's a painful tone, it hurts: the spirit of the dead cat howling in the strings."

To Boon's relief *sensei* did not seem offended by this description. He repeated the phrase to himself, sharpened his nose with his forefinger and gave a dry chuckle. Corn Flower retired behind her hand and giggled, the breath snicking jerkily out of her nostrils with a rat-a-tat-tat, tit-for-tat, very snide little rhythm.

"Then I will play for you again," *sensei* announced with dignity, "just for you, Bun-*san*. Perhaps I can convert you. The *shamisen* is usually played as accompaniment, but not merely that. There is also an extensive repertoire for the solo instrument, which you will probably not have heard."

"Bun-*san* would be highly honoured," said Ichimonji. "If I might be allowed to make a suggestion, *sensei* . . ."

And he drew him aside into one of those thickets where Boon was again unable to follow.

For the first time he became aware of a fragrance, a quiet feminine emanation on his right side, which until now he had neglected, and turning towards it he asked

"And what is your name?"

"Ayako," whispered the fragrance. She was so fragile that Boon wondered she had managed to acquire the substance of a body at all. He felt gross and brutish beside her. Ayako and Boon: the mere conjunction of their names was absurd.

Corn Flower said:

"Ayako and I are friends. We're both from Tohoku. We were classmates there."

"How long have you been in Tokyo then?"

"Two years."

"Like it?"

She shrugged. "At least there's work here."

"I liked your dance very much. And if you'd stayed in Tohoku I would never have seen it," said Boon, imagining to himself a dancer with Corn Flower's body and Ayako's bloom.

"Aya-*chan*, Aya-*chan* – "

"Bun-*san*!"

"– why don't we look in at Mitsukoshi tomorrow morning? We might be able to get it there . . ."

"Yes?"

"I'd like to introduce my nephew . . . Shinichiro!"

"*Hai!*"

Get what? Corn Flower put her hand on Boon's shoulder and leaned behind him to talk to Ayako, her body pressing – pressing her body? – lightly against him.

"Pleased to meet you," he said with great feeling, bowing to the young man in the chequered gown. He could hear the two girls chirping away behind him.

"I hope we're going to hear you play later on."

"Er . . . well, I'm afraid I don't play an instrument, but . . ."

"I mean sing, of course," Boon corrected himself hastily. "You sing, don't you?"

"Yes, that's right," said the young man, his face lighting up, pleased to be identified. "But your Japanese . . . how on earth? . . ."

He stared at Boon in blank amazement, his eyes fairly starting out of his head, as if he had encountered a talking dog.

Boon felt his shoulder become warm. He performed another trick, and the nephew's eyes grew as large as saucers.

Ichimonji caught his eye and said with a grin, apparently for the *shamisen* player's benefit but loud enough for the others to hear,

"*Marude uguisu no tani-watari no yo desu na –*" jerking his chin in the direction of Boon and the two girls.

"Ichimonji *sen-SEI!*"

Indignant shrieks from Corn Flower, who shot bolt-upright and glared across the table.

Gosh, what was this? Boon reached for the envelope under the table and pulled out a sheet of rice-paper.

"What was that? *Uguisu –*" taking out his pen, "what does that mean?"

"*Iya-a!*" wailed Corn Flower, bouncing up and down.

"It means," said the *shamisen* player in fluent and quite unexpected English, "a bush warbler crossing from one valley to another."

"I beg your pardon? Bush warbler? What exactly – ?"

"I leave to your imagination. If you will excuse me now . . ."

And picking himself up elegantly he wandered over to the stage.

Ichimonji hugged his knees and roared with laughter. Then he sat back on his heels and performed a ridiculous pantomime, fluttering his arms, puffing out his chest and straining his neck forward to show the singing bush warbler (Boon) coming to rest first in one valley (Ichimonji closed his wings, laid his neck on his shoulder and looked coyly at Corn Flower), and then in the other (addressing himself to Ayako). He enjoyed his pantomime so much that he went through it a second time, smacking his thighs and crowing with delight.

"Disgusting," said Corn Flower.

Ichimonji pulled out a handkerchief and wiped his eyes.

"And yet it seems that the phrase wasn't new to you . . ."

Corn Flower opened her mouth and shut it again.

Meanwhile the *shamisen* player had perched himself on a stool at the front of the stage and was tuning his instrument. Gradually the hubbub in the room began to quieten down. The player sat composed, drawing the audience into his concentration, with all the time in the world, waiting until long after everyone was silent. Then he began to play.

It was music straight out of nature, unravelling before Boon's eyes a mountain landscape, arid mountain scenery: rock, flint and pebbled streams, capsized hills and precipitous hanging scree drifting into the valleys, crag, spur, tree bark and clear water, one by one the sounds of wild objects were elicited from the rasping strings and revived in a sentient paradigm of the mute existence of natural things. The *shamisen* player picked out this world with closed eyes and impassive face, his hands mechanical, dissociated from his body and carrying out a will of their own. The sweat welled out from the roots of his hair and ran over his forehead in copious streams; it was like a face made out of porous stone. At the end of twenty minutes he jumped exhausted to his feet; tumultuous waves of applause broke over the hall.

Boon was again overwhelmed. It was not so much the music as the terrific physical force of its performance that seized him. The admiration he felt for the *shamisen* player was akin to the respect he might have felt if he had seen a man wrestle with a bull or perform some extraordinary feat of strength. All on three strings! It was a *tour de force*.

He descended from the summit of this craggy world to find himself left with only one valley to warble in. Fragrance had been wafted away to serve drinks at another table. The saucer-eyed nephew was having his palm read by the female singer. Corn Flower was cleaning her ears with a hair-grip and a paper napkin. Ichimonji had disappeared.

"Where's *sensei*?"

"Over there," said Corn Flower carelessly. She was sulking, and the ear-cleaning was meant to be understood as a reproach.

"No, not him."

"Oh that one, you mean." She pointed across the table.

Boon still couldn't see him.

"Where is he then?"

"Underneath," said Corn Flower with the hair-grip between her teeth, "asleep."

Boon peered under the table. Sure enough, there lay Ichimonji-*sensei* flat on his back and fast asleep. Apparently the fourteenth rank hadn't been quite good enough to keep him awake.

For the next ten minutes he made desultory conversation with the men he had met earlier in the evening. Dancers and players trooped back on stage for their last performance. A customer tripped over Ichimonji's feet and fell on top of him, waking him up. He rubbed his face and looked at his watch. It was half past eleven,

"Bun-*san*, let's go home."

It was no such easy matter though. The Local Politician first had to take his leave; by the time he had completed his elaborate farewells it was already ten to twelve. Despite what he had said to the contrary Ichimonji clearly relished ritual. Fortunately he was unaware of a large tear in the seat of his trousers, prominently on view whenever he knelt forward and performed a bow. The tear was right in the middle of his trousers and it reminded Boon of a mouth, laughing at Ichimonji behind his own back.

He had no opportunity of telling him about this until they were in the entrance hall putting on their shoes. Ichimonji grinned and said in coarse Japanese "When I bow to someone I show him my face and not my arse. Bun-*san*, you can get away with whatever you like so long as you show some respect for the proper form. *He o shite shiri-tsubome.* Go ahead and fart, but mind you keep your arse shut – it doesn't matter what you do if you know how to look innocent."

They came out onto the street and Ichimonji hailed a taxi. Boon, taking out his pen to note down this intriguing new phrase, suddenly realised that he had forgotten the envelope of rice-paper.

"I've left something behind," he said to Ichimonji.

"Then go and get it. This guy'll wait."

Boon hurried back downstairs, opened the sliding door to the hall, closed it again, cursed, sat down, unlaced his shoes and put on a pair of slippers.

"No more shoes with laces," he said to himself, pushed the door open again and went inside.

He found the envelope still lying under the table. On his way out he bumped into Corn Flower.

"My goodness!"

She had changed out of the white *kimono* into a blouse and slacks. With her hair down she looked quite different. Corn Flower had gone, and in her place stood Naomi, with stocky legs and plump hips.

"I forgot this."

"And you forgot to say goodbye to me."

"But you'd gone. I looked everywhere. You must have been changing."

"Really?"

"Really."

He o shite shiri-tsubome.

Boon saw the shape of her generous breasts and suddenly felt lustful.

"We could give you a lift."

"Where are you going?"

"Kita-ku."

Naomi thought for a moment and then shook her head.

"I must wait for Aya-*chan* in any case."

When he had once more changed out of his slippers and laced his shoes Naomi gave him a card.

"You can always reach me here – any time after six except on Sundays."

"Don't you have a home number?"

"No."

Boon said goodbye to Naomi and reluctantly made his way back up to the street. As he got into the taxi it occurred to him that they had not paid.

"What about the bill?"

"I daresay that'll be all right," said Ichimonji airily. Boon didn't like to ask, but this sounded very much as if Ichimonji hadn't paid either. Business acquaintance in Shinbashi, the nephew with the saucer eyes in Ikebukuro – *carte blanche* all over town.

"What a place!" he enthused. "And the *shamisen* player was terrific. I've become a convert."

"How about the girls?" asked Ichimonji matter-of-factly. "Anything to your taste there?"

Boon mentioned the dancer whom he called Corn Flower, which in his Japanese came out as *mugi no hana*. Ichimonji didn't think much of this name, saying that it sounded more like wheatmeal or some kind of oatcake.

"Is that a good name for a dancer? Oatcake?"

Rather crestfallen Boon admitted it was not.

"What you've got in mind, I think, is the flower we call *yagura-magiku*. How about that? Try saying *yaguramagiku* tenderly. Just have a try."

Boon tried and failed.

"I tell you what," said Ichimonji, who found this sort of detail irresistible, "you might abbreviate it. What about *yagu*?"

Boon thought *yagu* didn't sound very lyrical.

"D'you know what *yagu* means? No? Well, it's a counterpane – a bedspread. Stick a diminutive on the end of it. *Yagu-chan*. How's that? A little bedspread. A quiltlet."

Ichimonji creaked forward in the seat, shaking with laughter.

"Well anyhow," he said at last, recovering, "why on earth did you think of *yaguramagiku* in the first place?"

"It was the colours, you see," explained Boon guardedly, feeling a bit piqued, "the white *kimono* and the yellow hat."

"Yellow and white? But the flower we're talking about is red and blue."

This was a serious blow. Unless he put a stop to Ichimonji soon Corn Flower was going to be talked clean out of existence.

Ah now, wait a minute. Your *yaguramagiku* may well be red and blue – that's a poppy. But I'm not talking about poppies. Perhaps I didn't express myself clearly when I said corn flower. What I mean is a flower, one among others, that grows in the corn. And there are plenty of flowers growing in the corn that are yellow and white."

Ichimonji shook his head.

"Well, I won't insist. The trouble with this lyrical business is that so often the facts are wrong. You do as you please, Bun-*san*. But why all this naming paraphernalia? Isn't the woman enough?"

The taxi-driver asked his *o-kyakusan* where he wanted him to stop. "Here."

"A feeling is a fact," said Boon, but Ichimonji didn't hear this because he was asking the taxi-driver if he could change a ten-thousand yen note. The driver scratched his head, and Boon asked him how much the fare was. Six hundred and fifty yen. Boon had exactly that amount left in his wallet. He paid and they got out of the taxi. Ichimonji knocked over a dustbin. A dog started barking somewhere.

Boon followed his companion into a maze of narrow streets. It had turned unexpectedly cold. An early morning wind jostled the great red lanterns and plucked at the tails of the dragon-like banners hanging outside the shops. Ichimonji crossed from one side of the street to the other, ducking under the fringes of the shop-curtains to get a glimpse of the company inside, explaining, criticising and giving Boon a brief commentary on the qualities of the individual hostesses which ranged from bawdy abuse to pious sentiments reminding Boon of the horoscopes sold at shrines. "Takes time, but patience richly rewarded," he would announce, or "Don't touch this one with a barge-pole!", giving it a wide berth. In this way they finally arrived at the end of the street.

"Here we are," said Ichimonji, stopping outside a tiny shop and pointing upwards, "*Tsuru*."

Tsuru, the Sign of the Crane: auspicious omen, the bird of good luck. Boon had read the character on a wedding invitation only the day before.

"This is for us," he said, thinking of the providence of their meeting.

"So it is," agreed Ichimonji, adding unexpectedly "with a bit of luck we shall have the girls dancing naked on the counter for us before the evening is out."

And with this introduction to the Sign of the Crane he slid open the door.

They entered a mean, cramped, dirty little room smelling of tobacco and burnt oil, much less like a bar than somebody's private kitchen. It was Boon's first visit to a red-light bar, and if he had been alone he would not have stayed there voluntarily a moment longer, let alone paid money to sit there for a couple of hours. Presumably it had attractions which did not meet the eye. From one glance at the extremely low blackened ceiling Boon was quite sure that women dancing naked on the counter would not be among them.

The Sign of the Crane was half full. Two customers lounged at the bar; altogether there was room for about six. Ichimonji and Boon installed themselves at the other end of the bar, their backs to the street. Two or three more and the place would be packed.

"You're in early tonight, aren't you?" said a blowsy woman as she lifted a steaming kettle off the gas-ring. She didn't even look at Ichimonji, and Boon was startled by the very familiar tone of the pronoun she used, which he had otherwise only heard between man and wife. Perhaps she *is* his wife, thought Boon, prepared for all. His suspicions mounted when Ichimonji asked the woman for a packet of cigarettes and she told him to help himself from the basket hanging behind the counter. Perhaps it was his house.

"Where's Emiko?" asked Ichimonji.

"Gone next door to borrow some soya sauce. Should be back any minute. I was out shopping this afternoon but forgot to buy it. Terrible rush all day. My sister went into hospital this morning and I had to go out to Omiya to look after the children. Poor little mites."

"What's wrong with her then?"

"Her liver, they say."

"She shouldn't drink so much."

"You know how difficult that is. The customers don't like it and they stay away. Never gets home much before two in the morning, up at six to make the breakfast and see the children off to school, it really is no wonder. If you had to do it you'd be in hospital inside a week."

"And her husband?"

"He's in Hokkaido at the moment, on tour. Playing with a different band. They've got an engagement there in . . . where was it now? . . . well anyway, one of those resorts. Staying there over the new year. Hand to mouth, but that doesn't worry him. Happy-go-lucky, that's how he is. Tomorrow's wind will blow tomorrow . . ."

"Yellowtail!" said one of the customers at the other end of the bar.

"*Sake!*" trumped the other.

The woman wiped her hands on the corner of her apron and opened the fridge.

"Is there any whale?" asked Ichimonji.

"There is."

"For two. And *sake*."

"*Hai hai.*"

She took four blue-and-white flasks down from the shelf, filled them from a two-litre bottle of *sake* and placed them in the kettle. Then she lit the gas-ring, fetched a large greasy pan from under the sink and began to heat it, shaking it until the fat ran. The four men watched her in silence. At that moment the door grated open and a woman's voice said brightly

"Sorry I was so long, *mama*. I just couldn't get away next door – goodness, it's cold!"

The young woman who had just come in closed the door hurriedly, stamping her feet and rubbing her arms. When she stooped to duck under the counter Boon saw the bottom of her T-shirt slide up her back, revealing a few inches of bare skin. No wonder she was cold.

"Cucumber," said the other woman, "and two cups. Did you get the soya sauce?"

"It's there."

"Emiko . . ."

"*Hai.*"

"I've brought someone along to see you."

"Me? Really?"

Emiko was squatting on the floor with her head in a cupboard, her voice muffled, showing a margin of white skin. She took out two bowls, stood up and said again, her back still turned to them,

"Someone to see me?"

Mama dexterously flipped over the yellowtail in the frying-pan and stood back as it began to crackle and spit. With cat's-paw fingers she lifted the four flasks out of the kettle, wringing her hands, wiped them one by one and placed them in a steaming row on top of the counter. Boon watched the mirror on the wall slowly mist over. It was beginning to get really quite snug.

Emiko turned round and set two bowls of radish and pickled cucumber on the counter in front of them.

"Here we are, then – "

"His name is Bun. Comes from England, and is altogether a rather remarkable fellow. This is only his first night out, you know, but he's already fallen for a bedspread . . ."

"A bedspread?"

"Only a small one – a quiltlet. Still, he thinks it'll do to keep him warm."

Ichimonji choked on a slice of radish which he had unwisely put into his mouth before beginning to speak. He spat it out on the floor, laughing so much that he had to get down from the stool and loosen his belt. He took Boon by the shoulder and shook him affectionately.

"Bun-*san*, forgive me . . . you know how silly and noisy we Japanese can get when we've had a bit too much to drink. From my heart, I beg your forgiveness!"

His face suddenly became extremely solemn, and placing his hands on his thighs he bowed formally to Boon. There was no doubting his sincerity. He could laugh one minute and weep the next. Ichimonji was that kind of man.

Emiko dispensed piping hot *sake* and steered the conversation back to herself.

"My hair's different. Do you like it?"

"What's different about it?"

"You've had it cut," said Boon edgeways.

"*Ara!*" ·

She rapped the counter with her knuckles and looked at him in astonishment.

"How do you know that?"

"It just looks cut. As if your own head still hadn't quite got used to it."

"*Araa . . .*"

"And apart from that, the skin under the hairline is pale, whereas the rest of you is tanned."

Boon had been studying necks and napes with close attention throughout the evening.

"As if my own head still hadn't got used to it . . ." repeated Emiko to herself. "What strange things you say. There you are, *sensei*. Some people have eyes to see."

"If Bun-*san* had known you as long as I have he probably wouldn't bother to look either."

"Horrid man."

Emiko set down in front of them two saucers of whale.

"Do you like garlic?" she asked Boon. "This is garlic sauce."

"He's probably more worried about the whale," said Ichimonji. "Foreigners don't go in for whale very much, and they don't much approve of those who do, either. Can't understand what all the fuss is about, personally. Are we barbarians, Bun-*san*? Perhaps you can explain."

"Let him try first," said Emiko. "I expect he's never eaten whale."

"I haven't."

Boon pried loose a sliver of the red meat, dabbed it in garlic sauce and raised it to his lips. Everyone was watching him intently, as if he would now pronounce the binding verdict of an international whaling commission. *Tsuru no hito-koe*: straight from the horse's mouth.

"It's rather good."

Emiko clapped her hands.

"But the thing is, these whales are dying out."

"You've just contributed your share," said Ichimonji. "Isn't it the same thing as butchering pigs and cows?"

"Pigs and cows can be bred. You can't breed whales."

"Well of course. But the point is, whales are as important for us as pigs and cows are for you. They provide a staple Japanese diet. Foreigners don't seem to realise that."

"Then all the more reason, I would think, for whale conservation to be in the national interest of the Japanese. If you kill them all, and at this rate that's not going to take very long, what's going to happen to your staple diet?"

"But, look here . . ."

Ichimonji tried to ward off this simple argument, but he was obviously stumped.

The customer who had eaten the yellowtail pushed away his plate and said

"*Sake!*"

"Yellowtail!" said the other, not to be outdone. They were like twins playing snap.

"Perhaps one could breed whales," ruminated Ichimonji.

"Who cares about politics," said Emiko with the cropped hair.

"Not politics – food," Ichimonji corrected her.

"Would you give me a little *sake*, please . . ."

"Of course, how rude of me. Fetch yourself a cup," replied Boon with the eyes to see. And Emiko reached up behind her, allowing him a glimpse of a strip of white belly.

Boon and Emiko drank one, two, three, four little flasks of *sake* within an hour. He stood them on their heads and arranged them in patterns on the counter as Emiko told him the story of her life.

She came from Kyushu. At eighteen she had married and gone to live in Osaka, divorced four years later and had since worked in Tokyo. Her daughter, now aged seven, had been sent back to Kyushu to live with the grandparents. Emiko wasn't in the least bit sad about the turn that her life had taken and she seemed to have no worries about the future. "I'm only twenty-seven," she said, and in three years' time she was confident she would be running a place of her own. She had saved quite a bit herself; and as for the rest, *she* wouldn't have any problems finding a "sponsor". She invited Boon to judge for himself: what was her body like? Having discussed the finer points, Boon concluded that it was a sound investment and would take her a long way. Emiko was quite unembarrassed by this intimacy, and not coquettish either. After all, she had a practical mind and was discussing her business capital. But by the end of their long conversation Emiko was sitting beside Boon on his side of the bar, and eight upended flasks of *sake* were standing on the counter in tight formation, hip to hip and neck to neck.

The two stock jobbers had long since disappeared; drink had made Ichimonji maudlin and *mama* sentimental, and for the past two hours they had been listening to each other's troubles. The panels of the glass door had steamed up, the smoke from the frying-pan drifted up to the ceiling and shrank into the walls, outside a gale was blowing and Boon could hear the shop-curtains thumping and the tin signs crackling all the way down the street. Four under the Sign of the Crane sat warm and drunk.

"Sing a song!" Emiko commanded Ichimonji suddenly.

"Sing a song? Why should I sing a song?" he asked blearily.

"Because I want you to."

He made an effort to control his wandering speech.

"Emi-*chan*, I'll sing a song if you'll dance for Bun."

"All right."

"Wait a minute. I want you to dance like you danced in . . . where was it she danced, *mama*? Wake up! Wake up! Oh never mind. Yes! In April this year, after we'd been to see the flowers, Emi-*chan*. Remember? You danced on the counter . . . naked, remember?"

"Me? Naked?"

Ichimonji made a sweeping gesture with his arm and toppled off his stool. He picked himself up and grabbed Boon's sleeve.

"Bun-*san*, d'you want Emiko to dance naked on the counter?"

"D'you want to?" asked Boon, turning to Emiko.

She drew circles in his beard with the tip of her finger.

"Do you want me to?"

"Yes," said Boon.

Emiko stopped drawing circles and put a full stop in the centre of his chin.

"All right then, if you want me to I will. But you must sing first, *ne, sensei* . . ."

So Ichimonji sang, and when he had finished Emiko went outside, took down the pole with the *noren* from the shop-front, closed and locked the door and hung the dark blue curtains over the glass panels so that no one could see inside. Then she chose a cassette from the pile in the corner, slipped it into the recorder, turned down the volume and began to undress. Nobody said a word. Emiko stood beside Boon, folded her clothes and draped them over his knee. Naked she sat on the counter, swung her legs up and rose to her feet, standing with not more than a couple of inches between her head and the ceiling. She smiled down at Boon and said "Well?", quite unselfconscious, with her small, shapely breasts and slender hips, and began to dance.

When Boon and Ichimonji parted on the main street it was four o'clock in the morning. Newspapers, cartons, yesterday's debris rolled helter-skelter past them down the deserted morning streets. Elated, spent, no longer minding the cold, Boon watched his friend set out along the gusty pavement with coat tails fluttering and tie flying, like a pennant, behind him in the wind.

*A*bout the house. The following morning, three months after leaving Europe, Boon woke up to find that overnight he had arrived in Japan. Until then he had never really believed that he was there. Having made up his mind that it would benefit his Japanese if he avoided all contact with people who spoke his own language, he had isolated himself from one world without gaining access to the other and for a long time he remained uneasily suspended between the two. Celibate, studious, his intellect committed but his heart undecided, he might have stood wavering for quite a bit longer had Ichimonji not seized him by the scruff of the neck and pitched him into the magic circle where words and sentences became palpable events, a clamour of voices, faces and sensations, no longer a dumbshow but a glittering stage where the actors walked and talked, abruptly waking him out of his dream.

Boon went to Japan because he had once seen a Japanese actor walk across a stage in a way that deeply impressed him. It was not a big stage, not more than a dozen yards across, but the actor moved so slowly and with such controlled tautness of muscle that the stage itself seemed to become progressively bigger; it took him a full minute to pass from one side to the other. The distension of space and time in this performance on the stage likewise characterised Boon's decision, made in the course of this minute, to visit Japan, for when he did eventually get there he was to stay for almost three years – far longer than he had originally intended when he took that decision.

Asked why he wanted to go to Japan, Boon had at first tried to explain the remarkable impression left on him by this actor's walk across the stage, how it had ignited his imagination and made him curious to know more about the country. It seemed that this answer didn't really satisfy people; they wanted to believe there must be more to it than that. Surely not just an actor walking across a stage? Japan was on the other side of the world, after all. There were foundations which might sponsor serious academic research, but they would not be prepared to indulge a private whim. He was advised that the sort of thing he was interested in was generally known as cross-cultural studies; why not apply for a scholarship? Boon cautiously agreed, and so it was for this purpose that in 1973 the Japanese Ministry of Education invited him there for a period of eighteen months. Boon felt gratified at first but then rather uneasy; he was not at all sure what cross-cultural studies were.

The arrival in Tokyo was not promising. In late September the weather was still unpleasantly sultry. For two hours he had sat sweating and silent in the back of the car, driving through level, unprepossessing streets. He had no idea where he was being taken and no way of finding out. He didn't speak the language. He would have to learn it. His first glimpse of a vast city, sprawling outwards without any sense of plan or apparent end, like a scattered pack of cards, struck him ominously as being a measure of the task he had vaguely undertaken, in its own way just as vast, because just as unplanned and limitless.

It was not until the driver stopped the car and the other man had placed his bags on the steps in front of the building that Boon realised he must have finally reached his destination. He looked around him and didn't much relish the idea. After a journey of several thousand miles he found himself inside a walled compound with the inhospitable atmosphere of a barrack.

"Here?"

The driver leaned out of the window and spoke to him rapidly in Japanese. With a slight bow the other man turned and got back into the car, and they immediately drove off.

Boon understood that he had been told to wait. Perhaps because this was the first thing he had understood since his arrival at the airport several hours earlier he waited longer and more patiently than he would otherwise have done, for it was already one o'clock in the morning and very unlikely that anyone would come out of the building to look for him.

After ten minutes, however, the place still looked just as deserted; it occurred to Boon that he might have misunderstood the man. Perhaps he had not told him to wait. Perhaps he had said that somebody was waiting for him. Boon went up the steps into the building and looked into the office where the lights were on, but there wasn't anybody there.

"Nobody here," he said out loud, and pressed a buzzer on the ledge in front of the office window.

About a minute later he heard shuffling sounds from the far end of the corridor leading off the entrance hall. He peered into the corridor and saw a man coming towards him carrying a large white bundle. He went back outside to fetch his bags.

He found the man waiting for him in the hall. The man said something to him, but Boon couldn't understand. He was dressed in what appeared to be long white underwear, with a piece of yellowish woollen material wound round his stomach. He was carrying a sheet and a blanket.

Realising that Boon could not understand him, the man nodded slowly a number of times and pointed down the corridor, indicating that Boon was to follow him. They set off in silence.

The man shambled rather than walked, toes turned out, feet scuffing the floor. The muffled slap-slapping of his sandals made

Boon aware of the very different sound his own shoes were making – a hard-heeled, definite, in these new surroundings somehow alien sound.

He followed the man up a flight of stairs and along an identical corridor on the floor above. The lights were still on up here, and the first thing that struck him were the rows of shoes lining the walls on either side of the doors all the way down the corridor. The sight of these rows of shoes also seemed very alien. He felt increasingly depressed.

The man stopped outside a room where there were no shoes, unlocked the door and turned on the light. Boon went in and put down his bags.

On one side of the room there was a basin and a cupboard, on the other side a table, a chair and a bed, leaving just enough room in the middle for one person to pass in and out. The light bulb hung unshaded on a knotted strip of flex in the middle of the room. It was hot in the room, and when Boon opened the window it seemed to become even hotter.

The man rolled back the mattress and put the sheet and blanket he had brought with him on the bed. Then he opened the cupboard, took out a hanger, replaced it, pulled the drawer out of the table, patted the bed, turned on the tap and let the water run, as if Boon had never seen any of these things before and needed to know what they were for. Or perhaps the man simply wanted to indicate to him that he should feel at home; perhaps, for lack of any other communication between them, it was a demonstration of welcome.

"Thank you," said Boon.

The old fellow nodded gravely and shambled off down the corridor.

Boon took off his jacket and sat down on the bed. He could hear someone talking in the next room. He prodded the wall with his thumb and could feel it give way. It seemed to be made of thin hardboard that had simply been papered over.

The low hum of voices from the room next door continued without interruption until three o'clock in the morning. Boon took off his shirt, shoes and finally his trousers and sat on the bed naked, still sweating, smoking cigarette after cigarette, watching the cockroaches clamber in and out of the holes in the floorboards, and wondering why on earth he had come.

Boon did not like the Foreign Students Hall where it had been arranged for him to live, and on the same evening he moved in he decided he would move out. He committed this resolution to his diary.

> Been here a week now, another week to go. Similarities to English boarding-school too close for comfort.
>
> Must say that the Asian contingent, notably the Koreans, make a much better impression than the Europeans or Americans: informed, committed, excellently organised.
>
> There seem to be two reasons for this. The South East Asians are perhaps naturally more group-conscious, and from the odd remark one gathers that they also need to be: apparently they are subject to discrimination in Japanese society. The second reason is that whereas the Americans and the Europeans, almost to a man, are here to poke around in literature or the fine arts, and lack either skills or a goal (*viz.* Boon), the Asians are all in Japan to prepare for later professions, take their stay here more seriously and are thus perhaps more alert to everything going on.

Such diary entries became less and less frequent in proportion to Boon's growing command of Japanese and therewith his ability to communicate with those around him. This would never have happened if he had stayed on at the student hall of residence. But the decision that he did not want to live there was one thing, finding somewhere else to stay was quite another, and this in turn would have been impossible or at least very difficult if he had not happened to meet Sugama a few days after arriving in the country.

The introduction was arranged through a mutual acquaintance, Yoshida, at the private university where Boon was taking language courses and where Sugama was employed on the administrative staff. They met one afternoon in the office of their acquaintance and inspected each other warily for ten minutes.

"Nice weather," said Boon facetiously as he shook hands with Sugama. Outside it was pouring with rain.

"Nice weather?" repeated Sugama doubtfully, glancing out of the window. "But it's raining."

It was not a good start.

Sugama had just moved into a new apartment. It was large enough for two, he said, and he was looking for someone to share the expenses. This straightforward information arrived laboriously, in bits and pieces, sandwiched between snippets of Sugama's personal history and vague professions of friendship, irritating to Boon, because at the time he felt they sounded merely sententious. All this passed back and forth between Sugama and Boon through the mouth of their mutual friend, as Boon understood almost no Japanese and Sugama's English, though well-intentioned, was for the most part impenetrable.

It made no odds to Boon where he lived or with whom. All he wanted was a Japanese-speaking environment in order to absorb the language as quickly as possible. He had asked for a family, but none was available.

One windy afternoon in mid-October the three of them met outside the gates of the university and set off to have a look at Sugama's new apartment. It was explained to Boon that cheap apartments in Tokyo were very hard to come by, the only reasonable accommodation available being confined to housing estates subsidised by the government. Boon wondered how a relatively prosperous bachelor like Sugama managed to qualify for government-subsidised housing. Sugama admitted that this was in fact only possible because his grandfather would also be living there. It was the first Boon had heard of the matter and he was rather taken aback.

It turned out, however, that the grandfather would "very seldom" be there – in fact, that he wouldn't live there at all. He would only be there on paper, he and his grandson constituting a "family". That was the point. "You must *say* he is there," said Sugama emphatically.

The grandfather lived a couple of hundred miles away, and although he never once during the next two years set foot in the apartment he still managed to be the bane of Boon's life. A constant stream of representatives from charities, government agencies and old people's clubs, on average one or two a month, came knocking on the door, asking to speak to grandfather. At first grandfather was simply "not in" or had "gone for a walk", but as time passed and the flow of visitors never faltered, Boon found himself having to resort to more drastic measures. Grandfather began to make long visits to his home in the country; he had not yet returned because he didn't feel up to making the journey; his health gradually deteriorated. Finally Boon decided to have him invalided, and for a long time his condition remained "grave". On grandfather's behalf Boon received the condolences of all these visitors, and occasionally even presents.

Two years later grandfather did in fact die. Boon was thus exonerated, but in the meantime he had got to know grandfather well and had become rather fond of him. He attended his funeral with mixed feelings.

Sugama had acquired tenure of his government-subsidised apartment by a stroke of luck. He had won a ticket in a lottery. These apartments were much sought after, and in true Japanese style their distribution among hundreds of thousands of applicants was discreetly left to fate. The typical tenant was a young couple with one or two children, who would occupy the apartment for ten or fifteen years, often under conditions of bleak frugality, in order to save money to buy a house. Although the rent was not immoderate, prices generally in Tokyo were high, and it was a mystery to Boon how such people managed to live at all. Among the lottery winners there were inevitably also those people for whom the acquisition of an apartment was just a prize, an unexpected bonus, to be exploited as a financial investment. It was no problem for these nominal tenants to sub-let their apartments at prices well above the going rate.

Boon had never lived on a housing estate and his first view of the tall concrete compound where over fifty thousand people lived did little to reassure him. Thousands of winner families were accommodated in about a dozen rectangular blocks, each between ten and fifteen stories high, apparently in no way different (which disappointed Boon most of all) from similar housing compounds in Birmingham or Berlin. He had naively expected Japanese concrete to be different, to have a different colour, perhaps, or a more exotic shape.

But when Sugama let them into the apartment and Boon saw the interior he immediately took heart: this was unmistakably Japanese. Taking off their shoes in the tiny box-like hall, the three of them padded reverently through the kitchen into the *tatami* rooms.

"Smell of fresh *tatami*," pronounced Sugama, wrinkling his nose.

Boon was ecstatic. Over the close-woven pale gold straw matting lay a very faint greenish shimmer, sometimes perceptible and sometimes not, apparently in response to infinitesimal shifts in the texture of the falling light. The *tatami* was quite unlike a carpet or any other form of floor-covering he had ever seen. It seemed to be alive, humming with colours he could sense rather than see, like a greening tree in the brief interval between winter and spring. He stepped on to it and felt the fibres recoil, sinking under the weight of his feet, slowly and softly.

"You can see green?" asked Sugama, squatting down.

"Yes indeed."

"Fresh *tatami*. Smell of grass, green colour. But not for long, few weeks only."

"What exactly is it?"

"Yes."

Boon turned to Yoshida and repeated the question, who in turn asked Sugama and conferred with him at great length.

"*Tatami* comes from *oritatamu*, which means to fold up. So it's a kind of matting you can fold up."

"Made of straw."

"Yes."

"How long does it last?"

Long consultation.

"He says this is not so good quality. Last maybe four, five years."

"And then what?"

"New *tatami*. Quite expensive, you see. But very practical."

The three *tatami* rooms were divided by a series of *fusuma*, sliding screens made of paper and light wood. These screens were decorated at the base with simple grass and flower motifs; a natural extension, it occurred to Boon, of the grass-like *tatami* laid out in-between. Sugama explained that the *fusuma* were usually kept closed in winter, and in summer, in order to have "nice breeze", they could be removed altogether. He also showed Boon the *shoji*, a type of sliding screen similar to the *fusuma* but more simple: an open wooden grid covered on one side with semi-transparent paper, primitive but rather beautiful. There was only one small section of *shoji* in the whole apartment; almost as a token, thought Boon, and he wondered why.

With the exception of a few one- and two-room apartments every house that Boon ever visited in Japan was designed to incorporate these three common elements: *tatami*, *fusuma* and *shoji*. In the houses of rich people the *tatami* might last longer, the *fusuma* decorations might be more costly, but the basic concept was the same. The interior design of all houses being much the same, it was not surprising to find certain similarities in the behaviour and attitudes of the people who lived in them.

The most striking feature of the Japanese house was lack of privacy; the lack of individual, inviolable space. In winter, when the *fusuma* were kept closed, any sound above a whisper was clearly audible on the other side, and of course in summer they were usually removed altogether. It is impossible to live under such conditions for very long without a common household identity emerging which naturally takes precedence over individual wishes. This enforced family unity was still held up to Boon as an ideal, but in practice it was ambivalent, as much a yoke as a bond.

There was no such thing as the individual's private room, no bedroom, dining- or sitting-room as such, since in the traditional Japanese house there was no furniture determining that a room should be reserved for any particular function. A person slept in a room, for example, without thinking of it as a bedroom or as his room. In the morning his bedding would be rolled up and stored away in a cupboard; a small table known as the *kotatsu*, which could also be plugged into the mains to provide heating, was moved back into the centre of the room and here the family ate, drank, worked and relaxed for the rest of the day. Although it was becoming standard practice in modern Japan for children to have their own rooms, many middle-aged and nearly all older Japanese still lived in this way. They regarded themselves as "one flesh", their property as common to all; the *uchi* (household, home) was constituted according to a principle of indivisibility. The system of moveable screens meant that the rooms could be used by all the family and for all purposes: walls were built round the *uchi*, not inside it.

Boon later discovered analogies between this concept of house and the Japanese concept of self. The Japanese carried his house around in his mouth and produced it in everyday conversation, using the word *uchi* to mean "I", the representative of my house in the world outside. His self-awareness was naturally expressed as corporate individuality, hazy about quite what that included, very clear about what it did not.

Ittaikan, the traditional view of the corporate *uchi* as one flesh, had unmistakably passed into decline in modern Japan. A watery sentiment remained, lacking the conviction that had once made the communal *uchi* as self-evident in practice as it was in principle. This was probably why people had become acutely aware of the problem of space, although they did not necessarily have less space now than they had had before. A tendency to restrict the spatial requirements of daily life quite voluntarily had been evident in Japan long before land became scarce. When the tea-room was first introduced during the Muromachi period (early fourteenth to late sixteenth century) the specification of its size was four and a half mats, but in the course of time this was reduced to one mat (two square metres). The reasons for this kind of scaling down were purely aesthetic. It was believed that only within a space as modest as this could the spirit of *wabi*, a taste for the simple and quiet, be truly cultivated.

The almost wearying sameness about all the homes which Boon visited, despite differences in the wealth and status of their owners, prompted a rather unexpected conclusion: the classlessness of the Japanese house. The widespread use of traditional materials, the preservation of traditional structures, even if in such contracted forms as to have become merely symbolic, suggested a consensus about the basic requirements of daily life which was very remarkable, and which presumably held implications for Japanese society as a whole. Boon's insight into that society was acquired very slowly, after he had spent a great deal of time sitting on the *tatami* mats and looking through the sliding *fusuma* doors which had struck him as no more than pleasing curiosities on his first visit to a Japanese-style home. *

Sugama, Yoshida and Boon celebrated the new partnership at a restaurant in Shinjuku, and a week later Boon moved in.

The moment he entered the apartment a woman who was unexpectedly standing in the kitchen dropped down on her knees and prostrated herself in a deep bow, her forehead almost touching the floorboards, introducing herself with the words "*Irrashaimase. Sugama de gozaimasu . . .*"

Boon was extremely startled. He wondered whether he should do the same thing and decided not, compromising with a half-hearted bow which unfortunately the woman couldn't even see, because she had her face to the ground. She explained that she was *o-kaasan*, Sugama's mother.

Sugama had a way of springing surprises – or rather, he indicated his intentions so obtusely that Boon usually failed to realise what would happen until it was already in progress – and so for quite a while Boon assumed that there must have been a change in plan, that the mother had perhaps joined the household as a stand-in for the grandfather. He greeted her in fluent Japanese (he had been studying introductions for the past week) and promptly fell into unbroken silence, mitigated by the occasional appreciative nod. Boon for his part hardly understood a word of what Sugama's mother was saying but she, encouraged by the intelligible sounds he had initially produced, talked constantly for the best part of an hour, and by the time Sugama eventually arrived Boon had become resigned to the idea that his talkative mother was going to be a permanent resident.

The misunderstanding was swiftly ironed out. No, *o-kaasan* had only come up to Tokyo for a few days (from whatever angle of the compass one approached Tokyo the journey to the capital was described as an elevation) in order to help with the move.

Sugama's mother was a small, wiry woman in her late fifties. Her teeth protruded slightly; like most Japanese women, even those who had very good teeth, she covered her mouth with her hand whenever she laughed. She was a vivacious woman and laughed frequently, so one way and another, with all the cooking, cleaning and sewing she also did during the next four days, her hands were kept continually busy. She was of slight build but very sound in lung, with the effect that when she laughed it resounded throughout her whole body, as if the laugh were more than the body could accommodate. Perhaps this laughter drew Boon's attention to a girlish quality she had about her, despite her age and a rather plain appearance. He often watched her working, and in the spare, effortless movements of a woman who has performed the same tasks so many times that not even the tiniest gesture is superfluous there was also something unexpectedly graceful.

On the far side of the *fusuma* Boon often heard them talking late into the night. Night after night she sawed away at him with her flinty, abrasive voice. In the mornings Sugama was moody, the atmosphere in the house increasingly tense. Boon was left guessing. Gradually, in the course of weeks and months, Sugama began to take him into his confidence, and in retrospect he learned what must have been the subject of those nightly conversations.

O-kaasan's most pressing concern was that her son, at the advanced age of twenty-eight, was still unmarried. Boon couldn't see what the fuss was about, but Sugama was slowly coming round to his mother's view, who was quite sure it was a disaster. "The wind blows hard," he announced mysteriously, apparently by way of explanation – Boon himself had to blow pretty hard to keep up with conversations on this level. He said it was up to Sugama to decide when and whether he wanted to get married. It wasn't anybody else's business. Sugama would clearly have liked to be able to agree with this facile advice and just as clearly he could not, entangled in a web of sentiment and duty of which Boon was wholly ignorant.

The promptings of filial duty which caused Sugama such heartache and which to Boon were so alien demanded of Sugama a second, even more painful decision. He was the *chonan*, the eldest son, thereby inheriting the obligation not merely to provide for his ageing parents but to live with them in the same house. There were two alternatives open to him. He could either bring his parents to live with him in Tokyo or he could return home to his province in the north. A house in Tokyo large enough to provide room for grandfather, parents, Sugama and – sooner or later – a fourth generation family was out of the question; on his present salary he would have to work for several lifetimes in order to pay for it. A one-way ticket home came a great deal cheaper, which was just as well, since the only job awaiting him at the other end would be poorly paid and with even poorer prospects. Such was the path of righteousness.

Boon shuddered at the enormity of it. However, Sugama's easy-going nature and irrepressible optimism allowed him to keep a third card up his sleeve, on which he was secretly putting his money: that something else might turn up. The problem was real enough. Intermittently, in the course of the next two years, Sugama tossed and turned between these bleak alternatives, always finding the solution in the third. For two years, with great skill, tact and dogged perseverance, Sugama maintained the *status quo* by doing absolutely nothing.

The well-spring of Sugama's fertile optimism was his naivety. This naivety was really a capacity for trust. He was far from being a fool, but his intelligence filtered through the generosity of his nature and was applied without the benefit of caution or suspicion: he had a completely trusting intelligence. Somewhat to his surprise Boon later discovered that these trusting qualities underlay a great many Japanese attitudes. Sugama possessed them in a high degree; there was something of the daydreamer about him.

O-kaasan had only just packed her bags and gone home when – as usual without any forewarning – Sugama turned up late one evening accompanied by an old man, his wife and an enormous cardboard box. Boon was sitting in his pyjamas eating noodles out of a saucepan when these unexpected visitors arrived. Consternation. The old lady caught sight of him and dropped her bag (very probably she had not been forewarned either), immediately prostrating herself on the floor in the deepest of deep bows, old-style obeisance with the added advantage of concealing momentary shock and embarrassment. The old man was no slouch either. Palms on the floor and fingers turned inwards he bobbed his head up and down several times in Boon's direction, apologising profusely every time he came up for air. All this happened so quickly that the astonished Boon didn't even have the presence of mind to put down the saucepan he was holding, and he sat there in his pyjamas uneasily aware that he was the most unworthy object of the visitors' attentions.

Sugama came forward rather sheepishly, stepping in cavalier

fashion between the prone bodies on the kitchen floor, and explained who they were.

"My grandfather's brother – younger brother – and wife."

"Not your grandfather?" asked Boon doubtfully, always alert to the possibility of misunderstandings when Sugama ventured into English.

"No, no, *not* my grandfather."

"Your great-uncle, then."

"Ah! Great-uncle? *Great* uncle?"

Sugama paused to digest this new word, mustering his ancient relative with pursed lips. It was clear what was passing through his mind.

Boon was still not reassured. He kept an eye on the ominous cardboard box, quite large enough to accommodate a third, perhaps enfeebled relative, and wondered what else was in store for him.

"What are they doing here?"

"Earthquake," said Sugama simply. Boon fetched his dictionary and Sugama, reverting to Japanese, sat down to explain the situation.

At about nine o'clock that evening his great-uncle had called him in his office (Sugama worked a late shift) with the startling news that a major earthquake was imminent. How did he know? His wife had told him so. How did she know? A fortune-teller she regularly visited and in whom she placed absolute confidence had seen it in his cards and crystal ball. She was terrified, and having personally experienced the Great Kanto Earthquake of 1923 in which over a hundred thousand people had died she was not taking any chances. Her fortune-teller couldn't predict exactly when the earthquake would occur, but it might be at any time within the next three days; the greatest likelihood of its occurrence was forecast for midnight on the following day. The two old people ran a little shop in the downtown area of Tokyo where many of the houses were flimsy wooden structures which tended to slump and collapse very easily, even without the encouragement of an earthquake. But their great-nephew, they heard, had just moved into a marvellous modern building that was supposed to be *earthquake-proof*. Could they come and stay for a few days? Of course, said Sugama. So without more ado they bundled their worldly goods into the largest available box and Sugama brought them over in a neighbour's truck.

As a matter of fact there had been a slight tremor the previous evening. It was Boon's first. He had been standing in the kitchen helping himself to another glass of whisky when the floor unaccountably began to sway and a set of irreproachable stainless steel ladles, which until then had given him no cause for complaint, started rattling menacingly on the kitchen wall. Boon had replaced the whisky and made himself a cup of tea instead.

Great-uncle and his wife knelt on the *tatami* listening to Sugama's recital, wagging their heads and smiling from time to time, as if allowing that there was something rather droll about the situation, but also wanting to be taken absolutely seriously. However, with every moment they spent in the apartment this became increasingly hard to do, for the eccentric old couple seemed to be guided by a mischievous genius – they belonged to nature's blunderers, everything they touched turned to farce. Their great-nephew had just finished his dramatic account when there was a shrill call of *ohayo!* (Good morning) from the kitchen, and all eyes turned to the neglected cardboard box.

"Oh dear! The poor thing!" crowed the old lady, getting up at once and pattering over to the box. She pulled open the flap and gently lifted out a bright yellow parrot. The indignant bird rapped her knuckles a couple of times with the side of his beak and settled frostily on the tip of her finger.

Sugama, Boon, the elderly couple and the yellow parrot housed together for the next three days. Once he had provided his relatives with a roof over their heads Sugama took no further interest in them and was unaccountably busy for as long as they stayed there, leaving the house earlier and returning later than usual. His prodigiously long working hours impressed great-uncle and worried his wife, who took to preparing nutritious cold snacks for the labouring hero before retiring for the night. Sugama did justice to these snacks with the same appetite he applied himself to his work, warding off their anxieties with careless equanimity.

"You've got to hand it to him – he certainly works hard," said great-uncle at breakfast one morning, just after Sugama had left the house.

"Ah," replied Boon non-committally. He knew perfectly well that Sugama's overtime was not spent at the office but at mahjongg parlours in Nakano and Takadanobaba.

In the meantime Boon was left to study the evacuees and the evacuees Boon with mutual curiosity. On the whole he had the impression that they were rather disappointed in him. At first they looked at him as if he had descended from another planet, but when it became obvious that he was not going to live up to these expectations their interest declined into an attitude of gently reproachful familiarity. For Boon did not sleep on a bed, he dispensed with bacon and egg, he knew nothing about baseball, ate rice and drank green tea with relish and was unpardonably fond of dried cuttlefish and raw squid, foods which foreigners were commonly supposed to regard with horror and loathing. Altogether Boon was not as Boon should be, and they were rather disconcerted.

This attitude – a national prejudice, really – that foreigners and the Japanese way of life must almost as a matter of principle be wholly incompatible was something Boon encountered time and again. Under the cover of courtesy, of polite consideration for differences in tastes and customs, many Japanese would gleefully reveal their own select cabinet of horrors, confronting their guest with fermented bean curd or prawns drowned in sake not as something he might care to sample but as a kind of ethnological litmus test: if he found it indigestible and swiftly turned green this would be taken by them as confirmation of their own cultural and racial singularity. With barely concealed triumph the host would commiserate with his victim, invariably remarking *Yappari, nihonjin ja nai to* . . . (Ah well, unless one is Japanese . . .).

Great-uncle's day was leisurely, marked off by a series of alterations to the state of his dress and a gradually heightening luminescence in the texture of his skin. His night ended and his day began in the same long white underwear, unofficial national costume known as *suteteko* whose acquaintance Boon had already made on the night of his arrival in Japan; it was much loved by elderly men and for a neighbourhood stroll on summer evenings definitely *de rigeur*. After he had taken the air on the balcony and pottered around in the apartment for an hour or so, watering his imported plants and spoiling the prodigal bird with morsels of tuna fish, he settled down on the *tatami* to a long, methodical scrutiny of his feet. This completed, he eased himself under the *kotatsu* and polished his spectacles, a sign to his wife that he was ready for the newspaper and that she could bring him his happi-coat. Change number one, smoothly, according to plan.

It wasn't until great-uncle had slipped on his happi-coat that his face also began to unwrinkle and shed its muddy morning pallor, acquiring that taut consistency and discreet shine which so fascinated Boon. In the course of the afternoon, with each additional layer of clothing, and in the evening, the process cyclically reversing, with each depletion, great-uncle's luminescence rose by perceptible stages, transfusing his face. Boon never forgot that face. It was a comic masterpiece, at once beautiful and absurd, like the moon viewed through the skin of a drum.

Great-uncle's energies were almost completely taken up by the demands of his remarkable daily illumination. His wife was a devoted assistant, fully appreciative of the fact that his work could only be accomplished with undisturbed concentration and in a composed state of mind. She was constantly scurrying back and forth with happi-coats, blankets, freshly strained tea and crackers or anything else her husband might happen to need.

All these different articles were conjured out of the mysterious box in the kitchen. It was like magic. The box which had begun by yielding the yellow parrot continued for the next few days to produce an apparently inexhaustible inventory of household goods – clothes, bedding, pots and pans and mountains of food. Life for the elderly couple was centred around this box. When Boon later visited their tiny home and recognised many of the objects around him it was merely as if the box had expanded and that they lived not only out of it but in it.

On the fateful morning great-uncle took cover under the *kotatsu* earlier than usual and sat tight for the rest of the day. His wife went about her household tasks as briskly as ever, but when there was nothing left for her to do and at last she knelt down beside great-uncle at the little table it became evident how restless she really was. From time to time she laid down her sewing, listened intently, sighed and picked it up again. As the evening wore on and the tension began to mount, Boon couldn't resist cracking a few jokes, which great-uncle good-humouredly deflected at his wife. It was only to set her mind at rest that they had come to stay, he assured Boon. Women couldn't resist fortune-tellers, but it was just a lot of nonsense after all; and for good measure he made a few jokes himself at her expense. Boon was not deceived. Throughout the evening great-uncle helped himself to the bottle of fine old malt whisky, originally intended as Sugama's present, much more liberally than he otherwise did and by midnight he was in true fighting spirit, his face shining with such particular splendour that his wife's attention was diverted from the impending destruction of Tokyo to the threat of great-uncle's imminent collapse.

There was no earthquake that night, but the old lady couldn't quite believe this and for two more days she sat it out in her great-nephew's apartment waiting for the dust to clear. Sugama was dispatched, like a kind of dove from Noah's Ark, to report on the state of the world, and it was only after he had personally confirmed that the house in downtown Tokyo was still in perfect order that she consented to their departure. Boon particularly regretted the loss of the parrot, which spoke few words of Japanese but those very frequently, thus improving his pronunciation of the language.

*T*he old lady's chopsticks. The rooms in which Boon spent most of the next two years had something it would have been hard to find anywhere else in the Tokyo Metropolitan area – a view. From his window he could watch the industrial barges plying up and down the Sumida river, and a couple of hundred yards beyond lay a second river, the Arakawa, which was the boundary between Tokyo and Saitama prefecture. The view across these two rivers stretched uninterrupted for a couple of miles.

On the slender finger of land dividing the Sumidagawa and the

Arakawa enterprising businessmen had laid out a golf course and a driving range, but it was on a tiny piece of fenced-off wasteland directly beneath Boon's window that the beginners living on the housing estate practised their first erratic swings. Boon knew some of these men by sight, and in the course of the next months he was able to follow their progress from this patch of wasteland to the driving range across the river and finally to the golf course itself. One dedicated group laid down a simple, if occasionally hazardous, procedure for graduation to the awesome professionals across the river – the ability to drive a ball over to the opposite bank.

What surprised Boon about these would-be golfers was their equipment: it was superb. Men who had never hit a golf ball in their lives swaggered out to the miserable little piece of turf kitted out as if embarking on the most gruelling international tournament; cap, shoes, pants, gloves and a cartload of new clubs were indispensable for any beginner who really meant business.

Golf was only one outlet for this spirit of grim professionalism. The same kind of thing was true of tennis. On the asphalt enclosure between the two wings of the block where he lived couples would periodically stride out in immaculate whites, sternly challenge a section of wall, claim victory after half an hour or so and retire to a flat on the tenth floor. Where the tennis players rallied by day, other, more sinister practitioners appeared at night. Sometimes Boon would arrive home in the early hours of the morning to find a solitary white figure repeatedly springing up and kicking the wall. This might continue for ten or twenty minutes, in absolute silence. Naturally the man was dressed in the loose judo blouse and breeches, and sometimes he would be barefoot, even in winter.

All these sportsmen lived in a society in which uniforms held an honoured place. The training began very early. When Boon first saw three- and four-year-old children trundling around inside the wire pen of the housing estate kindergarten all dressed in the same mauve smocks and wearing the same yellow plastic hats he was horrified, but he soon became so used to seeing uniforms that they ceased to bother him. And as he learned more about the country he was able to see the point about uniforms in a more subtle perspective, revising the facile conclusions which he, like many foreigners, had immediately drawn.

One afternoon, when he strolled out to see how his golfers were getting on, Boon was distracted by the sight of a middle-aged man kneeling on the bank of the river fishing a kite out of the reeds. No sooner had the man retrieved his kite, however, than he turned his back on it and ran as fast as he could in the opposite direction. After a hundred yards or so he stopped, his back still turned to the kite, raised both arms and began tugging gently, very much as if he were pulling two invisible lavatory chains. The kite at Boon's feet remained inert. He was about to step forward to help get it airborne when he caught sight of three other kites, dipping and bobbing several hundred feet above him. The two renegade kites having been coaxed up on a buoyant air-stream, the man hurried back to the river to attend to the fourth.

Boon thought about helping him and decided not, for it was obvious that the man's pleasure in the sport lay in flying his four kites simultaneously and single-handed. After several abortive starts and a great deal of rushing back and forth on the part of the kite flier the watery, long-tailed paper frame staggered into the air and soared cleanly up to join the others. The man sat down by his anchor on the grass, lit a cigarette and gazed up at his flock of kites with an expression of grudging satisfaction.

In Boon's experience this kite flier was someone rather unusual in Japanese life: he played. Kite flying cost next to nothing, required no membership in a club, no special equipment, head-gear, gloves, shoes or anything of that kind. It could claim tradition, but certainly not social status. It was something done solely for its own sake. Most activities usually had to be *for* something, however woolly, like improving one's mind or one's powers of concentration.

Golf players and their kind were legion in Japan, the overwhelming majority. Recreational activities almost had to become indistinguishable from work in order to qualify as pleasure. Grit your teeth and enjoy yourself. The ordeal of pleasure in Japanese society was compounded by another difficulty which had nothing to do with personal attitudes – the lack of space for recreational facilities and inadequate access to such as were available. For the urban Japanese (i.e. most Japanese), who did not have a golf course or tennis courts on their doorstep, the attention to stylish appearance and the wholesale purchase of classy equipment sustained a world of make-believe. The men standing in tiered decks on top of an office building in central Tokyo, driving their quota of golf balls into a net not more than ten yards away, could not have found it easy to imagine they were teeing up at a country club, but perhaps it was a little bit easier, particularly for those who had never played and quite possibly never would play on a real golf course, if the outfit they wore and the clubs they used were, at least, "the real thing", the best that money could buy.

These rooftop cages and their solemn devotees presented a sight that Boon found both sad and ludicrous. There was little to be said for taking one's exercise on top of a building, let alone underneath it, but in Tokyo it had to be either the one or the other. Every day for a year Boon walked over a vast subterreanean sporting facility without even being aware of its existence. The golf cages and underground sports palaces were one aspect of a modern civilisation which Boon rejected as monstrous only for as long as he remained unaware of the desperate congestion that made it inevitable.

There were many things he found offensive but which he learned to accept because they were necessary, and equally a number of things that were unacceptable because they were offensive without being necessary. The worst of these was noise. Hour by hour and day after day columns of vans and cars, loudspeakers blaring, circled the estate laying a cordon of noise from which there was no escape. Occasionally there were political announcements, but on the whole they dealt with the price of fish and vegetables or some forthcoming attraction in a local hall, always couched in the most effusive courtesy language; a futile palliative, for the damage had already been done. Most Japanese had become resigned to this violation of their peace and assured Boon that he would soon get used to it, but he didn't. In fact it became steadily worse. The first jarring notes of the tinny melodies that were always churned out before these announcements were enough to drive him to fury.

Later, when he moved out into the country, these raiders on wheels duly followed him. Here they were more or less tolerable, however, because there were fewer of them and they offered more variety, including the traditional chants of itinerant fishmongers who had long since vanished from central Tokyo. *Shijimi'asari, a-sári!* Boon had to practise this difficult chant (advertising clams) several times in the bath before being able to reproduce it convincingly. The rise and fall of the little ditty reminded him of the responses he had sung as a boy, and it occurred to him that the texts as well were perfectly compatible.

Oh Lord, open thou our lips:
And our mouth shall show forth thy praise.

He was sure that the clam crier would have been gratified to learn this, but unfortunately the point was too subtle for him to be able to communicate.

On one occasion, only an hour or so after the ancient fish crier had passed through the village, a van with loudhailer drove up and down the street warning the inhabitants that it was about to rain and that on no account should anybody go out without suitable protection. By this time Boon was sufficiently familiar with the indulgent, paternalistic attitudes of public corporations to be only mildly surprised by this curious announcement, but when he attempted to go out for a walk later in the afternoon – naturally without an umbrella – he was pounced on by his watchful landlady and scolded for his foolhardiness. He had only partly understood the announcement; it was not just rain but *acid* rain, borne on clouds from a nearby chemical plant.

If the Japanese had become immune to noise sources outside the building, their sensitivity to noise inside the building, where the culprit was easily identifiable, could sometimes lead to extreme violence. Boon read a terrifying newspaper article about an event on another housing estate which he would not have believed if he hadn't happened to know someone who lived there and who could confirm it for him.

Arriving home one evening and finding himself increasingly irritated by the yapping of a dog in the next apartment, a man had apparently gone over and rung his neighbour's bell, forced his way into the apartment and hurled the offending animal from a balcony on the seventh floor. Shortly afterwards the owner of the dog himself arrived back and was told by his distraught wife of what had happened. Seized with rage, he in turn rushed over to the neighbour and without more ado threw *him* over the balcony. People in Tokyo were generally phlegmatic and very long-suffering, but when occasionally the pressure of their cramped living conditions became too much for them and the lid blew off, outbursts of such violence were not altogether surprising.

One of Boon's greatest pleasures during the first months of his stay was that whenever he went out for a stroll he would discover something novel and arresting; the longer he stayed the more he lost the capacity for this pleasure, the things that had once delighted him would seem dowdy and commonplace, or he failed even to notice them at all. Washing-lines, for instance, he often stopped and inspected with wondering curiosity. Happi-coats and *yukata*, which he had often enough seen people wearing on warm autumn evenings, only revealed their true form when hung out on a washing-line to dry. The broad-sleeved cotton gowns hung on balconies or in gardens like great birds with spread wings, pinned back and captive, struggling faintly against the breeze.

The men who had tamed these splendid birds and nonchalantly wore them on Saturday morning shopping excursions, clacking up and down the aisles of the supermarket with the short, slightly feminine steps characteristic of *geta* (clogs), never seemed in the least self-conscious, or their appearance incongruous. The *geta* added a few inches to their height, of course, and the swathe of the *yukata* made them look broader; but, as Boon discovered when he tried it out himself, an element of *gaki-daisho*, a robust, cock-of-the-walk swagger, was as inalienable from the man's *geta* as a quality of subdued grace from the woman's *kimono*. Whenever the Japanese male discarded his crumpled suit, in which he easily looked puny and downtrodden, and slipped on a broad-sleeved robe, he underwent a truly Phoenix-like transformation: out of the ashes of urban man rose an exotic creature of proud plumage, not just impressive, but even majestic.

It was sometimes pointed out, as one index of the fundamental change that had taken place in Japan during the last hundred years, that whereas in pre-Restoration days a person's social rank or trade had immediately been apparent from the way he dressed, in modern Japan it was impossible to say from a glance at the average man on the train whether he was the company director or the store-room clerk. This disappearance of outward distinctions in the structure of a society which still preserved many of the inner distinctions led to some interesting side-effects or compensatory measures that were peculiar to Japan's social evolution. The most notable of these was the almost universal use of business cards. The exchange of cards at even casual meetings having nothing to do with the business interests of either party might on the surface appear to be a sophisticated and convenient modern practice, but its real significance ran much deeper. Business cards endorsed not merely the identification of a person, his name and the organisation to which he belonged, but also his rank and function within it. They supplied the social context of the individual that was considered indispensable to his dealings with others. Without this information many Japanese were at a loss to know what attitude and tone they should adopt towards the other party.

The way people dressed, Boon decided, might have lost its classical function of defining rank in feudal hierarchy, but it was still a factor of significance, now associated with a new set of values. People in Japan adhered to a standard of Appropriateness, vague in theory but rigorously observed in practice.

Appropriateness was distinct from the common requirements of etiquette, those marginal social inconveniences to which some people voluntarily aspire and others occasionally have to submit. It would be straining the meaning of the word unduly to say that the appearance of the wasteland golfers and the backyard tennis players conformed to "etiquette". It was not etiquette. They were Golfers and Tennis Players, and they dressed accordingly; partly, perhaps, to bolster their own confidence, but also in order to make themselves immediately recognisable as such to others. Ah, Golfer! Ah, Tennis Player! Here was appropriateness, the world was in order.

The Californian hippie and the London businessman were also recognisable by dress, of course, but there was much more personal taste and whim about it. In Japan, where lateral relationships between strangers, meeting casually and parting without obligations, were still far from common, dress signalling constituted an unwritten social code which could be interpreted less freely. Differences in dress did not occur by accident but according to a social arrangement and for a social purpose, to make unmistakeably clear what sort of creature you were.

Wherever possible, uniforms were available to provide this function, from kindergarten to college and, at least on the premises, in many professions. Boon once spent a summer teaching English at a company in northern Japan. He appeared regularly every evening in a succession of coloured shirts, although always wearing a tie. He became friendly with one of his pupils, and occasionally they went drinking together. From this man he learned that his appearance in class had met with strong disapproval. Coloured shirts were worn "for play", and hence reflected a lack of seriousness in Boon's attitude towards his job and his pupils. He should have worn a white shirt. Otherwise he was – categorically – not a Teacher.

His favourite example of Appropriate Dress was furnished by the Artist, who was unmistakable in his beret and (an optional extra) drab-coloured mackintosh. Boon met a few artists who were serious and also distinguished, and a great many more who were neither serious nor distinguished, but they all wore berets. Ah, Artist! It was a recipe for instant recognition, and Boon occasionally made use of it himself.

A very common specimen was the Holidaymaker. Holidays in Japan were short and nasty, jammed between one weekend and the next, one traffic congestion and another. But the Holidaymaker's outfit was always on show to challenge any lingering suspicions that here was a man who just possibly might not be enjoying himself very much. As the behaviour of holidaymakers in Japan tended to diverge from their normal behaviour even more radically than was the case in most countries, their uniform dress had the added advantage of mollifying policemen and landlords, who could read the code and knew what it implied: here is a man on holiday, be lenient, let it pass.

The standard of Appropriateness was applied with equal consistency to the solemn and the trivial, the important and the peripheral. Sugama and a group of enthusiastic friends, for example, made up a casual baseball team that trekked off to a distant sports-ground every other Sunday morning for matches with other amateur teams. Sometimes they would be a man short, the equipment had to be shared, and so on; it was an improvised sort of affair. However, not only did all the members always turn up in full baseball gear, their shirts and caps were even emblazoned with the team colours. Impromptu football matches of the kind to be seen anywhere in Europe, where the players grab anything to hand, could not easily be conceived in Japan, because they would be *basho-gara wakimaezu* – not in keeping with the nature of the occasion.

The notion of Appropriateness, or *basho-gara* (literally, the "character of a place", hence behaviour and appearance in keeping with the place), encompassed Japanese society with a universality which Boon otherwise associated only with collectivist doctrines or religious beliefs. It was not a doctrine or a belief, however. Dress was one index of Appropriateness, but it could be traced just as clearly in a number of other forms, notably the use of language: men's language, women's language, deferential and familiar language – the range was both broad and subtle.

Although the attitudes which *basho-gara* underlay were firmly established, the word itself did not occur frequently in idiomatic Japanese. The common term for "appropriateness" or "suitability" was *tekito*. When Boon could follow conversation better he was likely to hear this word at least once a day. It gradually became clear to him that for people to be able to think in terms of "appropriate" behaviour there must somewhere be a remarkable consensus not merely about the abstract or model on which such behaviour was based but about the need for there to be any model at all; and to the extent that one's behaviour was based on a model it must naturally contain an element of imitation, which in turn entailed a comparison between oneself and what one measured oneself by.

In *Nihon no Shiso*, a book which Boon did not read until much later in his studies, the political philosopher Maruyama Masuo had this to say about role identification and the tendency of the Japanese to qualify the image they presented of themselves in terms of the function they performed at any one time: "(In contrast with the rigid hierarchy clearly defining the rank and obligations of members of a feudal society) nowadays the same person is simultaneously bound into a network of very different relationships and has to carry out a number of functions whose nature varies with the circumstances in which he finds himself. Thus, even when visiting an acquaintance, it is common to open by saying 'Today let's speak as friends', or 'Today I have come in my capacity as head of the department'."

The constant alertness of the Japanese to the appropriate image to present, the appropriate thing to do or say, was conditioned by this involuntary qualification of oneself "in terms of" or "in the capacity as" some previously established, instantly recognisable stereotype. Without stereotypes, social communication based in this way on specification of supraindividual roles would obviously not work.

Not merely were sportsmen sportsmanlike and managers manager-like, there were also implicit ideals of "likeness" for Man, Woman, Mother, Father and so on to which very few Japanese were not in their hearts susceptible. *Otoko-rashii, haha-rashii*. These ideals were still very potent in Japanese life.

Women, in particular, underwent a spectacular metamorphosis, illustrating susceptibility to role identification more clearly than anyone in Japanese society. The bevies of eligible girls between the ages of eighteen and twenty-five that passed Boon in the streets were better turned out, or at least more conscious of their appearance, than almost anywhere in the world. Whether as a result they were also smarter and more attractive was a matter of opinion, but there was no mistaking the amount of time, care and hard cash that must have gone into their making. With bright lipstick and soft curls, faces painstakingly put together, they eagerly set out on the hunt; at first just for pleasure, later in search of a more settled company of acquaintances and friends among whom they would find their eventual husbands.

Unfortunately there were very few of these bright young things where Boon lived, because government housing estates catered for brave young couples and not single girls. This environment did however allow him to find out what happened to bright young things when they got married. The transformation was immediate and drastic. Suddenly these brilliant creatures began to moult, shedding all their glitter and coloured plumage.

It was almost as if a married woman, and especially once she had children, no longer had any business to be attractive. Later, much later, perhaps; but in the long years of suckling, rearing and keeping a home for her brood her personal attractiveness was not a quality either expected or, apparently, desired. For several months Boon lived in a house where one such young woman occasionally went out in the afternoons to work as a hostess at conferences and receptions, dressed in a *kimono* and looking (as her husband pointedly remarked) very much as she used to do before they got married. The couple needed the extra money and the wife obviously enjoyed her part-time job, as it gave her an excuse to get out of the house, but under the combined pressure of husband and mother-in-law her afternoon excursions were soon brought to an end. *Konna kakko de!* – dressed up like that! It was not appropriate.

In and about the house, going shopping or walking out with their children, even attractive young women managed to be dowdy in their appearance. There was an almost Cinderella-like quality about them: besieged by children, sitting in drab smocks and shapeless trousers at home among the ashes, forgotten by their princes. Nearly all young mothers were like this, because this was what young mothers were supposed to be like. A permanently harrassed look belonged to the part. They did not merely accept this role of household drudge, they cultivated it and sought fulfilment in it, because there was no alternative anyhow. The Japanese very seldom entertained at home, and it was extremely unusual for a husband to take his wife out in the evening, to dinner, a concert, a party or whatever. Baby-sitting facilities didn't exist. For a mother to leave her child in someone else's care even for an evening was tantamount to desertion.

There seemed to be two explanations for the studied unattractiveness cultivated by young wives. Once she had procured a husband and borne him children a woman's chief motivation for making herself attractive – at least in terms of a rather crude social mechanics – abruptly ceased to exist; and as the social life of a couple was severely curtailed after marriage there was no other incentive either. The capacity which Japanese society had nurtured in woman from early childhood she now turned into a career – self-sacrifice.

At first Boon was in no two minds about the manifest injustice of such a situation. Women simply got a rough deal, and that was that. Without ever basically changing his opinion he did come to modify it, however, as he gradually found out how much more demanding were the standards of service that prevailed everywhere in Japanese life; almost no quality was as highly regarded as readiness for self-sacrifice, that classic Japanese quality.

As in many parts of Asia, women in Japan carried their children on their backs. For children from about two or three upwards collapsible push-chairs were the usual means of conveyance, but in three years Boon didn't see a single pram. For baby it was mother's back (and father's too, occasionally), or *onbu*, as this form of carrying infants was called. In a country which was notable for the alacrity with which it adapted to more efficient or convenient methods Boon was struck by the universal popularity that the archaic and uncomfortable custom of *onbu* evidently still enjoyed.

When he first arrived at the housing estate in October the weather was very warm, and the curiously top-heavy forms of mother and incumbent child were everywhere on view. Hands resting on the mother's shoulders, legs dangling, neither fully joined nor disjoined, like an organism encroaching on the life-system of another without quite being a parasite, incumbent child and encumbered mother presented a rather ungainly sight in which the natural ambiguity of symbiosis was at the same time beautifully epitomised.

On the first cold morning Boon went out to find all this gone. All the women had put on their *onbu*-capes and acquired a winter hump; swaddled in the folds of this cape, in a kind of front-to-back pouch ideal for hibernation, no more could be seen of their charges than their heads peeking out. The cautious disengagement of mother and child which yesterday had still been in process seemed all at once, with the onset of winter, to have been brought to a halt.

Apart from the discomfort to the mother, the practice of *onbu* was sometimes criticised on the grounds that it caused children to grow up bow-legged, but Boon was unable to get scientific confirmation of this view. He was in any case less interested in the possible effects on the child's legs than on the child's disposition and general sense of well-being.

From this perch on his mother's back every Japanese made his first acquaintance with the outside world. The strange objects in his field of vision were first glimpsed through the familiar screen of her hair, the odours of the world around him compounded with the more immediate and reassuring scent of her body. It seemed to Boon that such a child must grow into a very special world, one in which each new discovery must have been favourably conditioned by the peculiarities of the seat from which the child had first made it; familiar despite its strangeness, constant despite its variety, from the very beginning. He expected of a child who for a long time had been entrusted to the world only on his mother's back to have above all a trusting disposition: and very often he did, even if this particular identification of cause and effect went the way of all other bow-legged theories.

It sometimes seemed to Boon that the self-insufficient Japanese remained suspended *onbu*-style throughout the course of their lives, always bearing and always borne by others, equally indulged and imposed upon, as ambiguous in the terms of their mutual dependence as the entire Japanese archipelago itself, sprung on a buoyant volcanic cushion between the Pacific ocean and the Sea of Japan.

In course of time, after putting together the jigsaw of many casual observations, Boon groped his way towards the formulation of an *onbu* psychology, which he later discovered had already been proposed by the psychologist Doi Takeo in his theory of *amae*, essentially a study of the morality of dependence in parent-child relationships.

At first, for example, when he began to disentangle intelligible bits and pieces of information from the garbled whirl of voices commanding, warning and exhorting at every station and on every·

58

train, he merely considered them a tiresome interference, adding yet another increment to an already substantial level of noise, but later he fancied he detected in these voices evidence of the *onbu* system writ large.

The same kind of solicitous concern a mother showed for her child was embodied in the person of the National Railways and extended to the millions of helpless passengers whom it temporarily had in its charge. Passengers were told the name of the next station, the transfer connection available there, not to forget anything when they got out (in wet weather umbrellas were given a specific mention), to open or not open the windows as this car was or was not air-conditioned; they were requested, always in the most courteous tones, to be patient when there was a delay, when it was crowded they were offered apologies, when it was hot commiseration, when tired they were soothed and comforted, and in fact very well looked after twenty hours a day all days of the year, not including strikes. Boon was surprised that the management had not yet thought of providing their customers with weather forecasts and the baseball scores.

The Japanese public seemed wholly indifferent to these unseen controllers, but Boon increasingly listened to train announcements with avid attention. On routes that he travelled particularly frequently he came to identify individual voices, distinguished by unmistakable mannerisms, pitch and style of delivery. From some of these voices he gained the impression that a few announcers really enjoyed their job; within the limited scope available they could perform with virtuosity, turning out little masterpieces of cadence and phrasing, quite undeterred by the repetitive and pedestrian nature of their theme.

For a long time Boon's staple diet of announcements was provided by train controllers on the Yamanote line. This had both advantages and disadvantages. It was one of Tokyo's busiest lines, shaped like a wobbly loop, which a train could have kept on going round and round theoretically until the crack of doom. With its intimations of, if not quite immortality, at least a kind of cyclic permanence pleasing to the Buddhist mind, the Yamanote line was appropriately enough the place where old railway staff were put out to grass, contemplating their karma between completion of one lap and resumption of the next. On this famous loop line the veteran train controllers, the old warriors who in the space of forty odd years had literally announced themselves to death, ground out their swan-song. These announcers knew their stuff all right, but they were also the hacks, professionals by habit and not vocation; they no longer had the time or the heart for the frills and fancy bits. The one exception was when pulling into the three great railway terminals on the Yamanote line – Ueno, Shinjuku and Tokyo. More sentimental announcers invariably rose to the occasion, calling out these stirring names in unequivocal tones of rich, full-throated fortissimo. Others preferred a deadpan style. They left it as late as possible, even waiting for several seconds after the microphone had been switched on, giving the impression that they had forgotten the name of the next station or that they were due to make an announcement at all. *Aaaaa . . . . . . Shinjuku . . . . Shinjuku.* Throwaway line, delivered in a drawl. It was gripping stuff.

On the long-distance suburban lines such as the Odakyu-sen a very different type of train controller operated. Unlike the lines in central Tokyo, where the average journey was short and the passenger population constantly turning over, the operators on the long-distance services could be sure that a fair proportion of their clients would be with them to the journey's end. They had what was every entertainer's dream: a captive audience. This provided them with the incentive to develop a much more personal pitch; they could spin it out, play a broad register, confident that its merits would be judged from the performance as a whole. Some of these performances were masterly.

Particularly memorable for Boon was one announcer on a south-bound line that had only recently opened. Boon listened for him in vain during the day; it seemed that he only worked nights. Perhaps this was the time to which personal inclination or specialist training best suited him, for it was at night that passengers were most irritable and sensitive, and this particular announcer's repertoire left Boon in no doubt that he was dealing with a consummate psychotherapist.

The tone of voice seemed to be regulated in accordance with an exact barometer of the atmosphere in the car. It could be chatty but not intrusive, brisk but not hectoring (for example after an unusually long interval between stations, when the announcer judged that there were a number of passengers who needed to be roused from sleep), soothing without ever becoming bland or ingratiating.

Station staff in Tokyo, including those whose unenviable task it was to stand by the train doors during the rush hours in order to shove passengers in, worked under as difficult conditions as could be found anywhere in the world, yet they were probably the most helpful and considerate. They were of course assisted by an equally cooperative and patient public, but their job motivation, their attitude of always doing more than the bare minimum, could only be explained in terms of a remarkable professional ethos.

This was something that appeared to exist everywhere in Japan, and wherever it was in evidence, and however menial the task of the person concerned, it commanded respect. Perhaps the word "respect" missed the mark, as it implied a process of conscious reflection that in practice did not occur. It was taken for granted that wherever people were at work it was always with the intention of providing as complete a service as possible. That in itself, however, already describes an attitude of respect; it shows what high expectations you have of the person and the work concerned. In Japan this sounded self-evident, but in most countries it was very far from being so.

Later on Boon acquired enough knowledge of the country to be able to trace the origins of this professional ethos. He was struck, for example, by the sight of railway staff who walked along the tracks collecting refuse on pointed sticks and who always set about this task wearing white gloves. Boon could think of nothing less practical than white gloves for carrying out such a dirty task; he could make no sense of it until his attention was drawn one day by a woman on the platform who happened to be wearing *tabi*.

Tabi are short white socks (occasionally blue) worn with open sandals as part of traditional Japanese dress, and to Boon's mind, envisaging the filthy condition of the roads at the time when *tabi* had still been in everyday use, just as dotty as the railwayman's gloves. To resolve this question he conferred with Sugama, who in turned referred it to his girlfriend, and at length they came up with an answer. The point about these white socks, it seemed, was precisely that they showed the dirt. Naturally a woman must own many pairs, and these would of course have to be washed very frequently; but a woman's pride and joy was in being able to show a pair of clean white heels and a set of clean white toes whenever she went out, thus giving proof of neat habits, feminine delicacy and (at least in earlier days) a measure of prosperity.

Illustrations of this mentality were carried to Boon from other quarters. In some factories workers were issued with white overalls as part of an ingenious if somewhat fiendish policy to encourage them to acquire (*mi ni cukeru*: literally to attach to the body, i.e. make one's own) careful working habits, to work cleanly. This ruse took some beating. A worker who left his assembly position at the end of the day with spotless overalls must be either very efficient or very lazy.

So what about the railwayman's gloves? Were they also to remind him to work cleanly? Obviously not. But the whiteness of his gloves gave him a wholly unexpected touch of dignity, they dissociated the man from the meanness of his function, the glove itself literally so, the colour symbolically. And more, they drew *attention* to his work. Boon might not have given the man a second glance, or his work a second thought, but for the incongruity of his gloves. This was the kind of detail in which professional ethos resided, and which probably achieved more in the cause of harmonious industrial relations than an entire bureaucracy.

Perhaps the national railways had training programmes for their employees to inculcate the qualities of calm and phlegmatic patience they most needed for their work, for they all seemed remarkably self-possessed. Boon once sat in a train that was held up for ten minutes (in Tokyo not just a delay but a disaster) as railwaymen wrestled on the floor of the car with a violent epileptic. No impatience, no abuse, not even any indication of distaste. Before the stretcher-bearers arrived to carry the man off, one of the staff leaned over him and wiped the effusions from his mouth with a clean handkerchief, which he then replaced, quite unselfconsciously, in his own pocket.

If the odd epileptic or suicide was all in a day's work for railway staff, a much more significant percentage of their working time at night was taken up dealing with drunks. From about nine o'clock in the evening until the railways closed down at one in the morning probably more drunks could be counted on the platforms of Tokyo's several hundred stations than in any other city in the world. Boon knew what he was talking about, because for a year or so he was himself very frequently among them.

Yoi-dore kega sezu – drunkards break no bones. So says one of the innumerable Japanese drinking proverbs, and from his own experience Boon was perfectly satisfied it was true. He once fell off the platform at Oji station, which probably did him more benefit than harm, for it immediately and permanently restored him to his senses. Trains passed in and out of Tokyo's stations every two or three minutes, a calculation that was not lost on Boon.

He was out many nights and he saw all manner of drunks, but never once did he see a Japanese fall off the platform. It was difficult to explain why they did not, unless what was true of most skills applied equally to drinking – early training and constant practice make for mastery. The performance of drunks on platforms was miraculous. A platform ten yards across and often with as much as fifty yards to go to the next exit presented a more formidable challenge to a drunk than a tightrope did to an acrobat. Within this lethal margin Japanese drunks did everything and went everywhere but over the edge, staggering in a series of hair-raising zigzag manoeuvres from one side to the other until they reached the relative safety of the exit. Relative safety, because this was where most accidents usually happened, on the stairs leading down into the street. Just get to the exit, the drunk instinctively told himself, and so it was no further than to the exit that his residual powers of concentration and self-discipline managed to last. Here he disintegrated and gave up the ghost, entrusting his body to the wise discretion of the proverb. The fall might be painful but at least not fatal; and pain, in any case, was an account that would not have to be settled until the following day.

By no means all of Tokyo's stations were transformed into this regular nightly battlefield. One advantage of being rich was that your drunken stupor could be brought on and allowed to pass off in conditions of relative privacy, incoming on the arm of a discreet hostess at your club and outgoing in the arms of a taxi driver, who could be trusted to perform the additional services for which he had additionally been paid. It all went down on expense account anyway. The stations where these same rich men boarded the train in the morning were therefore relatively deserted at night. Boon did not even get a glimpse of this world behind closed doors until he had won his spurs in Tokyo's seedier districts by running the gauntlet of many last-train platforms very many times.

One cluster of these "bad" areas was served by the Keihin Tohoku line, on which the prodigal Boon was often borne back to his native station of Oji in a semi-conscious condition. A lot of Boon's early, less mature drinking was done in the squalid bars of Ikebukuro, and the journey home entailed a change from the Yamanote to the Keihin Tohoku line at Tabata. It was at this station that he once witnessed a classic encounter, illustrating that quality of almost saintly patience he so often had cause to admire, between a member of the national railways staff and a drunk who had to be dislodged from the station premises.

Having missed the last but one train, Boon was now having to wait ten minutes or so to catch the last, and he was able to follow this memorable episode from beginning to end. Enter left, from the staff room in mid-platform, a bright young signalman in his twenties. He carried out the series of routine checks that were standard practice before closing up for the night (Boon knew the movements although he could not name the parts), looking up and down the platform a couple of times to make sure that nobody was about to fall off. His eye came to rest on a prone figure stretched out on a platform bench close to where Boon was standing.

The signalman approached the bench and quizzed the recumbent figure with his flashlight. Step number one. No response whatsoever. Step number two. Solicit the attention of the subject in a firm tone of voice, but do not yet touch. *Ne, okyakusan, sore wa dame da yo*, or similar words (usually these), to be repeated several times and with increasing sternness should this be necessary (the formula could be translated as "Come on, this won't do, you know" – the tone was as mild as that). The figure still lay on the bench ominously inert, and at this point it evidently occurred to the signalman that his honoured customer (*okyakusan*) might have passed out.

Putting his flashlight down onto the platform, he started patting the man's cheeks with the flat of his hand, continuing for about half a minute, until eventually the figure stirred and gave a faint groan. Then he grasped the man by the shoulders, sat him upright on the bench and lowered his head between his knees.

"Where are you going, then? Where d'you live?"

No reply. The man groaned and coughed and suddenly vomited between his parted knees, spattering his shoes and the insides of his trouser-legs. The signalman stepped adroitly aside, his hand still grasping the man's shoulder, reproaching him in the same set of phrases which he repeated over and again, but gently, almost as if he were talking to a child. When the man had recovered somewhat the signalman again asked him "Where are you going?"

"Dunno . . ."

"What, you don't know? Come off it!"

And so it went on. The man repeated that he didn't know where he was going and couldn't remember where he lived. The signalman said this was nonsense, a man couldn't forget where he lived, that he ought to be ashamed of himself, getting so drunk that he couldn't even say where he was going. By the time the last train arrived the man still didn't know where he was going, but having cajoled him back into, if not sobriety, at least a condition in which he could talk and more or less stand, the signalman bundled him into the train notwithstanding. Boon got off a couple of stops later, so he never knew what eventually happened to the man, who had fallen into a cataleptic sleep the moment he sat down.

After days of wandering on foot and interminable train rides through the arid metropolitan landscape Boon had gained the impression that Tokyo was not so much a city as a dense cluster of urban villages. He missed the occasional open spaces, the parks, squares and avenues typical of European capitals. In many quarters the streets were so narrow that cars could barely pass, residential and industrial areas sprawled indiscriminately into one another, jostling for space. Tokyo had little to offer the conventional sightseer. It was an ugly city which took great care to keep its attractions hidden.

Disappointed by the dismal panorama of the city as a whole, Boon began to suspect that he might be looking at it in the wrong way, judging it by standards that did not apply. And he recalled an incident that he had experienced about a week after his arrival.

He had seen an old lady kneeling by the side of the road, cleaning out the gutter in front of her house. As he passed by he noticed to his astonishment that she carried out this task with a pair of chopsticks. Most Japanese would themselves have regarded this use of chopsticks as eccentric, but the scrupulous attention to detail which it demonstrated would probably have gone without comment. On Boon it left a lasting impression. Discarding those large-scale expectations which the city failed to live up to, he set about exploring Tokyo with the old lady's chopsticks. He ignored the general and searched for the particular, in time discovering that for the loss of a spectacular urban panorama he was richly compensated by an inexhaustible fund of detail. It was a city made interesting solely by its people, customs and the terrific vitality of its street life.

Echoes and shadows. After Boon had been precipitated by Ichimonji into the steamy life of the water trade his Japanese suddenly flowered. He began to understand patterns and trace contours in the map of the language which until now he had acquired piecemeal and quite arbitrarily. He learned, as his first and most important lesson, the astronomy of the many satellite words and elliptical sounds which circumscribed the primary matter of the Japanese sentence without apparent meaning or purpose. No reference to this cosmology was to be found in the handbooks; it could only be gleaned from the style of discourse and casual remarks, having nothing to do with the subject of the lesson, of those who purported to be his Japanese instructors. Diffuse, arcane, and thoroughly misleading as this cosmology was, it still provided the only approach to the language: crab-wise, by a combination of intuition and divine stealth.

Before learning to speak he must acquire the art of the preamble, tentative, oblique, hedging his bets, and before the preamble a palate of anticipatory sounds indicating agreement, encouragement, surprise, doubt, boredom, attention, excitement, discouragement and disagreement, or whatever the pre-speech posture required. The wealth of these speech initiation sounds compensated for the relative poverty of the body language of the Japanese. They possessed an extensive sign language or code, but those spontaneous gestures which accompany speech, the movement of the hands and facial muscles in particular, were usually absent from conversation. The same results were achieved by a judicious regulation of wind and vocal pitch, sounds which conveyed attitudes or moods rather than meaning.

These sounds usually prefaced one's own attempts at speech, but they were equally important when promoting the speech of others, a technique known as *aizuchi*, borrowed from the forge, meaning to strike the anvil in turns. The reason for producing these agreeable chimes, coaxing or prompting a reluctant speaker, could probably be sought in the caution and self-effacement of the Japanese, whose use of speech in many situations would approximate about as close to silence as it is possible for a talking man to do. They appeared to mistrust eloquence. Men who were naturally fluent cultivated rhetorical penury, a shambling, diffident mode of speech, as the best recommendation for integrity and shrewd judgement. Careers are made, Boon was once advised by a senior executive, by men who have learned to keep their mouth shut. This kind of mentality clearly had little use for body language. The raised eyebrow, the wagging finger, the face as a book where men may read strange matters, all this would be far too explicit, disturbing that delicate balance of ambiguities essential to the speech posture of the Japanese. A sound still inside one's own body at the back of the throat, lips closed or barely parted, was less intrusive than the manifest hand which violates unseen borders and changes without warning the spatial configurations in which the speakers are arranged.

Boon ignored these sounds at his peril, for they contained information, hints rather than statements, which would not be given elsewhere. He was accepted as a speaker of Japanese only as he became, to his own ears, progressively inarticulate. By personal choice and cultural prejudice he believed in speaking to the point where his own language was concerned; and as a beginner at Japanese, struggling to communicate and grateful to be understood at all, he was left with no other option anyway. In many cases, of course, he had been misunderstood, even when his sentence, at least by the textbook, seemed irreproachable. It would elicit a reaction he had not expected. This was because the Japanese ear instinctively sought the meaning of a statement in the medium through which it had been filtered; they apprehended the significance of what had been said from how it had been said. Allowances were made for foreigners, but this making of allowances introduced a factor which was fundamentally at variance with the natural speech habits of the Japanese, like playing a game of cards while showing one's hand, thus confusing the issue still further.

Sentences which the Japanese broached with these demonstrative, low-content sounds might frequently end with a conjunction. Boon first registered this practice when he saw it in print. "Perhaps I'll be able to make it next weekend but." Not a dash or a series of dots but an unequivocal full stop. "But", "however", were the words most commonly used in this way, with conjunctions of time putting in an occasional appearance. In literary Japanese one could also often find sentences that closed with the particle introducing the object, omitting the verb. He had some trouble understanding such sentences until he realised that they were only apparently, or according to his own understanding of grammar, incomplete. They provided the rhetorical disclaimer, that retracting device without which no incomplete Japanese sentence is complete. A high percentage of spoken sentences were of this kind, their open-ended structure providing a logical analogy to the reticence and ambiguity which the speaker displayed physically and his sound-words semantically. It was all of a piece – and very much of a piece.

The result was often just what one would expect – a hopeless muddle. At first Boon debited lack of clarity to his own inexperience; his ears were not yet attuned. But after a couple of years, when he had acquired a more than competent understanding of the language, he saw that lack of clarity was an objective fact of the language, or at least of the use of it, reflecting an endemic Japanese belief in the expediency of being devious, in the value very generally of allowing things to remain implicit rather than making oneself clear and taking responsibility for whatever consequences were incurred.

Boon's attention was first alerted during a conversation with a young man whom he met casually in a restaurant. Apart from this man and himself the place was empty. In the course of their elementary and quite harmless conversation an exchange occurred which Boon thought distinctly odd at the time.

Boon: (Have you got) any brothers and sisters?

Man: Do you mean me? (Touching his nose).

Boon: Well, there's nobody else in here (laughter from Boon, not shared by young man).

As he had been asking this man questions about himself for several minutes leading up to this exchange and could not possibly have been asking him about anybody other than himself, the question "Do you mean me?", popping out at him as if he had inadvertently released the spring in a Jack-in-a-box, rather startled Boon. What sort of blunt instrument was this?

Perhaps the young man was neurotic or deaf. Boon made a note of the matter in his book of curiosities and forgot about it until some six months later, by which time he had heard the same rhetorical question put to him in similar situations by dozens of people, men and women, young and old alike. Clearly all these people were not neurotic or deaf. He found that the response was most often elicited when they had been asked a personal question, invited to state their own preference or to give an opinion on some matter that was still under discussion. In such cases they were really playing the game of sound-words, here disguised as a question, behind which one could detect a reluctance that in other cultures might have been expressed by shuffling one's feet or blowing one's nose. They had been singled out, and for whatever reason it made them feel self-conscious.

The framing of questions in Japanese was an art, an instrument to be handled with great delicacy and care. A direct question at an untimely moment could prove very destructive, merely by virtue of its directness. Direct questions (with obvious exceptions in professional, business life and so on) were not much liked. The typical question was really a feed line, what in a court of law would be disqualified as suggestive, full of loop-holes, offering escape-hatches, and in fact as unlike a question as it was possible to be. The person who had been asked the question could thus be indicted on no more serious charge than of aiding and abetting the person who had asked the question; an accessory to the answer, as it were, not the principal malefactor. He had merely *conspired* to answer.

Somewhere in the more remote, archaic regions of the Japanese soul there must have been an uneasy feeling that when you asked a person a question you were somehow putting him on the spot. It was only fair then to try and make it as discreet, as painless as possible. He had been challenged to emerge and declare himself, and this was a disservice, for few Japanese willingly detached themselves from the symbiosis of the collective in which they lived and had their being. The fact that in roughly sixty percent of spoken Japanese sentences the subject was omitted could also perhaps be accounted for in similar terms; but, as Boon was later to discover, there were other, more complex reasons for this characteristic of the language.

In idiomatic Japanese statements of feeling and conjecture were often qualified by such phrases as *nantonaku, nantomoienai*, – "I just think/I somehow have the feeling". Professions of not knowing or not being able to say were commonly to be heard from people who did not want to say what they knew, but they received a sympathetic hearing despite or perhaps precisely for that reason.

The tentative, self-effacing, ambiguous use of language was known in Japanese as *aimai*. It enjoyed a certain tradition. Throughout two hundred and fifty years of autocratic rule under the Tokugawa shogunate (1603–1867) and no doubt in the centuries of civil war preceding Ieyasu, the first Tokugawa shogun, who enforced the peace his successors consolidated, life was in general short and violent, but probably less short and less violent for those who, like Boon's executive, learned expediency and kept their mouth shut. There was no shortage of Japanese proverbs testifying to the advantages of silence; the naturally voluble man was squeezed from two sides, by draconian laws reminding the civilian population to keep a civil tongue in its head and by the example of the warrior caste, noted for its taciturnity and sangfroid. The ideal was still relevant in modern Japan, the spirit by no means quenched. Sayings such as "a defeated warrior does not speak" or epigrams like *sannen kata-ho*, meaning that a warrior should not allow himself to show emotion more than once in three years, were quoted to Boon with approval, not frequently, but often enough to show that they were still knocking around in Japanese heads.

This explanation of *aimai* was the one always offered Boon. Historically, it was true, the Japanese had not enjoyed the advantages of free speech, without restriction and over a sustained period, until after the Second World War; and perhaps that was their own fault. In a society where it could be dangerous to express oneself unequivocally, so the argument ran, the genius of the Japanese language had responded with *aimai*, a means of communication which allowed one to understand and be understood without ever being explicit. Boon's chief objection to this was that although the feudal system and later (less repressive) social containment which the argument identified as the underlying cause of *aimai* had long since ceased to exist, the phenomenon of *aimai* itself had not. Eighteen-year-olds talked less circumstantially, but on occasion could be just as ambiguous as their parents, who themselves, in many cases, could have been only marginally exposed to the influences of a repressive political climate in the years before the war.

A more subtle and for Boon the fundamental explanation of *aimai* could be derived from a remark made by the psychologist Okonogi Keigo in a discussion of *haji*, the Japanese concept of shame. "*Haji* is the characteristic feeling of people who are dependent on a group, taking the form of a vague fear of rumour, gossip, of possible ostracism. In the day to day life of people who are sensitive to this kind of shame the essential thing is accordingly *not to express oneself unequivocally*." There were still groups in modern Japan – specialised trade guilds, for example, or the *yakuza* who ran the underworld – whose use of language could be not merely equivocal but unintelligible. These groups had developed their own argot, like the Cockneys in London or gypsies anywhere, for a reason which applied equally if less obviously to the Japanese population as a whole: in order not to be understood by outsiders. The source of *aimai* lay here.

The common Japanese term for outsider was *tanin* (literally, another person) or occasionally *yoso no hito/mono* (person from another place). The neutral meaning, therefore, corresponded to the English word "stranger", a person of different blood or who comes from different parts, but the unmistakable hostility with which the use of *tanin* was infused in the Japanese language made the factual description (stranger) indistinguishable from the moral judgement (outsider). He was the person outside the *uchi* (loosely, household), a social unit originally constituted by relationships of blood or a common locality, but also covering any group of persons brought together physically and spiritually in a common cause, typically their work. All Japanese were members of various *uchi*, ranging from their own immediate family to the firm in which they were employed. In very simple terms, members of one's own *uchi* were familiar, trustworthy and above question; inversely, those who did not belong to the same *uchi* were unfamiliar, their trust untried, and therefore faintly suspect. In short, it was not the outsider as a possible Tokugawa spy who was suspect; it was the outsider *per se*. This seam of thought ran through the entire structure of Japanese society.

It was Boon's impression that the Japanese subtly regulated their use of language according to the particular insider-outsider constellation which happened to prevail. He regarded the courtesy language which was adopted between rival *uchi* as itself a form of *aimai*. Courtesy language was not entirely devoid of content; the incantation of some time-honoured formula, the circumspect phrases, the studied avoidance of sensitive areas, this itself conveyed a message; namely, that one wished to take a conciliatory attitude. The main concern in exchanges between outsiders was to neutralise any potential conflict, *butsukaranai yo ni*, "taking care not to clash", as they constantly reminded themselves. It struck Boon that this very concern gave testimony of a deep-rooted suspicion that such conflict could and did very frequently occur. Underlying the apparent conviviality and polite effusions there would be on both sides a keen awareness of their separate group identity, and therewith the seed of discord. Indirectly, in fact, by a rather circuitous route, the deployment of courtesy language was more likely to reinforce one's own group consciousness and solidarity with the *uchi* than to promote understanding of one's common interests.

A second form of *aimai* comprised the use of language within the *uchi*. To any outsider who happened to be listening, insider talk would often be unclear, occasionally impenetrable, but for fellow insiders it was telegraphic, communication by omission. A very common example was the use of demonstrative pronouns, notably *are* (that). It was possible to carry on quite long conversations without openly referring to the persons, objects or events in question; unless he had already been let in on the secret, the casual eavesdropper would go away none the wiser. In the sound-travelling world of *fusuma* and *shoji* there were cogent reasons for the evolution of this kind of speech. More generally, language supplied yet another application of the truth that the *uchi*'s corporate sense of belonging depended as much on a capacity to exclude outsiders as on any intrinsic unity of its members.

When confronted with Boon the *uchi* which the Japanese represented became their nation and the insider language they used was Japanese itself, which in the context of a foreigner could now serve as shield and barrier. Hence the dramatic, the unfailing consternation when the foreigner turned out to be able to speak that language; the defences were suddenly dropped down. Boon often stopped someone on the street and asked him the way. Such people, accosted by a foreigner, sometimes failed to register that he was speaking to them in Japanese. *They did not hear.* They even struggled bravely to find English words. Confronted with a foreign face, they did not recognise their own language, as if momentarily they had been disabled by some kind of neurological short-circuit.

In part Boon attributed the notorious inability of the Japanese to speak foreign languages to a deeply-engrained perception of language as a means of retention and exclusion rather than as release and expression. Language can have two functions, to say and not to say. The relative importance attached to these functions depends upon the values of the culture as a whole, of which language is only a part. So far as Japan's traditional culture was concerned, the function of not saying, of leaving implicit, open-ended, obscure, enjoyed as honoured a place in classical aesthetics as did ideals of abstinence and self-negation in the Japanese soul. But students of a foreign language do not have the option of strategic vacillation, of artfully keeping suspended; the function of not saying is already a mark of linguistic expertise. They can only blunder out, hoping for the best, where angels fear to tread; and this is against every instinct of a people whose inalienable perception of speech has been conditioned by a protective insider language.

Only after longer exposure to Japanese did Boon begin to appreciate what a formulaic language it was. In any language, he realised, not only Japanese, formulaic expressions most frequently occurred in two kinds of situation: broadly, commencement and termination. The arrival of a guest or a letter, telephone calls, intrusions, the resumption of things laid aside, and, less obviously, attitudes adopted for the purpose of initiating something, for example a request, a command, a hypothesis and so on, could all be regarded as forms of commencement. Conversely, any kind of departure, farewell, attitudes adopted for the concluding of something, such as an apology, a refusal, an admission and so on, could be regarded as forms of termination. Frequently they might overlap, needless to say.

Although the use of formulaic expression in Japanese shared some resemblances with established idiom in European languages, i.e. was not so different in kind, it was very different in degree. This was apparent in the much greater strictness of, the almost verbatim adherence to speech formulae, and in the frequency of their occurrence, the manner in which they dictated speech habits and took over whole tracts of language which in Europe were still wild and where an individual could hunt as he pleased. It required an unusually vigorous and independent mind to bypass these conventional speech patterns, stockpiled to meet every conceivable situation in daily life. There were interesting parallels Boon sometimes felt tempted to draw between fixed speech and shared thought habits. The concensus about the Japanese state and nation, economy, language, culture and so on that emerged from his casual interviews with the inmates of Tokyo's bars struck him as uncanny. These people were not giving him an opinion; they were repeating a formula.

Boon's study of speech patterns in domestic life benefited from stays in several *uchi*, and through television he was given access to several hundred more. Phrases which at first caught his fancy later returned to become the plague of his life as a translator. It was often quite a riddle-me-ree business. A person leaving his house, for example, would pronounce *itte kimasu!* (I go and come), eliciting the gnostic response *itte 'rasshai!* (Then go and come), which a cynic might say only served him right. Someone's return to the house was heralded with the cry *tadaima!* (Just, – presumably a contraction of "I have just got back"), to which the inmates replied in laconic chorus *o-kaeri nasai!* (Return!), in a language which reminded Boon more of prayer than command. Something akin to prayer was indeed in the woof and warp of these runic sayings.

No alternatives were available. For someone leaving and returning to his house it was either these words or none at all, and in Boon's experience it was not just some people who sometimes said them but all people always. This struck him as very remarkable.

He spent a lot of time studying the textbooks used in primary school for Japanese instruction. The formulaic nature of the language was very much in evidence here. Among other things children were taught how to write letters. A letter should never begin with oneself but with an enquiry into the health and general well-being of its recipient. Then there followed a remark about the weather. For each season and even month a set phrase was provided. Boon came across these same phrases, or very similar ones, in letters written by representatives of three generations; and the fourth, very clearly, was now on its way. Only after these overtures had been dutifully completed was it considered proper to broach the real subject of the letter. The same applied to telephone enquiries and responses. As with letters, there would be no variation from established use of language until the real purpose of the call had been broached.

There was an element of superstition in this use of language, which Boon had hitherto only noticed in dead languages such as Anglo Saxon and Latin. Relics of archaicism, of course, are to be found in all languages. Goodbye is archaic, and so is any liturgy; speech which has become fossilised, which has acquired its power or nourished a belief in its power as a result of unvarying repetition over many centuries: speech with talismanic properties. It was Boon's impression, however, that the function of language as prophylaxis and invocation characterised Japanese on a much grander scale.

When the emperor made his famous broadcast announcing the capitulation of the Japanese at the end of the war his speech was unintelligible to the majority of his people. The special use of language evolved for the imperial family, of what might be termed imperial *aimai*, was grounded in the belief that a form of speech so removed from the language of his common subjects as to be virtually impenetrable was a proper symbol of the emperor's inaccessibility. Sustained euphemism making up a distinct language, isolating the emperor from verbal contamination, supplied a clear example of the superstitious use of words.

There were things which analysis should not presume to explore. The too rational approach was frequently disparaged as *rikutsuppoi*, or "smacking too much of a logic that ignores reality". When Boon once inquired if there were any particular reason why male and female students usually sat apart in the university canteen he was answered with a proverb. "Boys and girls over the age of seven mustn't be allowed to share the same seat." That was why, he was told, but in effect this meant no more than that they did so because traditionally they had always done so. This was a characteristic Japanese answer, identifying a precedent as a cause, following an established feeling rather than "a logic that ignores reality".

The formulaic use of language, a superstitious belief in the power of words, a declared trust in intuitive feeling and distaste for the logic that ignores reality: what was then this ultimate reality which superstition sought to appease, which only feeling could discern and with which logic was allegedly unable to cope? Boon decided that an answer to this question would have to allow for the unpredictability and violence of the natural conditions under which the inhabitants of the Japanese islands had always lived.

The climate was not at all accommodating, with extremes that compared unfavourably with most civilised parts of the world. In more recent times the worst of summer humidity and winter cold had been relieved by modern technology, but no technology would ever contain the arbitrary destruction caused by earthquakes, floods and typhoon. Boon's housing-estate, the spectacular, almost defiant skyscrapers in Shinjuku, had been built to withstand the frequent tremors and occasional severer quakes, but only time would tell whether these buildings would stand or fall under the impact of a second Great Kanto Earthquake. The Japanese themselves remained, for the most part, phlegmatic but doubtful; some of them, like Sugama's great-aunt, more doubtful than phlegmatic.

Because of the volatile world in which they lived the Japanese traditionally built in wood rather than stone and continued to do so right up until the Second World War. Wooden structures had the disadvantage of collapsing easily, but the advantage of being more easily rebuilt. A volatile world is also an inflammable world. More severe earthquakes were accompanied by fire which could turn whole towns into holocausts; the wooden houses burning like funeral pyres, their inhabitants roasted. Buildings which escaped fire succumbed more gradually to erosion. Wood naturally draws moisture, and the humid Japanese summers accelerated the process. Temples, pagodas, imperial villas, all were made of wood: the monuments rotted or were razed to the ground. Japan was thus left with few original monuments to demonstrate the historical standing of its culture.

One could speculate that a people so completely exposed to an environment unpredictable only in the length of the intervals between one act of destruction and another should seek continuity and permanence in forms more likely to remain inviolable. One such form was an aesthetic, later fashioned by Buddhism, which drew its vital inspiration from the discontinuity and impermanence of its native world, *ukiyo*, a transient, ephemeral world. Without labour of paradox notions of constancy derived naturally from the constancy of change, eternity from the copious, fugitive instant. Nature was indeed a Heraclitean fire, not by the edict of aloof philosophy but as a matter of plain common sense. Was it this common vulnerability that had given Japanese society its egalitarian cast? Fire, flood and earthquake were the great natural levellers, and perhaps the disintegration of feudalism and the devolution of power were unleashed later rather than sooner partly because of the community of mind these natural levellers had long since shaped.

According to Ono Susumu in his book *Nihongo no nenrin* (The year-rings of the Japanese language) the inhabitants of the country which two thousand years ago was known as Yamato had originally not known any word for nature. The term *shizen* was only later imported from China. The fact that there was no word for nature, Ono argued, justified one in assuming that there was no very clear concept of it either. In the Japanese understanding, nature had never constituted a discrete entity "out there", something to which man stood in opposition, but the world in its entirety, embracing all things, organic and inorganic alike, a great symbiosis of which man was an inseparable part. Despite their reckless invasion of the natural environment in the twentieth century the Japanese still cherished this view of man-in-nature with feelings akin to reverence. It was strikingly epitomised by a remark, quoted in Tanaka Yasumasa's *Gendai Nihonjin no ishiki* (The consciousness of contemporary Japanese), to the effect that man at work in the rice fields seemed "less like an animal than a plant endowed with reason".

The people of Yamato feared their violent natural world, and from this fear evolved respect. Nature was the prime mover, nature itself set in motion what nature was, through the agency of the verb *naru*, meaning "to become". Expressions of respect for the actions of others, on a direct analogy to this fundamental respect for events in the natural world, combined *naru* with other verbs: arrive-become, depart-become and so on. The semantic element of becoming, contained in the suffix *-ru*, could likewise be attached to common verbs, for example *nasu – nasaru*, meaning "to do". These forms of courtesy language, originating in a reverence for the power of the natural world, survived intact in modern Japanese usage.

In this way actions needing respectful treatment came to be

described as actions which "naturally occurred". The onus of sentences reporting such actions without specifying the agent would accordingly appear to lie less on the person responsible for the action than on the manner of its occurrence. In the terms of a *Weltanschauung* which endorsed the view of man-in-nature rather than man-and-nature, an attempt to isolate the one from the other by clearly identifying the instigator of an action in a syntactically discrete subject would seem paradoxical, perhaps incomprehensible. The suspension of subjects that was such a profound characteristic of the Japanese language might thus be regarded as proceeding inevitably from the integration of man and nature, of man's actions and self-moving natural occurrences.

Whether in the origins of courtesy language, the stealthy appropriation of intuited but unnamed natural powers as the implicit begetter of man's actions; in the suspension of subjects and objects, allowing the agent to be no more than *inferred* from verbs with qualifying functions; in the frequent use of demonstrative pronouns, typical of *aimai*, to stand in for absentee nouns, or in those many unfinished sentences which the listener was left to extrapolate, it seemed to be a fundamental characteristic of the Japanese way of expression to take as its point of reference something that was not itself there but only by implication: the echo, not the sound, the shadow, not the light.

Such at least was Boon's impression, the impression of a foreigner, an outsider. Perhaps the Japanese themselves heard those sounds and saw those lights which for him would always remain inaccessible. If so, their language supplied powerful evidence of a mutual understanding that subsisted beyond the use of words.

Dragon country. The sheaf of rice-paper which Boon had purchased at a shop near Shinbashi station on the evening he met Ichimonji accompanied him a week later on his second visit to his calligraphy teacher, Suzuki Kazuko. Under her stern eyes he negligently took the envelope out of his portfolio and placed it face up on the table, complete with the patchwork of ribald inscriptions which Ichimonji had penned for him under the Sign of the Crane in the reckless hours before dawn. Hastily he transferred the envelope to the floor, but Suzuki-*san* had already seen and understood, conveying her disapproval by a slight compression of her lips.

Boon had originally sought out a calligraphy teacher in order to discipline his erratic, crab-like hand, but he soon found that the strokes, points and spatial composition of the characters he laboriously began to copy exerted a fascination entirely for their own sake. They were not mere letters, the flat, inert transcriptions of sounds; they were living things. Sprawled across hoardings, rampant in the snarled vertical folds of cloth signs flagging the narrow streets, they reminded Boon of dragons and he regarded them with awe. His teacher Suzuki Kazuko was accordingly the dragon-slayer, and his first visit to her house in Nakano a foray into dragon country.

The appearance of the large *tatami* room, bare of all ornament and furnished with no more than a low black lacquered table, was certainly austere but by no means forbidding. Here, every Saturday afternoon, Suzuki Kazuko taught Boon and other small children the abstruse art of calligraphy for a fee of two thousand yen per month, to be paid in advance. Sometimes the children would arrive as Boon left, sometimes they did their exercises together, and on these occasions their teacher showed herself capable of dealing with two or three embryonic dragons all at the same time. With a careless ease that Boon envied, seven year-old children produced dragons of great natural splendour, but none of them satisfied the dragon-slayer and they were consigned ignominiously to the waste-paper basket.

On Boon's first visit he was received by Suzuki Kazuko alone. Dressed completely in black, with jet-black hair, she knelt at the glossy lacquered table in the centre of the eight-mat room, her hands in her lap and eyes fixed on the floor, withheld in a dark pre-scriptural trance, an attitude of concentrated repose, from which Boon's entry into the room abruptly released her. Somehow he felt the need for an apology.

"I hope I haven't come too early . . ."

"Oh no!"

Suzuki-*san* smiled brightly and ran her fingers over the polished table. "How are you? And Nakamura-*san*? Is he well too?"

Nakamura was the friend who had arranged their introduction. Suzuki-*san* invited Boon to sit down opposite her, and after they had chatted for a couple of minutes she produced a black plastic case and pushed it over to him.

"I bought this case for you. It contains everything you will need to begin with. And – well, I thought we'd start by going through the names of the things we shall be using."

She opened the case and took out a large brush.

"All brushes used for calligraphy are called *fude*. There are all kinds and all sizes, but for the time being we shall be using only two: a small one, the *kofude*, and a large one, the *ofude*."

Suzuki-*san* spoke the word and held up the object she was naming in front of her eyes. Inserting her forefinger into the loop attached to the base of the bamboo shaft, she dangled the *ofude* between them, bushy tip down, and invited Boon to touch it.

"The tip of the brush is surprisingly hard, isn't it," she said.

"Shouldn't it be?"

"Later, you see, when you dip the brush into the *sumi* and knead the tip until it is moist it will gradually become soft. A good brush, depending upon the skill with which it is used, possesses both hardness and softness. In this way you can achieve contrasts, balance . . ."

Suzuki-*san* laid the brush down and asked Boon to repeat what she had said. In the cold air of the room a perfume, or the natural scent of her body, began to warm and unwrinkle, like melting frost.

Then she showed him the *sumi*-stick, coal-black and three inches long, looking like a chunk of sealing wax or solidified resin; and the smooth slate-like inkstone with a trough at one end into which she poured a dash of water. Moistening one end of the resin stick she began to rub it against the inkstone with steady, unhurried movements, lubricating the stone with a sprinkle of water whenever the stick jarred. After a short while the surface of the inkstone began to dissolve under the abrasion of the stick; coagulating with the fine dark grain of the inkstone, the water gradually thickened, pricked with tiny glistening bubbles, into the dense black fluid called *sumi*, blacker than any substance Boon had ever seen.

"What I am doing is called *sumi o suru*," said the young woman softly.

"When will the consistency be right?"

"It is right."

"But you still go on. How long should one go on?"

"Until the heart becomes quiet."

After a minute or two she laid down the *sumi*-stick, took out a piece of felt, a sheet of paper and a bronze paperweight. She placed the felt on the table, arranged the paper square in the middle and weighted it at the top. Boon was startled by the sudden whiteness of the paper. The case, the felt, the resin stick, inkstone and *sumi*, Suzuki-*san*'s hair, even her sleeves resting on the table – everything else was black. Greyish, jet-black, grained matt, glossy: a conspiracy of shades of black.

It was very still in the room, from the street outside only a faint murmur.

Arm outstretched, she held the brush poised over the paper for a second and then plunged it down like a sword. Moist, fat, black, lustrous in the instant but still spreading perceptibly, even after her hand had passed on, as the ink soaked into the fibre of the paper, suddenly all kinds of forms started up out of the whiteness in front of her: the woken dragons snarled. She wrote like a woman in her sleep, her hand moving with magical certainty, as if it had merely to trace the shapes that were already latent in the paper in order to make them apparent on its surface. Lines as straight and clear as pure sound, the slabby joints and hinges of the characters where the brush turned in its own damp track and swung down into the vertical; gnarls, loops, and sometimes a breathless emptiness, the brush skimming the paper as a stone leaps water, leaving no trace. All these forms to Boon were sounds, and it did not occur to him that they also had meaning. Nevertheless Suzuki-*san* asked him if he were able to read what she had written.

"I'm afraid not."

"It's an old saying . . ."

Placing the sheet on the floor beside her, she took out a fresh piece of paper.

"You know the *kana*, don't you?"

"Yes," said Boon.

"Well, we shall only be using *hiragana* here. Once you have mastered the *hiragana* we can go on to the characters. Then it becomes a question of composition. But the basic technique, brushstroke and so on, which you will acquire as you learn *hiragana*, applies equally to the writing of *kanji*. So one ought not to hurry at the beginning. The *hiragana* are the foundation of *shodo*."

Beside the more common Chinese characters, or *kanji*, as they were called, Boon had also been required to learn the two *kana* syllabaries, *hiragana* and *katakana*, consisting of forty-seven letters apiece. *Kana* were the contracted forms of characters that had gradually been systematised and developed into a phonetic syllabary much like any other alphabet. *Katakana* were used less frequently than *kanji* and *hiragana*, but all three scripts were indispensable for even elementary Japanese writing.

"And do you know the order in which they come?"

"Vaguely. It begins *i ro ha* . . ."

"Then we shall take those three first today. Just those three."

In her teacher's red ink Suzuki-*san* swiftly executed the three forms and spread them out on the table for him to copy. It looked quite easy. Meanwhile Boon plied the *sumi*-stick vigorously back and forth, watching the dark *sumi* well up out of the inkstone and waiting for his heart to become quiet.

But his heart refused to become quiet. For whatever reason, it knocked around terribly inside him, shying and rearing like a startled animal. He spent an hour spoiling good paper and returned home chastened.

The sheaf of rice-paper he had bought in Shinbashi would not be nearly enough to practise the three symbols. In the kitchen he unearthed a pile of newspapers as high as his knee, quality newspaper on coarse material whose texture was similar to the cheaper brands of paper used for *shodo*. Settling down on the *tatami* he immersed himself in newspapers and ink for two hours that evening and every evening throughout the following week.

Once or twice in an hour he could produce a form with a tolerable resemblance to the model which Suzuki-*san* had turned out in thirty seconds, but he never knew beforehand when this would happen. It was a fluke. Once or twice was not enough, not even eight times out of ten was competence, and real skill lay far, far beyond that. At even a basic level *shodo* demanded nothing less than unbreached consistency. Neither more nor less gifted with a brush than the average person, Boon would probably require at least a year of regular daily practice in order to approach such consistency. In fact for as long as he remained in Japan Boon never really embarked on the superior Way of Writing (*shodo*) but kept company with its poor relation *shuji*, meaning simply the Practice of Letters.

And that was exactly what it was. Boon practised not in order to become a master but to be able to claim familiarity, to acquire a taste for and therewith some understanding of a form of art which lay completely outside the terms of reference of European culture. The word "calligraphy" was merely a convenience of translation for the controlled explosions on paper which occurred in true *shodo*. All decorative function, ideas of the smooth, pleasing composition that does not jerk the eye, were alien to the aesthetics of *shodo*.

As a foreigner, new to the line and curve of the Japanese script, Boon lacked the essential precondition for *shodo*: sleepwalking, unconscious familiarity with the letters he was shaping. This lack of familiarity with the forms of letters could be compared to the differences between Japanese and European music. Boon had been trained as a singer when he was a boy, and he did not have much difficulty whistling or humming correctly any tune he heard. The harmonics of traditional Japanese music, however, were quite unfamiliar to him; it surprised him to find how hard it was to learn folk songs accurately or reproduce even quite simple melodies. He discovered that his ear was as prejudiced as his eye, hand or any other sense organ.

That apart, nightly practice of *shuji* on the *tatami* floor acquainted him with two basic principles: pressure of the brush, and rhythm of the hand between those moments when the brush was actually touching the paper. One might even say that the "bloom" of *shodo* emerged not from the apparent shapes but from the white spaces they left on the paper. In *shodo* as in all Japanese art this shaping of the negative form, the suggesting of enclosures and continuous lines by ostensibly unrelated parts, was characteristic and important. It could likewise be detected in everyday attitudes and the use of language, as Boon had already discovered.

Boon's first letter, the *i* which he had begun to practise, was a good example of the two principles. The symbol consisted of two separate, approximately parallel diagonal strokes. The tip of the brush had to strike the paper softly but full-on, broadside as it were, allowing the whole body of the brush to rest momentarily on the surface of the paper and creating an initial line at an angle of forty-five degrees to the top of the paper. Almost simultaneously with the impact the brush was gradually retracted as it was drawn downwards, until towards the base of the stroke only the tip of the brush was feathering the paper. At this point the line would be roughly half its width at the top, curving gently at first and then sharply down to the right. Again the body of the brush was brought to bear fully on the paper and swept vigorously up towards the right, relaxing the pressure so as to finish on a sharp point. Here the brush left the paper, having drawn a shape roughly similar to a capital L whose base is not horizontal but diagonal, at an angle of about forty-five degrees to the vertical.

The suspended brush continued to draw an invisible upward diagonal in the direction of the top right-hand corner of the page, until its tip again just pricked the surface of the paper and pulled firmly down, the full brush splayed. The brush was finally retracted from the page by doubling the tip back upwards into the line it had already drawn. When the *sumi* had dried, this overlap, the down-up of the brush, was naturally darker than the rest of the stroke in which it was contained and could be seen clearly. The finished stroke resembled an inverted comma, slim at the top and broad at the base.

Attenuation of line, variation between the flat body of the brush and its tip, were the stock-in-trade of the *shodo* artist's technique. Accomplished calligraphists performed with the arm fully extended, but Boon's hand was not steady enough to do that; unless his forearm were supported by his left hand it began to waver. This posture was more typical of a rather delicate task, such as the painting of miniatures or ceramics. It was a cautious posture, and Boon felt that this already disqualified him, for caution had no part in *shodo*. Beyond the discipline and concentration one would naturally have expected, *shodo* also called upon resources or qualities that were less obvious. The moment the calligraphist set his brush to the page he was committing himself to something hazardous. However good he might be he was always taking a risk. He had to be bold, he must have moral courage. Boon accepted the truth of this partly because it coincided with his own experience and, more importantly, because it was only within such terms of reference that the profound respect, even awe, extended to the *shodo* artist, and the ethical claims made on behalf of *shodo* could be properly appreciated.

At this time Boon still had no inkling of the breadth and resonance of *shodo*. For him it was largely the sensual friction of contrasts, black and white, wet-dry, hard-soft. The dark illicit sexuality with which *shodo* was flush, the rampant brush spilling onto the page, all this had excited him from the very start, and by chance it clashed with a discovery he made at about the same time he took up *shodo*. After three or four inert months he had awoken to the attractiveness of Japanese women.

There was nothing complementary in the nature of this attraction. It came to him as an awareness of unmistakable sexual antagonism; the male sought his opposite in the female, the female in the male, opposite not in type but gender. Language, custom, education, superstition, everything in Japanese society bred artificially what may or may not have been natural to woman but was at any rate believed to be so: woman as repository, the pliant, concave element, a hollow acquiescence receiving the brunt of the extended male as space receives body or dry earth soaks up rain.

What man imposed woman bore. In Chinese philosophy he had been represented by the *yang* principle; heaven, daytime, the positive charge. Boon knew nothing of this. He saw only that Japanese women showed themselves beautiful where they were also most vulnerable: the nape of the neck.

Boon's sensual friction of contrasts, the vertical brush on the supine page, dark stain on porous whiteness, was a paradigm of this antagonism between male and female. The aggressive sexuality that lodged in *shodo* might not have been so clear to him had his teacher Suzuki-*san* not been a woman. She was an attractive woman; and she wore her hair fastened at the crown of her head, uncovering a fragile indentation at the base of her neck. In the cold room of the apartment where Boon knelt on the *tatami* practising his letters with numb hands this image generated a kind of ardour, not in Boon and not for any person, but in the feelings that materialised outside him on the page. For when he had done as best he could with *i* alone he coupled it with *ro*, a consort of syllables vertically arranged: *iro*. And by chance these first two symbols in the Japanese syllabary constituted a word meaning shade, colour, love, libido.

At first he botched it. *Iro* staggered miserably through an entire month of newspapers, the November issues of the *Asahi Shinbun*, superimposed on the faces of ministers, cancelling summits and mocking crises with a few brush-strokes, just as it pleased. In early December, as he became more sure of its form and found the dense print of political backgrounds rather distracting, Boon transferred *iro* to the advertising pages. On the whole they were emptier. Beside suits, aeroplanes and automobiles *iro* had more room to develop, and as it acquired maturity of form the need for successors became apparent. For basic technique it was enough to practise letters individually, but for flow and composition they would have to be rehearsed in combination. Accordingly he scanned his character dictionary for compound words with which *iro* could be eked out. It was an amazingly fertile word and not in the least fastidious, compatible with any partner, it seemed. Thus it could be drawn out into love affairs, dyed leather, crayons, coquetry and unbridled lust. All these words were the progeny of *iro*.

Boon did not show these exercises to his teacher, but when he returned the following week the marked improvement in his draughting of the first letters of the Japanese syllabary made it clear that he must have been courting *iro* with single-minded dedication. Suzuki-*san* was mildly surprised, calling her mother in from the kitchen to watch Boon wreak black mischief with his dripping lance.

"*Ara!*" crowed the old lady, guarding her lap with folded hands. Unfolded, knees parted, her daughter quivered.

What Boon had undertaken facetiously and as little more than a pastime became a serious occupation during the following year. His darting forays into dragon country led to wary encampment there; reconnaisance patrols developed into nightly skirmishes. His confidence grew, and finally he was stalking dragons in broad daylight.

He never spoke to Suzuki-*san*, even obliquely, of the admiration he felt for her or of the subtle fascination that flowed like a tide to him out of her darkness. There was no need. Everything that passed between them was already explicit, there, on the slab of paper that lay in front of them. The carnal Boon at her side she did not even see perhaps; but the dusky incubus who descended from the tip of his brush and dragged his spoor across the page she could admit into herself, to that she acquiesced; and more, she guided him to his mark. Side by side at the lacquered table she would sometimes get up and kneel behind him, reassuring his blind hand with two fingers pressing lightly just above his wrist. Week by week he knelt in the hush of her room, barely exchanging a word with her, the blunt winter light seeping through the paper screens, aware of a very slight cadence in the contours of her breasts beside him, rising faintly and falling.

Occasionally she broached herself to him.

"I am told my writing is masculine."

"Why?"

"It is strong, vigorous."

And she took out a long slim copybook with concertina leaves. Subdued marks and very fine lines, apparently fragmentary and to Boon utterly meaningless, like the descent of a spider with inky pads. He was disappointed.

"Is this you?"

"Oh no!"

She sounded horrified.

"This is *sensei* . . ."

Suzuki-*san* allowed him no more than a glimpse of her own work. It was not secret but sacred, her final intimacy. She would sooner have taken off her clothes and shown herself naked.

In this intimacy of her own calligraphy the *shodo* teacher was inaccessible. Some time, no doubt, she would marry, but Boon could not imagine her giving herself to any man. She talked, laughed, drank tea and shared biscuits with him, grinding the crumbs between her fingertips, but she was not really there. Her face was somehow shuttered, like a window netted with muslin. She was of impenetrable chastity, for in secret she had already taken her vows and become the bride of *shodo*. Not for any man.

The first Boon heard about *shodo* was from his barber. He astonished Boon twice, first by shaving his forehead and his earlobes, although Boon had only asked for a haircut, and then by remarking that for the past ten years he spent two hours every evening improving his calligraphy after he had closed up the shop. Why did he do that, wondered Boon.

"I find it very relaxing," said the barber, detaching the apron and shaking it out so vigorously that Boon was persuaded there must be more hair on his forehead than he had previously supposed. When he brought up this matter of shaving the forehead and the earlobes the barber seemed hurt and went on the defensive. What about the honoured customer's own country? Was it not common for barbers to shave the forehead and the ears? Boon assured him it was not. And he admitted to the honourable barber that when he first laid razor to ear he, Boon, had had a nasty fright.

The barber was now completely at a loss.

"But it's a haircut, isn't it? The hairs must be cut, the face must be clean."

Boon assured him that this was logical and true, pointing out that differences in barbering practice might well be accounted for by the fact that many men in Europe, like himself, wore beards. Consequently they were sensitive to distinctions between hair on the head and hair on the face, and barbers were careful to respect that distinction. For a client whose facial hair had been removed, whether by misunderstanding or otherwise, might in circumstances consider himself an injured party and claim damages for which the barber would be held liable. Boon said this as a joke, but the barber unfortunately took him at his word. The notion that compensation might be forcibly levied for hair that had been cut off went so utterly against his professional instincts that for a while he was speechless.

Boon changed the subject back to calligraphy.

"I've finished for today," said the barber, "so if the honoured customer has time I would be very pleased to show him some of my work . . ."

Boon duly followed him upstairs into a tiny apartment where he was shown specimens of the barber's other work. He practised an unusual form of *shodo* – moulding characters in wax or carving them in wood and making prints. This naturally entailed a reversal of the image, an immensely complicated process which for Boon did not bear thinking about. But beyond the bland statement that the cultivation of *shodo* "relaxes the mind and makes the heart quiet" the barber was unable to say anything that satisfied his curiosity.

Just how far Boon was from a proper understanding of *shodo* was well illustrated by an episode during one of his Saturday afternoon classes. He brought along a well-known poem which his calligraphy teacher had asked him to copy out as his homework. In the terse, contracted language typical of classical Japanese poetry the poem described the destruction by fire of Kyoto; the author, weeping, watches a skylark rising over the burnt land. In the Japanese original there was a deft contrast between the rising skylark and the weeping poet (his tears fall), which Boon had in mind when he copied out the poem. The lines being arranged vertically on the page, it occurred to him that the contrasted motions of rising and falling essential to the effect of the poem might also be given a reflection in the calligraphy.

Suzuki Kazuko was extremely startled when she heard this suggestion.

"What a funny idea! Oh no, that's got nothing to do with it, nothing at all."

"But surely the meaning of the words must have something to do with the calligraphy," insisted Boon. "Otherwise I might just as well write the first thing that comes into my head. Instead of something like Man is One with Nature, I could write Shut the Window . . ."

"You must choose a suitable text, of course," said Suzuki-*san* stiffly, and with that the discussion was closed.

Occasionally Boon raised the subject of *shodo* with Ichimonji, who was himself a skilful if lazy practitioner.

"She's right," he said, "you must select a suitable text. Beyond that, however, *shodo* isn't much concerned with the meaning of the words. Words and texts selected for *shodo* all have a certain resonance, because of literary or Buddhist traditions or whatever. The more conservative calligraphists prefer a classical text; others are prepared to use more modern writings, from post-Meiji literature.

"It's true that ideographs were once pictures, simplified pictures of the world, but in the course of time they have become pure abstractions; ideas about *shodo* accordingly changed too. In the medium of *sho*, of the written character, these abstractions acquire plastic form. It's this process of abstraction-becoming-plastic that is decisive . . ."

"And just what is it that is decisive?"

"The rhythm of the *shoka*'s heart when his brush touches the paper."

"I'm not sure that I understand," said Boon.

"Be patient, Bun-*san*, you are not a *shodo* artist; you are not even Japanese. The artist's brush, the speed and pressure of its handling, make the rhythm of his heart transparent. That is the business of *shodo*. If he is a true artist what he has created on the paper in front of him will seem to us beautiful. We acknowledge its taste, its bloom . . . the abstraction becomes plastic, something palpable. The artist's heart becomes apparent.

"This requires great strength of spirit. After all, what emerges from *shodo* is something quite abstract, detached from the material world. And the less need there is to reproduce the material phenomena of the outside world, the more necessary it becomes for the inner life of the individual, the spirit of the artist, to emerge in their place."

Sometimes Boon would bring along specimens of *shodo* (not his own) for Ichimonji to comment on. In this way he learned that, leaving aside the many highly specialised differences, there were two basic schools of thought among practitioners of the art: the classicists, or those who sought the perfect harmony of "Form" and "Heart", and those who gave preference to the expression of Heart, to which they believed formal considerations should be subservient. "This here," Ichimonji would say, "this looks really quite spectacular, doesn't it. In fact it's rather vulgar. Flashy. The form is imperfect, the composition shoddy. Typical example of Form neglected in the interest of Heart. Take care not to overrate this kind of work! Yes, it does have heart. But what I see above all is lack of competence."

"What should the *shodo* artist be seeking to express?"

Ichimonji named two qualities which could be translated as "gravity and austerity of soul". Perhaps the Latin word *gravitas* came close to describing what Ichimonji wished to convey.

Although few modern Japanese were serious practitioners of *shodo*, the very widespread respect accorded good calligraphy was unmistakable, and this rather surprised Boon. When high-ranking politicians took up some office of state, for example, photographs would be regularly published in the newspapers showing them performing calligraphy. In casual conversation Boon often heard it said of someone that he wrote a good hand, and once friends and acquaintances learned that he had taken up lessons they never failed to mention this fact when introducing him to other people. At New Year a large number of people still knelt down solemnly to execute their ritual *kakizome*, or new year's resolution, in traditional style; and at several larger shrines in Tokyo he saw exhibitions of calligraphy done by schoolchildren from all over the country. Why was this extremely esoteric activity being taken so seriously by an evidently large number of people?

Perhaps a more or less conscious desire to preserve one aspect of Japan's national heritage played a part. Unlike flower arrangement or the tea ceremony, *shodo* was one of the very few traditional arts with an illustrious past that was still actually developing and would continue to develop in the future; it was a living tradition, still relevant in contemporary Japan because still capable of absorbing contemporary ideas, and indeed benefiting from them. In the cramped, unprepossessing apartment blocks that were the fate of most urban Japanese Boon very seldom saw flower arrangements, and under these conditions, he was told, it would be wholly inappropriate to hold a tea ceremony. The fossilisation of many traditional arts was the consequence of a failure to adapt; they lacked the flexibility that would have been required to effect the transition to contemporary Japanese society. *Shodo* was different; it could be done just as effectively in a two-and-a-half mat room as in the most spacious house, and because of its abstract nature its "relevance" remained quite unaffected by social change.

Shodo was a quintessentially Japanese form of art. The Chinese had invented the ideographs, they had *sho*, the Writing, but they did not have *shodo*, the Way of Writing. In what way *shodo* was "quintessentially" Japanese Boon discovered when he pursued the analogies to a number of other eminently Japanese institutions, among them *sumo*, *seppuku* (better known as *harakiri*) and the music of the *shakuhachi*. Often when studying examples of *shodo* Boon had the impression he could be listening to the feathery, rasping sound of the *shakuhachi* between marvellous dissonant shifts or when the volume of air in the player's lungs was almost spent. There was a quite unexpected affinity of musical tone and plastic form between the breathy sound the *shakuhachi* produced at the opening or close of a phrase, suspended, barely audible, the trace of a tone that was itself never quite apparent, and the rasping brushwork of *shodo* at those points where the ink had almost drained out of the brush. A miraculous, an indescribable quality.

Sumo (Japanese wrestling) is held in a small ring with a diameter of not more than a few yards. A bout is often over within less than ten seconds. It is won by forcing the opponent out of the ring, by causing him to fall or to touch the ground with his hand. *Sumo* is a lot more subtle and requires much more technical skill and experience than is at first sight obvious.

Boon became a keen student of *sumo* (which in Japanese would never properly be described as a sport) and gradually came to discern those qualities which helped to explain the hold it still exerted over the popular Japanese imagination: the ritualised prologue to the encounter, the extreme concentration required of the protagonists, the brevity of the encounter itself, the slightness of the error or advantage upon which defeat or victory depended, contrasted with the utterness of defeat, the humiliation, often the ridiculing of the wrestler who had lost.

What struck Boon as so Japanese about *sumo* were the narrow limitations of the conditions under which it took place. He knew no other form of sport – better, ritualised encounter – whose formal limitations were as severe as those which governed *sumo*. The specifications of the ring, the rule that the outcome is to be decided by one and only one encounter, demand an immediate all-out confrontation. There is no room to evade the opponent, no dodging and weaving as in boxing, and the loser will not get a second chance. By luck, main force or remarkable agility an initial disadvantage can be reversed, but it is typical of *sumo* that the tiniest error results in immediate defeat. The cathartic effect of this now-or-never, the moral rigour of this unequivocal either-or which Boon detected at the basis of *sumo* was in his opinion inimitably Japanese, and it was this that accounted for its fascination.

It seemed to him that *shodo* shared much of the aesthetic rigour of *sumo*. For a short space of time the calligraphist was required to commit himself utterly to a task which mercilessly exposed his strengths and his weaknesses. He had no second chance. He had no possibility of rubbing out a line and drawing another, of making any correction, of slurring a line in order to disguise a momentary uncertainty; it would at once be apparent. From the moment he thrust his brush downwards at the paper to the retraction from the final stroke he must concentrate on unbroken continuity of rhythm, on the faultless execution of the individual stroke and the perfect balance of the composition as a whole.

Naturally he could take a fresh piece of paper and try again; in this sense, of course, he did have a second chance. But this trivialises the essence of true *shodo* performed by a true artist, who has spent not merely years but decades perfecting his art. Each fresh piece of paper is a challenge to his formidable repertoire of skills and experience, his concentration of purpose and self-control. The artist himself will know if he has succeeded or failed. Either one or the other, nothing in-between.

This was what Ichimonji meant when he told Boon that "the rhythm of the heart becomes apparent". Quite apart from art and technique, *shodo* represented to the artist a forum of moral judgement.

Perhaps the reason why photographs showing newly-appointed ministers performing *shodo* were published in the national papers lay in this perception of its moral significance. The tradition of *kakizome*, the ritual inscription of new year resolutions, even though not observed by many in modern Japan, could be explained in similar terms. The seriousness associated with and the formal constraints imposed by *shodo* reinforced the resolution far more potently than when it was not ritually committed to paper but merely formed abstractly as an idea in one's head.

When Boon knelt on the *tatami* in his cold bare room (for some reason the cold had a beneficial effect on *shodo*) and began to prepare for his calligraphy exercises, images of the ritual performance of *seppuku* would spontaneously come to his mind. Tense, a little excited, like a coiled spring, he mentally went through the motions of the strokes he intended to put down on paper, waiting until he was sure what he wanted and for the moment when he could do it. Now – and without thinking that he had already made up his mind to begin he found the brush suddenly dropping down onto the paper, almost of its own accord. The tip of the brush struck the paper with a slight jar. With a sense of shock he watched it cut a dense black swathe on the blank paper, irreversibly, he could no longer draw back. His pent feelings were released and began to flow down the page in the wake of the glossy ink.

This transition from intending to do an act to implementing that act had about it a suddenness, a feeling of involuntary prompting, as if it were not possible unless the agent were momentarily suspended and the implementation of his act autonomous, which Boon otherwise knew only from acts of physical courage, like a forced leap into the dark. The surprise he invariably felt when the brush descended and the ink first stained the paper was for him one of the most powerful fascinations of *shodo*; and this surprise, although of course painless, seemed comparable to what must be experienced by a person performing *seppuku*. But maybe this was private to Boon's imagination, maybe this was not how the Japanese themselves felt about *shodo* at all.

*N*ew Year fare. At the New Year Sugama invited Boon to spend a few days with him at his home in Toyama, a couple of hundred miles north-west of Tokyo on the Sea of Japan.

"You will meet grandfather," said Sugama. "He was born in the Meiji era," which made grandfather sound really very ancient indeed. At the top of his suitcase Boon placed the stack of invitations and handbills which representatives of charities and old people's clubs, with growing mistrust, had left at the apartment for the phantom grandfather care of Boon. He also took along a few presents. Presents were very important in Japan.

Travelling on slow trains, as Boon had requested in order to see as much as possible of the countryside, they did not reach Toyama until late in the evening. From the station they took a taxi. It was dark, but very few lights were visible. Apparently Sugama's parents lived out in the country.

Snow was falling. Somewhere in the white-bordered dark the taxi stopped and they got out. Sugama walked up to a house and pulled open a sliding door on the raised wooden veranda.

"*Tadaima!*"

He began taking off his shoes. Boon followed suit. Sugama pulled open a second door and led him into a large *tatami* room where the parents were waiting to greet them.

Since his first meeting with Sugama's mother in Tokyo Boon had got used to the formal ceremony of Japanese greetings and was now able to prostrate himself on the *tatami* without self-consciousness or risk of injury. It was really no more than a sort of handshake with one's whole body, and when it had been done one passed on to informal behaviour and conversation with much the same ease. If anyone, it was Sugama who seemed a little uneasy to see Boon with lowered head and hands on the floor. "*Ii ii*," he muttered, waving his hand.

Over beer and cold snacks the hosts and their guest took the measure of one another. The Sugamas enquired about the Boon family, and Boon enquired about the Sugama family. Both families were rather large, so this took some time. Boon's account of his kin, their great numbers and broad geographical distribution, appeared to make a favourable impression. This could be rather useful in Japan, where it was usual to see a person in terms of his family, to extrapolate the individual, as it were, from his genealogical data. Sugama's father grew particularly intrigued and was pressing for details of one eighteenth-century branch of Boon's family when his wife reminded him that grandfather had stayed up specially to meet Boon and should not be kept waiting any longer.

The old gentleman was sitting beneath a large clock in the next room, warming his legs under the *kotatsu*. Boon was introduced to him and invited to sit down for a chat.

"He speaks Japanese," his daughter-in-law reassured him.

"What's that?"

"He speaks Japanese."

"Oh."

Grandfather duly turned to Boon and asked him a question that was quite unintelligible.

"Didn't you say he spoke Japanese?" he asked, looking puzzled and disappointed.

"Yes – just ask him again."

The old man cupped his ear.

"What?"

"Ask him again."

But despite all these good intentions, for as long as he lived and Boon knew him grandfather's speech remained wholly impenetrable. He was old, he had no teeth, he spoke dialect: an unbeatable combination. Grandfather, for his part, could understand Boon's standard Japanese quite well, although he was hard of hearing. This resulted in some odd conversations unsatisfactory for both parties. After several unsuccessful exchanges, in which Boon guessed what grandfather had asked him and grandfather failed to make any sense of Boon's reply, the old man became wary of asking any questions at all. On the other hand, when asked a question he was very willing to oblige Boon with an answer. Boon usually could not understand this answer, however. The rules of the game were soon established: grandfather was allowed to answer but not ask questions, and Boon, although asking lots of questions, was never expected to pay the slightest attention to grandfather's answers.

There are not many cases where language is an actual impediment, but this was undoubtedly one. It would have been much better if Boon had pretended he couldn't speak Japanese at all and relied entirely on signs when communicating with grandfather. Increasingly this was what they did. The old man had a graphic face and a range of very explicit gestures; his meaning was always clear.

Deprived of speech, at least of the privilege to initiate speech by asking questions, and being rather hard of hearing in any case, it was quite understandable that grandfather felt a strong need to touch things whenever trying to communicate with Boon. In this need to touch things grandfather gave the impression of wanting to be sure of his ground, of wanting to test the reality of Boon. Perhaps it was just the infirmity of old age, but Boon could well imagine that the mere presence of a foreigner in his house imposed quite a demand on the old man, requiring his hands to be more than usually active, as if groping around for additional means of support.

On the evening grandfather first met him Boon was bearded and wearing a mohair pullover, which in its colour and texture happened to look very similar to the beard. Boon never saw another such mohair pullover while he was in Japan, and he very seldom saw a beard. It would not be altogether surprising then, when grandfather first set eyes on the outlandish Boon, if the thought had passed through his mind that this strange beard and the unfamiliar garment it resembled both somehow grew on Boon or were at least made up of the same material. At any rate, such was Boon's impression when he sat down at the *kotatsu* and looked at grandfather's troubled face.

The old man was unable to suppress an exclamation and the involuntary movement of his hand in the direction of Boon's pullover.

"Yes, isn't it a nice warm pullover," said the daughter-in-law, but Boon could tell that it didn't interest grandfather to know that the pullover was nice and warm; he wanted to know what it was made of. Boon offered him his sleeve.

"Hor!" grunted the old man, leaning forward to examine it. After a while he raised his eyes and said *"Hige mo ii na!"*

Boon had been anticipating this reference to his beard and he understood it as a request: grandfather was asking for permission to touch his beard and compare it with the pullover.

"Doozo, kamawanai," he said with a laugh, sticking out his chin. *"E?"*

Startled by his own boldness, uneasily aware that he was overstepping the bounds of propriety, grandfather was none the less unable to resist this tempting offer. Gingerly he tweaked the beard.

"Hor!"

Boon would have much liked to know what conclusions the old man had drawn, but he carried this secret with him to the grave. No doubt those conclusions were in any case seriously complicated by the fact that Boon later returned to the house without his beard. If grandfather really had detected some mysterious collusion of beard and pullover he must have been very perplexed by all the variations he saw: Boon bearded but without pullover, Boon with pullover but no beard and finally Boon with neither beard nor pullover.

On that first evening grandfather gripped him by the arm whenever he spoke to him. It was an unexpectedly firm grip – he had spent the sixty odd years of his working life as a carpenter. Later he was content merely to touch or nudge Boon; always, it seemed, as if making sure that he was actually there. Whenever possible, he touched or pointed at any object that came up in the one-sided exchanges between him and Boon. In course of time he confined himself to only those subjects where such illustration was possible. Altogether he was a very solid sort of man, a carpenter with whom one would never have wanted to discuss Platonic chairs and tables. In recent years, Sugama confided to Boon, he had become more mellow or perhaps the will to dominate had merely faded, but until that time he had ruled his house with an iron hand, an unchallenged despot. Judging by the undiminished power of his grip, Boon was quite ready to believe what Sugama said about the authority the old man still wielded in his house.

How cold that house was! The cold penetrated his skin and sunk into the marrow of his bones, like a dull ache. During the week he spent in Toyama Boon never once felt really warm.

He awoke early the first morning because he was cold. On the *tatami* beside him Sugama was still enviably asleep. Boon rolled out of the *futon*, got dressed quickly and went to the window. The house stood in the middle of a snow-covered plain. Nearby there was a timber yard and a frozen stretch of water, and over the rooftops of scattered houses he could see the ragged outline of mountains in the distance. A strong wind was blowing. He could see it raking the surface of the bedded fields; the loose powder-snow rose and drifted in gusty veils.

Across the narrow landing was the second upstairs room, where Sugama's parents slept. The sliding door was open, the room empty. He peeked in. The bedding had already been rolled up, the *futon* stowed away. There was a cupboard and a dressing-table. How spare it all was, thought Boon, how simple! But the emptiness of the room made it seem even colder. He shivered and went downstairs.

The cold dark kitchen was deserted. On the *kotatsu* in the little room where grandfather had sat last night, screened off from the kitchen by a sliding glass-panelled door, breakfast things had been laid: soup bowls, cold fish, a thermos container for rice. There was no sign of Sugama's parents. The door to the *kyakuma*, the room where he and Sugama had been welcomed the previous evening, stood ajar. He could hear someone coughing and mumbling.

He pushed the door softly open and looked in. Grandfather was kneeling on the *tatami* with his back to Boon in front of a chest-like cabinet whose flaps had been opened outwards to reveal what was evidently a shrine. The old man was praying. Occasionally he clapped his hands, mumbled something and relapsed into silence. This continued at intervals for quite some time.

The prayer ritual he witnessed on his first morning in Toyama remained the one and only occasion on which Boon ever saw someone praying at an *ujigami* shrine (dedicated to the household gods). The custom still survived in rural districts, but it had long disappeared from the homes of urban Japanese. Sugama's grandfather observed the ritual every morning, communing with his deceased wife, whom he had lost several years previously. Quite what the ritual signified, whether the old man followed a set liturgy or did anything besides praying for the soul of his wife, remained unclear to Boon. Perhaps it didn't matter. Grandfather ritually tended the memory of his dead wife in much the same way that other people tend a grave. Ceremony gave his act an aspect of piety, but it was unlikely that grandfather himself was aware of either ceremony or piety. It was something much more straightforward, immediately human. He was merely thinking about his wife. The shrine embodied the thought.

In stockinged feet Boon tiptoed past towards the front entrance where he had left his shoes. Apparently grandfather slept in the *kyakuma*; his rumpled bedding lay in a corner of the room. The room was icy. Apart from the *kotatsu*, the small heated table in the room where the breakfast things were laid, there didn't appear to be any heating in the house. Boon wondered how anybody could voluntarily endure such cold. He pulled open the porch door and retrieved his shoes. Unfortunately the clatter of the sliding door disturbed grandfather at his prayers. He peered round the *shoji* screening off the shrine from the rest of the room. Boon wished him good morning and apologised for having disturbed him, but the old man didn't seem to mind. He grinned and pointed good-humouredly at the shrine, clapped his hands again and laughed, as if to say "Well now, and what do you make of all this hocus-pocus?" Boon realised that the old man probably felt embarrassed.

At that moment Sugama's mother appeared in the doorway and asked him if he would like some breakfast.

He found Sugama sitting in his pyjamas under the *kotatsu* watching television.

"You're up early," he said to Boon.

"I was cold. I'm cold all the time."

He sat down and stretched his legs out under the *kotatsu*.

"How does this thing work? It's not plugged in anywhere . . ."

"Old-fashioned *kotatsu*," replied Sugama. "Use warm coals. Here."

He lifted aside the rug and showed him a bracket fixed to the underside of the *kotatsu*.

"The warm coals are placed in here. Of course when they get cool you have to replace them – two or three times a day if you want the *kotatsu* to be really warm."

"And if you want to be warm you have to sit under the *kotatsu* – there doesn't seem to be any other heating in the house."

Sugama laughed.

"No. There's another *kotatsu* upstairs, of course. You could try sleeping with your legs under it. Then you'd be sure to keep warm. The point is, houses in Japan are traditionally constructed so as to be cool in summer. People don't worry so much about the cold. It's the heat they're afraid of."

"But how many months of the year is it really hot? Probably not more than three or four. Whereas the cold weather lasts much longer. Personally I'd be more worried about the cold than the heat."

"Ah, you haven't experienced the summer here. Very sticky, very uncomfortable. Just you wait!"

Through the glass door he watched Sugama's mother bustling around in the kitchen. He noticed that the door leading out into the back yard was wide open. The temperature in the kitchen could not have been more than a few degrees above zero.

"*Ocha!*" bawled Sugama.

"*Hai hai!*"

His mother came pattering over and pulled open the door, wiping her hands on her apron. As she cleared the table she saw that Boon had left his food almost untouched.

"Oh dear, haven't you eaten anything?"

"Well, I had some *misoshiru*," explained Boon cautiously. He had managed the bean paste soup without trouble, if not with particular pleasure, but he definitely baulked at fermented soya bean and cold fish. "It's still rather early in the morning . . ."

Grandfather cackled with delight. He had joined them at the *kotatsu* in order to watch Boon have his breakfast. Like many Japanese he had doubts about the compatibility of foreigners and local food, and now that he saw himself vindicated he seemed enormously pleased.

"Heh heh!" he chortled happily, "no point in giving him fermented soya bean – can't eat it!"

Sugama poured green tea into his rice-bowl and swilled it until the remaining grains of rice had been dislodged from the sides of the bowl.

"Perhaps you'd like an egg?" he suggested.

"Heh heh! Egg!"

Better and better, everything just as he had expected. Grandfather was getting his money's worth.

In deference to his tender stomach Boon conceded moral defeat and gratefully accepted. Under the old man's approving eyes he dispatched a boiled egg and three slices of toast.

But at lunch he got his own back. Knowing how partial Boon was to *sashimi*, Sugama's mother had prepared a very special Toyama delicacy: *shiromi*, or fillet of raw white fish, wrapped in fresh leaves which changed the natural colour of the meat and imparted an exquisite flavour.

"Heh heh! Raw fish!" announced grandfather gleefully as the family burrowed under the *kotatsu*. And turning to his daughter-in-law he said reproachfully "You've forgotten Bun-*san*'s egg. Where's his egg?"

"He's not having an egg. He's going to eat fish with us."

"What?"

But there was no doubt about it. Boon really was going to eat fish. To his consternation he saw Boon mix horseradish with soya sauce and swallow a slice of the red-stained *shiromi* with every appearance of pleasure.

"Is it all right for him to eat raw fish? Bun-*san*, please, don't eat it just for our sake ..."

"Delicious! The tastiest *sashimi* I've ever eaten," pronounced Boon.

"Really? Heh heh!"

But it was clear that the old man wasn't too pleased.

Most of his days in Toyama Boon spent sharing a corner of the *kotatsu* in this little room facing the kitchen, because it was the only warm place in the house; and for the same reason this was where the family gathered for their meals, to talk, watch television and sleep. By contrast he realised how the central heating he was accustomed to in Europe had a highly diffusive effect; the more generally heat was available the more it became an extension of privacy. But heat in the Toyama house was only available in limited quantities and only at one place. Like the obsolete village pump it was still a communal facility. The *kotatsu* was not just an alternative way of heating; it enforced a quite different way of life.

The Sugamas were not poor people. They could have got rid of the *kotatsu* and laid pipes. Maybe they just hadn't bothered to, or maybe they were inured to the cold and wouldn't have thought it worthwhile. But Boon thought there was more to it than that. The Japanese did not merely make use of the *kotatsu* to get heat; they were attached to it, in a way one could never become attached to one's central heating, however much one might enjoy warmth. The *kotatsu* was as rich in its associations for the Japanese as the hearth for an Englishman or the *Kachelofen* for people living in the colder parts of Europe. Most important, it allowed the Japanese to make a virtue of necessity and succumb to what the formality of social manners otherwise discouraged: physical intimacy and unstrained familiarity.

Hence, no doubt, the survival of the *kotatsu* in even the most modern apartments, where its presence could not be accounted for as an additional heating requirement. It was an irreplaceable cultural symbol.

Quite soon the family and neighbours grew used to Boon. He could submerge under the *kotatsu* and watch everything that went on as freely as if he had been invisible. In this way he acquired insights into the privacy of a household and the daily commonplaces of Japanese life to which an outsider normally had no access.

The attitude of Sugama to his grandfather was respectful but impersonal. Although he never said so in as many words, it was obvious that he felt little affection for the old man. Possibly he bore him a grudge on account of what Sugama saw as the harshness with which his mother had been treated in the past, and the jocular relationship mutually accepted by grandfather and Boon as their *modus vivendi* was not entirely to his liking. Sugama already saw in Boon an ally. Maybe he felt let down by the conciliatory, even friendly manner that Boon adopted towards his grandfather.

The position of the daughter-in-law in the household she entered was notoriously unstable in Japan, the butt of endless social comedies and an unflagging source of inspiration for serialised television soap operas avidly followed by tens of millions of people. Boon had first-hand experience of this problem in several families, but he first became aware of it during his stay in Toyama. The problem was by no means peculiar to Japan, but its ramifications, especially in those rural areas where the transition from the archaic family system had not yet been fully accomplished, were as complex and far-reaching as one might naturally expect of any process of fundamental social evolution.

Sugama's father being the *chonan*, the eldest son, it was inevitable that his wife would be expected to live with and look after his parents whether she liked it or not. As had been usual at the time, the young couple were betrothed in accordance with the custom of *miai kekkon*, or arranged marriage. The difficulty of the task confronting any daughter-in-law was exacerbated in the case of Sugama's mother by the fact that she did not come from Toyama. By the very parochial standards of the Japanese, intensely aware of insider loyalties and resentful of intruders, she was accordingly a stranger. Academic social commentators liked to point out that daughters who entered a house by marriage were treated much more as members of the family than natural daughters who married and left the parental home. Presumably this was true of marriage and exchange within the same region; but any person moving from one region to another where the dialect is so distinct as to be almost a different language is an outsider by virtue of that distinction alone. The privileges associated with being native to a place were exercised in the same way all over the world, and it was inconceivable that Sugama's mother had not had to contend with an element of regional prejudice when she first arrived in her new home.

This background information was indispensable to Boon if he hoped to interpret correctly what he observed in the casual ebb and flow of the Sugamas' daily life. Sugama, as Boon knew, was under pressure to get married fairly soon and to honour his filial duties by returning to his parents' home in the not too distant future. Naturally his parents would have preferred a local girl, but there wasn't much they could do about that. He had already set his heart on a girl born and bred in Tokyo; all he had to do was wait until she set her heart on him. Unfortunately this was taking rather a long time, which prejudiced his parents from the start. Any girl who took so long to make up her mind when an eligible young man made a serious offer of marriage was not a girl worth waiting for.

Over this question of his marriage the mother formed an alliance with his father and grandfather against the son, who otherwise, if less obviously, was allied with her against the grandfather for exactly the same reasons: the double burden of being wife and daughter-in-law in a strange household far from home and friends. During childhood Sugama had felt sympathy with his mother, whom he considered unjustly treated by her parents-in-law, and now that he was himself thinking of marriage he had no intention of letting the same thing happen to his future wife.

Though always restrained, the affection that mother and son felt for each other was unmistakable; theirs was the deeper, the long-standing alliance. Their present antagonism had a specific cause and would end as soon as that cause had been removed. In the meantime, however, the parlous state of her son, unmarried on the threshold of his thirties, was her chief concern, overriding all other loyalties.

Boon was drawn into this family squabble against his wishes. Sugama would certainly not have had any ulterior motives when he first asked him to come and stay over the New Year, but Boon's presence in Toyama undoubtedly suited him very well. Boon was a distraction, a woolly bearded manoeuvre whose mere appearance in a room neutralised conflicts and blunted edges. Behind this shield and buckler Sugama retired whenever the opposition began to throw stones.

On the other side of Boon was the counsellor and confidential informant. This side of him was frequently addressed by Sugama's parents, who importuned him for details and expert opinions whenever they could get him on his own.

"Tell me, Bun-*san*," said Sugama's father one afternoon, after he had lured him into his study on the pretext of showing him some pictures, "tell me what you think of this girl. You've met her, after all."

"She's a very nice girl. There's really no need for you to be worried."

"Then why can't she make up her mind? Why doesn't she say she'll marry him? Don't you think her behaviour's rather odd?"

"Not in the least. She's still very young, and she just doesn't want to get tied down too early. She needs more time."

"Really? Are you sure that's it? Just a question of time?"

He didn't sound very convinced. Varying his angle of approach he grappled with Boon on several further occasions, equally unsatisfactory, because equally inconclusive. At some point it must have occurred to him that Boon was not married either, and that it might be a good idea to sound out his views on this subject before pressing his son's case further.

His approach was very devious, starting in the seventeenth century with that branch of Boon's family which had originated in France. For quite a while Boon thought that he was just being taken out on another of those historical excursions which Sugama's father so relished, to be resumed where it had been interrupted on the evening of his arrival, but as the slant of his questions became increasingly tendentious, and the quirky parentheses, which at first Boon had put down to his rambling drag-net style of talk, began to pile up ominously, the drift of their conversation was plain for all to see: the weight of centuries, an entire Boonish dynasty rested squarely on this young man's shoulders. There was no question of him shirking his responsibilities, was there. No indeed. In irreproachably Japanese style Boon heartily agreed.

"I just wish my son would follow your example," said Sugama's father earnestly.

"Well, he is following it, isn't he?"

"What d'you mean?"

"I'm not married either."

"Ah, Bun-*san*, but you're younger. And besides, you know that you will."

"As a matter of fact, I'm not so sure about that. Maybe, maybe not. I'll wait and see."

"But . . . Bun-*san*, did you misunderstand me? What I said about the continuity of the family line – didn't you agree?"

"Oh yes, there's a lot to be said for it. But actually doing it, well, that's an altogether different matter . . ."

Sugama's father was stunned by the perfidy of Boon. After a while, realising that on Boon's behalf he had assumed as a matter of course convictions which Boon quite evidently did not share, he generously acknowledged that marriage need not after all be an inescapable event, a case of *force majeure*, but might equally well be the subject of free, individual decision. Boon was forgiven. Still, he had given him a nasty shock. Wasn't he worried about the future of the human race, because wouldn't there be dire consequences when too many other people started or rather stopped behaving in the same way? Boon said he wasn't and he didn't think there would.

He could never really bring himself to believe Boon's listlessness about marriage and indifference to procreation. With the unfailing civility of the Japanese the subject of Boon and marriage was converted into a standing family joke, teeth drawn, out of harm's reach. Boon and marriage! Heh heh – egg! It was much the same tone of voice.

About six weeks later Sugama's father was in Tokyo on business. He took the opportunity to have a look at the girl for himself. He stayed overnight in Oji and Boon had a long conversation with him. If Boon's opinions rather alarmed Sugama's father, his views too occasionally astonished Boon. After meeting the girl he cautiously agreed that she was not such a bad sort after all; still, but, however, there could be absolutely no question of marriage.

"Why not?" asked Boon.

"Here, you see."

He tapped his glasses significantly. Boon was puzzled.

"I'm afraid I don't follow you."

"Well, as you know, my son is very short-sighted too."

"And?"

"The girl has very bad eyesight, Bun-*san*. That makes two of them. A most unfavourable genetic constellation. Just imagine the effects it could have on their children! Poor eyesight is a hereditary fault among the Sugamas. No, I'm afraid he'll have to look around for a girl with really good eyes, to redress the balance, as it were."

The reasons Boon had offered to explain why Sugama's girl-friend was not yet willing to get married were true. Partly true. There was one serious obstacle which he thought it better not to mention: the girl didn't much fancy the idea of moving to Toyama to live with her parents-in-law. Sugama knew very well why he was a worried man.

Curiously enough, grandfather stayed out of this household war. Perhaps he agitated in the background, or perhaps he already had such a surfeit of great-grandchildren that one more or less no longer mattered.

For Sugama and Boon at one end of life, who thought they had all the time in the world, and for grandfather at the other, who knew his time was running out, they were lazy days. Sugama's father worked until midday on New Year's eve, and his wife continued to toil every day from morn till night without rest. She was indefatigable.

On the morning of New Year's eve she was unusually busy, trekking back and forth from the kitchen to the lumber-room that had once been grandfather's workshop with trays, boards and bowls of dough. A neighbour and assorted children began to emerge mysteriously from various corners of the house, as if they had been drawn out of a hat. The children romped; the neighbour kept his hands in his pockets, smoked and talked non-stop, all at the same time. He always stood in exactly the same attitude, the mark of the professional loiterer; Boon saw him like this in a succession of different rooms, without actually seeing him move from one room to the other. In the *kyakuma* he loitered talking to grandfather, in the kitchen to Sugama's mother and in the lumber-room to himself. He didn't mind. Talk for him was apparently much the same as standing with his hands in his pockets, something that could be done just as well with an audience as without.

Boon put on his coat and went to the lumber-room to find out what was happening.

"We're making rice cakes," said Sugama's mother.

She was kneeling on the floor in front of a row of bowls, kneading coarse-grained rice and water until the texture thickened and formed a paste. It was bitterly cold. The paste she was kneading drew the warmth out of her hands, and wisps of steam rose out of the bowl. Her hands and bare forearms had turned a rich pink, the colour of boiled crab meat.

When the last bowl of rice and water had been pummelled into a whitish paste she brought out a pestle and a wooden block with a smooth hollow surface. She scooped the tacky paste out of one of the bowls and slapped it onto the block. For a brief moment the chunky mass oozed, stretched and shuddered, almost as if it were alive.

Flicking elastic tentacles of paste from the tips of her fingers she rinsed her hands in fresh water and said "We need a strong man."

Boon, elected by unanimous vote, sheepishly took off his coat. There was an argument about the pestle. The loitering neighbour seemed to think it wouldn't be any good, and he dispatched one of the boys to look around for a wooden hammer. The diminutive boy promptly dived into the tangled wreckage of planks and sacking at the far end of the lumber-room and for a long time failed to reappear. A second boy was sent to look for the first, but at this moment he staggered out with a colossal sledge-hammer in tow.

Boon swung it by the shaft. It was made entirely of wood, much lighter than it looked.

"I'd forgotten we had that," said Sugama's mother. "I think it was used for mending fences."

"And now it'll be used for making cakes," said the boy.

She cleaned the hammer with a rag and moistened its blunt head.

"I shall turn the rice base between strokes, and keep on turning it until it has the real consistency of dough. Mind you don't hit my fingers."

Boon swung the hammer and flattened the paste to pulp. She folded the sides back into the centre, squeezed it, Boon swung the hammer down again. From blow to blow he could feel the texture of the rice base thickening, becoming harder and more resistant. It soon lost its tackiness and there was no need to moisten it; it recoiled under the hammer and sprang upwards, like a sponge, detaching itself from the block. The blows became rhythmical and faster. He swung down, she turned and kneaded the dough with quick movements, barely withdrawing her fingers between the blows.

Beating the rice base into dough went on for the best part of an hour. After a while Boon was relieved by Sugama, who in turn passed the sledge-hammer on to a succession of excited boys. Even the loitering neighbour was persuaded to take the cigarette out of his mouth and his hands out of his pockets and have a go. He pounded the dough with unexpected vigour, accompanying each stroke of the hammer with a barbarous cry, his eyes glowing. The clamour of voices and the resounding thud of a hammer, long forgotten in his disused workshop, awoke grandfather from his midmorning sleep. He stood in the doorway scratching his head, as if unable to cope with all the memories that had suddenly been dislodged.

Long after everyone had dispersed, Sugama's mother continued to kneel on the floor of the lumber-room moulding rice-cakes and laying them out on trays. There must have been a couple of square yards of cakes in all. Boon wondered who would ever eat so many cakes. He had sampled a rice cake and found it indigestible.

The character of this woman merged so completely with the ideal in whose service it had been formed that as a personality in her own right she was easily overlooked; perhaps the distinction was no longer possible. It was difficult to see how the woman could be separated from the function. Into selfless dedication she actually put a great deal of herself. The greater her sacrifice for others, the greater their dependence on her. And that was her reward: she became indispensable.

The person to whom she was least dispensable she most loved. She cared for grandfather like a baby. She had probably staked more on grandfather than on anyone else. He was her big investment; and after thirty years in his house she had at last secured his approval. Strain held her together. When the old man died some two years later she broke up, unable to change her design, like a boat laid up and no longer required to displace the pressure of water. In her understanding of the meaning of duty and service Sugama's mother was unusual only to the extent that she was old-fashioned. She was certainly not unrepresentative. Boon met many Japanese women who had a great deal in common with her.

In the late afternoon a fire was lit in the yard behind the kitchen to heat water for the bath. It was a cumbersome and wasteful system. The water in the boiler in the kitchen was heated, but nothing else, for the fire itself was outside. Because it was such a tedious business, bath days were usually fixed in advance and members of the household took their bath one after another in a set order. Senior males went first and guests were given priority. Boon was accordingly allowed to jump the queue and take second place, naturally after grandfather. Otherwise he would have been fourth.

Unlike Europeans, the Japanese did not actually wash in the bath but only wet themselves, squatting on a stool outside the bath in order to soap and sluice. Thus it was quite natural for as many as five or six people to use the same water at any one time. So long as the water was reasonably clean Boon was not fastidious. Not all housewives, however, were as scrupulous as Sugama's mother about emptying and cleaning the bath after each bathing session. He was invited to refresh himself in a number of private houses in water so murky that he couldn't see the bottom of the bath.

It had been Sugama's idea to set out with Boon at midnight on a tour of the local shrines, but gusty wind and driving rain that continued throughout the night persuaded them to stay indoors. Boon crawled under the *futon* in the upstairs room and listened drowsily to the storm spitting and crackling above the roof, while Sugama engraved a tiger on a piece of boxwood and began to print his *nengajo*. He always designed his New Year cards himself and he was as conscientious about sending them as he was unpunctual. It was quite a good tiger, and Sugama obliged him by sending one to their joint address. It arrived in February.

New Year's day began earlier for Boon than it had ever done before. At half-past five he was woken by the clanging of pans and the sound of running feet. He credited Sugama's energetic mother with a great deal, but being in three or four different places at once was beyond even her powers; and sure enough, when he arrived downstairs for soup and cold fish he found three ladies in white aprons chattering and drinking tea. They had come to help Sugama's mother prepare for the New Year banquet, which was to be held that afternoon.

These three women were all Sugama kin. They were quite fierce, in their clucking, goose-like way. Clucking and pattering, red-faced and short-stepped, with tight buttocks and smooth round bellies, they wore their aprons like badges of office, pouncing on all menfolk caught lingering in the downstairs rooms. Grandfather was allowed to sit in a corner of the *kyakuma* smoking his pipe, but when the talkative neighbour ventured into the house for a stint of loitering in the old man's company he was immediately shooed back into the street. Poor man! The storm had abated and now it was freezing. Fortunately he could get in at the back door and sneak upstairs unseen, where the diminutive boy who was his son had settled down to his New Year calligraphy.

Sugama explained to Boon the meaning of *kakizome* (New Year resolutions) and challenged him to try his hand. Boon, masking incompetence behind diffidence, said he would prefer to sit and watch. The small boy, with all the gravity his ten years could muster, knelt ceremoniously on the floor and wrote out *ningen kokuho* ten times on ten pieces of paper. The phrase meant "a living national treasure", a title conferred on outstanding craftsmen and performers in the traditional Japanese arts as a reward for service to the nation and, it seemed to Boon, for sheer staying power: most nominees were ongoing octogenarians. It was hardly an honour which could be conferred posthumously. Even for a boy as remarkable as the neighbour's son it seemed a premature resolution; he would have to wait half a century at least. But the boy explained it was not a resolution, he was just keeping his hand in over the school holidays.

Sugama meanwhile had still not managed to get anything down at all. Here Boon saw for the first time the characteristic effect of *kakizome* and other occasional *shodo*: the concentration of mind, the singlemindedness of purpose that was brought into focus by the challenge of having to put a thought down on paper in a technically very demanding form. What Sugama eventually wrote was as accomplished in its penmanship as the thought was apt: *kenkon itteki*, "heaven and earth at one stroke". This was how he chose to express the task confronting him in the new year. One way or the other, the question of his marriage must be brought to a final resolution.

The first guests began to arrive in the early afternoon. Sugama casually mentioned that the New Year banquet was always held at his father's house because he was the *chonan* and accordingly the symbolic head or – so long as grandfather lived – at least the heir apparent of the large Sugama family. It was on this occasion that Boon first heard the term *tateshakai*, meaning a society structured vertically according to precedence and rank, and the banquet held that evening in the house of the senior member of the Sugama family gave him a memorable introduction to how this kind of society operated in practice.

Most of the men wore Western-style clothes, a few preferred Japanese dress, but the women without exception appeared in festive *kimono*. The men lounged and the women knelt, so long as they were not attending to some household chore or other, around the *irori*, where grandfather sat in patriarchal style warming his toes and smoking his pipe. The *irori* had been specially lit for the occasion; it was about eighteen inches deep, sunk into the floor and filled with hot ash. It performed invaluable service, both to grandfather's toes and his pipe, which was long and slender and had a very small bowl that the old man constantly had to refill and relight. Watching him flex his toes and tap his pipe on the side of the *irori* as he received his seven sons and rustling daughters-in-law kneeling to greet him in their bright silks, Boon had the feeling of being on set for a period film in which he had been asked to take part wearing the wrong costume.

Boon's mohair pullover, although never again confused with his beard, was an object of almost greater curiosity than himself. The pullover was stroked, plucked and prodded, as if it were something not on him but in front of him, not a garment but a display, available for public inspection. It was an irresistible gambit, allowing him to be agreeably handled by modest ladies who would not otherwise have dreamed of approaching him. In this way he had an opportunity to speak to almost every person in the room.

At about five o'clock the guests were asked to take their seats, or rather their cushions, at the tables lined up along one wall of the room and now piled with mysterious foods which Boon never saw before or afterwards, but which he was assured were great delicacies. To his astonishment there was not a single woman among the company that sat down to eat. Throughout the meal wives and daughters pattered in and out, serving their menfolk; only when the meal was over and *sake* had been brought to the tables did they sit down and themselves begin to eat – not in the *kyakuma*, however, but in an adjacent room where they were on call whenever needed. Sugama was not surprised that Boon found this odd. The women were quite satisfied with this arrangement, he said, and on the whole tended to prefer their own company. Just as well, thought Boon.

Opposite him sat the second eldest son, who was a banker. Between furtive mouthfuls he engaged Boon with merciless tenacity in exchanges that were more like a duel than a conversation. He gave no quarter, interrogating Boon in the same blunt way he dealt with an obstinate piece of fish. He was the most worldly, the least prepossessing of the Sugamas. On either side of the banker sat two unsatisfactory capital investments, his teenage sons, with faces as white as radishes, very much in awe of their masterful father and anxious they might be inadvertently gobbled up. Neither boy spoke a single word the whole evening. The banker skilfully used Boon in order to goad his two meagre portfolios to greater capital appreciation, praising Boon selectively to prove to his sons that they were blockheads. Perhaps they were, but they were so cowed it was impossible to tell.

It was interesting to see how such very different personalities could be bound together by their common kinship. Most of those present that evening would probably not have voluntarily sought out the company of any of their relatives at any other time, yet not a single member of the family who was not prevented by mortal sickness failed to attend the New Year reunion. They did so out of duty, without any great show of pleasure, because the family was their original power base and a ritual demonstration of allegiance to it of great psychological importance as a means of reinforcing, almost, indeed, of blessing by proxy their membership in those other social groupings for which the family supplied the one and only original. Here was nourishment at the source and fount of all social harmony.

The atmosphere was never quite easy. *Sake* lent the graceful illusion of papering over the cracks, but in fact it only blurred the edges. As with so many convivial occasions that Boon attended in Japan, there was a rapid transition from diffidence to hilarity which omitted the intermediate stage of gaiety. There may have been physiological grounds for this. As soon as many Japanese began to drink they also began to get drunk; but in Boon's experience there was also a lot of self-persuasion about this, an element of self-intoxication that was purely psychological. Many drinkers badly wanted to be drunk, they drank in order to get drunk.

And so it was at the New Year party in Sugama's house. There was a duty to be merry, the stronger the duty the weaker the natural inclination. *Sake* duly flowed, faces reddened, songs were broached in warming chorus.

Unknown to Boon he had been placed at the table in the seat of honour with his back to the *tokonoma*, the narrow alcove in which the household displays its greatest treasures; in this case a superb hanging scroll depicting the rising sun. It was the result of a curious, long-forgotten evolution which had tossed up the paradox that the one place in the *kyakuma* from which one could not see these treasures should traditionally be regarded as the seat of honour. The veneration of a custom so far removed from its original cause as to be justifiable only by precedent, by the mere assertion that something was so because it had always been so, struck Boon in retrospect as peculiarly Japanese, a fitting end to the week he had spent as a guest in an eminently Japanese household.

Records of a cherry tree. Ichimonji Junichiro, self-appointed *sensei* and true son of Edo, had inherited an old-style wooden house in Higashi-jujo, on the outskirts of downtown Tokyo. The tiny house and still tinier garden accommodated the master himself, his wife and two children, a collection of *bonsai* and a pool of carp. The rooms were unfurnished and the decorations spare, in the quiet, almost chaste Japanese style. Ichimonji at home, enclosed in serene domesticity, preferred Japanese dress to Western clothes when cultivating his grandfather's trees or when engrossed in his historical studies of Toshima ward. Some of these studies, later intended for publication as a book, had already appeared in a learned journal not widely read. Ichimonji cared little for fame and was casual about money, although he would naturally have accepted a publisher's advance if one had been offered. In lieu of cash he pre-empted the publication of his book by accepting the honorary title of *sensei* which his dedication to scholarship allowed him to claim. The true son of Edo, proverbially spendthrift, neglected to make provision for the future, and by the same token would not defer until tomorrow the honours that could be enjoyed today.

This nimble man of many parts, amateur historian and occasional moralist, one-time cabaret owner and future candidate for a post in ward politics, was a builders' sub-contractor by profession, an actor by vocation and a rogue at heart. He was a realist sustained by the flight of his imagination, a born water trader, who lived one life and led a dozen others. Thirsty and venerous in the bars where Boon met him, loosening his talk with his tie, he slipped into a shabby, magisterial gown when he crossed his own threshold and sat obediently among his books and plants under the placid, redoubtable gaze of his wife. She spread quiet around her as a tree spreads shade.

From time to time Ichimonji would invite some of his more

reputable cronies to spend an evening in the shade that was cast by his beautiful wife. With that flair for dramatisation which underpinned his whole life he referred to these casual gatherings as the Ichimonji Circle, or, even more improbably, the Higashi-jujo Seminar. Boon sometimes attended too. He took along his tape recorder, not in order to record the event for posterity but for his own private review afterwards, as a means of improving his Japanese. Ichimonji saw this differently of course. In the simple fact that Boon was recording these meetings he already divined the historic significance of his circle. "Our chronicler," he would say proudly, when introducing Boon to a new guest.

The chronicler received another summons in mid-April, when the cherry tree in Ichimonji's garden had just begun to unwrinkle its pale pink blossom. Ichimonji had arranged a private flower-viewing party in its honour. "Do not go to the parks," he advised Boon, "at least, not until you have seen the blossoms in my garden first. There are too many people, too much noise and drunkenness in the parks. That is not the right frame of mind for *hanami*. You will find yourself distracted by the absurd spectacle of middle-aged men, who are unable even to stand properly, trying to sing and clap their hands and dance on tip-toe all at the same time. Not only that. Among so many trees with so many blossoms you will find it impossible to look at any individual flower. I have only one tree in my garden, so that is where you should start. Come and record my tree."

Ichimonji was engaged in a business discussion with two of his guests when Boon arrived, so his wife showed him out into the garden.

"That's Kenji," she said, "my husband's youngest brother. He's spent the last three years in London, and only got back here last week. I think you'll find him rather interesting . . ."

Boon found a young man of about his own age sitting cross-legged under the tree, his hands resting on his knees and his eyes closed. He appeared to have fallen asleep. Boon settled quietly on the lawn, the spring sunshine warming his shoulders, and admired Ichimonji's single tree. The cherry murmured with faint colours; the pinkish swarm in its leaves and the leaves' own humming green seemed almost like sounds. Remembering he had been asked to come and record the tree Boon dutifully switched the tape on. It really was a tree one could record.

After a while Kenji yawned and opened his eyes.

"Hello," he said in English, "you must be Boon. How very impolite of me. I'd been expecting you, you know, but . . . well, I only arrived in Japan a few days ago and I'm still rather tired. I must have fallen asleep."

"I've recorded your sleep," said Boon. "Would you like me to play it back?"

"What? Recorded my sleep? How – ?"

Kenji noticed the tape recorder and laughed.

"No, not unless it's particularly interesting. Did I snore?"

"I'd be more interested to hear what you've been doing in London," said Boon.

"I'm a sociologist. I was studying there to complete my doctorate. And now I've been offered a post at a university in Kyushu."

Boon took an immediate liking to Kenji and they were soon chatting away like old friends. He was eager, articulate, forthcoming, his experiences abroad still fresh on him, glossy like a dew, addressing Boon by his first name and shifting back and forth from Japanese into English with unselfconscious ease.

"You know, the so-called culture shock," he said, "is something we're supposed to feel when confronted by a strange culture for the first time. Has it ever occurred to you that this feeling is actually much more powerful the other way round, when one returns to one's own?"

"That's not a question I can answer until I get back home myself."

"Well, I'm still reeling. And I have the unpleasant suspicion that after three years' stay in a foreign country I have in fact learned much less about its culture than I have about my own. I used to take the underlying consensus in Japanese society for granted, but now, after three years abroad . . ."

"Now?"

'Well, I've woken up to it as something almost miraculous. The food we eat, the houses we live in, what we say and how we behave . . . the basic round of daily life is always the same. I can sympathise with the remark that someone once made to me in England: that he found the Japanese interesting as a people, but as individuals they bored him. There seems to be a quality of sameness, a quality of being Japanese, which goes all the way from the surface to the core. Membership in the same community of thought and feeling, the reassurance that even in the privacy of his thoughts the individual experiences what is common to others, is just as important to us as all formal, outward display of unity. This personal introversion of shared experience is how individuality is understood in Japanese society, in what one could describe as a centripetal society: the movement is always towards the centre."

"Where is the centre? What do you mean by centre?"

"The *uchi* of course."

Kenji was silent for a few moments, collecting his thoughts.

"In the old days it was a matter of course for individuals to subordinate their personal wishes to the interests of the family or clan they served. Unconditional loyalty to the head of the family or clan supplied the linch-pin of ethics in feudal society. This could and did lead to a conflict of ethics and the law. For example, those famous *ronin* – leaderless samurai – who committed a collective murder to avenge their lord were praised as the Glory of the age of Genroku for the noble example they set, but they were sentenced to death by the shogunate notwithstanding. That may strike us as paradoxical today, but it was fully approved of by society at the time."

"But these events took place three hundred years ago."

"Exactly. That's the point I wanted to make. The ideal exemplified by the forty-seven samurai has kept a hold on the Japanese imagination almost in perpetuity; at least until the Second World War, when it was celebrated as *messhi-hoko*: selfless patriotic service. In my opinion it's misleading to call it patriotic. Ostensibly those selected for the *tokko-tai* – kamikaze is the word that has become legendary – were dedicating their lives to their emperor and their country, but their private letters and diaries give a rather different impression. From these letters it emerges that the sacrifice has been made on behalf of the members of the *uchi*: fathers, mothers and sisters. These are the people the heroes were thinking of; it was their protection, not so much the protection of their country, which supplied the real motivation of the young suicide pilots."

"Could you wait a minute . . ."

Boon changed the tape in the recorder and labelled it carefully for future reference. Higashi-jujo, April 18. Recording of Ichimonji's cherry tree and of Kenji asleep. Kenji talking: *uchi*.

"What you say about the *uchi* as centre, and so on – I think that's clear. But how about outside the *uchi*? What provision was made for relations between one *uchi* and another?"

Kenji blinked and started massaging his knee.

"Well," he said, "that's exactly the problem. None at all. The five basic tenets of Confucian ethics, on which feudal society was founded, apply to relationships between master and servant, parent and child, husband and wife, brothers and sisters, and finally to the relationship between friends. There's no mention at all of the relationship between strangers, however; in feudal society the status or rank of a person was immediately clear from his appearance. One's behaviour towards this person followed the rules of etiquette prescribed for his particular status. A *moral* code, such as one finds in Christian teachings, applying to the association between strangers, doesn't exist and doesn't need to exist in a society of this kind.

"The archaic feudal *uchi* has evolved into the business and industrial concerns of modern Japan. The persistence of the word *uchi* when referring to the organisation to which one belongs is surely the clearest possible indication of the survival of the *uchi* mentality almost intact. This evolution is often regarded as something of a wonder, but it doesn't seem to me that it should surprise us in the least. Historically, the groundwork for any form of social structure other than the *uchi* was never laid. Anything in the nature of a public morality, even the concept of 'public' itself, has failed to materialise in this country, and we are badly in need of it."

"Surely that's an exaggeration. Some notion of 'public' is indispensable to a modern state. And there are words for it in Japanese, *oyake*, for example . . ."

Kenji smiled.

"Well, yes, *oyake* can sometimes have this meaning, but it's so much more restricted in usage than the word 'public'. Originally it denoted a large building; later it came to mean the imperial palace, the court and thus government. At no point does it share the original meaning of the word 'public', whose etymology embraces the common people and the idea of franchise. Nowadays, of course, the Japanese have adopted the word 'public'. We've imported the word but not the spirit."

"All right. But there must be some way of solving this problem in practice."

"Well, there are ways round it. Let me give you an example. As you probably know, the *Asahi* newspaper runs a famous column called *tensei jingo*. It also publishes an English translation, which I used to study when I was a student. At that time there were two cases which were very much in the news – the lawsuits on behalf of the victims of mercury pollution, known here as *minamata-byo*, and thalidomide. It'd be difficult to think of two cases more suited to be described as matters of public concern. And indeed, in the English version it was the word 'public' which most frequently occurred. In the Japanese original, by contrast, our imported word *paburikku* was not used once. There were references to the indignation of the *machi no minshu*, the 'townspeople', and very often to *ware-ware*, which simply means 'we'. Putting it rather harshly, these cases were not matters of public concern, because it is difficult to mobilise support for an opinion when those who support it remain unidentifiable, and this is unavoidably the case so long as you have no established word to address or refer to the general public."

"That's interesting," said Boon, ". . . astonishing, in fact."

Ichimonji's wife appeared on the veranda and asked them if their stomachs were empty. Yes, empty, said Kenji, breathing over his glasses and polishing them on the hem of his socks. From inside the house came the sound of breaking glass, followed by laughter. Ichimonji's wife hurried back inside.

"Who are those two men in there with your brother?" asked Boon.

"One of them is a man called Nakao, editor of some magazine or other, I think. I don't know the other man. My brother mentioned he was a designer."

Boon picked a blade of grass and began to chew it.

"D'you know," he said, "the blossoms on this tree are already much further than they were an hour ago. One can almost see them coming out."

"I hadn't noticed," said Kenji. He put on his glasses and peered at the tree. "To be quite honest, I'd never even noticed it was a cherry tree at all."

"Coming back," said Boon between mouthfuls of grass, "to your last point. If you have such problems with 'public', how do you handle the idea of private?"

Kenji pondered for a while and Boon chewed.

"We've also imported the word *puraibashi*, which seems to have taken much better than *paburikku* . . . the indigenous Japanese expressions for privacy turn on the word *hito*, meaning people: not among people, not in front of the eyes of people, and so on."

"Rather like the Latin *privatus*: withdrawn from public life," put in Boon.

"Quite. But don't let that mislead you into thinking that *hito* corresponds to public. It doesn't. The reason is that the word *hito* has always had extremely negative connotations which the English word 'people', to the best of my knowledge, entirely lacks. You'll probably have come across some of the many Japanese proverbs testifying to the hostility and suspicion which *hito* connotes. Now it strikes me as very remarkable that a word meaning people should so often be used in the much narrower, pejorative sense of 'stranger'. When members of an *uchi* refer to non-members – i.e. to the rest of mankind – as *hito*, an awareness of those people as outsiders who don't belong is automatically implicit in the use of the word. Naturally the members of the *uchi* in question are themselves referred to as *hito* by everyone else. Objectively everyone constitutes 'people', while subjectively it seems that nobody does.

"In these circumstances it's not hard to see why anything like the idea of public has failed to emerge in Japanese culture. There are the pair words *uchi-soto*, but these are very different from private-public. The word public, standing in creative opposition to private, has a positive meaning, whereas *soto* merely designates what does not belong to the *uchi*: it is a non-concept, a disastrous omission. In Japan the private-public axis is really an insider-outsider axis. This is the axis on which all the rival *uchi* of politics, business, industry and so on, collectively making up the national interest, negotiate with one another in the hope that the national interest can be served at the same time as their own."

Boon smiled.

"Was this the subject of your doctoral thesis?"

At this point they had to break off the discussion and join the others for lunch.

Ichimonji's wife had prepared a variety of cold snacks on the veranda – slivers of fish, grilled chicken and pork on cocktail sticks, rice balls and pickled vegetables.

"I'm afraid it's nothing much," she said. "Perhaps it's a little cold out here. No? I thought we'd eat on the veranda as Bun-*san* was specially invited to come and see the tree in flower . . ."

The men sitting cross-legged on cushions, only their hostess kneeling, they began to eat, all eyes on Ichimonji's modest tree. The blossoms visibly swelled and blushed, caught fire and softly detonated in a series of pink explosions. But for the trains that clattered up and down the nearby Keihin–Tohoku line every few minutes, the illusion of flower-viewing in a rural setting would have been complete.

"Does *otaku* have the custom of flower-viewing in his own country?" inquired Nakao politely.

"Unfortunately not," said Boon.

"Perhaps you could introduce it," suggested the nameless designer.

"Good idea," said Ichimonji, "take it home with you, Bun-*san*. In your luggage. Become a missionary of the Japanese spirit in foreign lands. Which reminds me. I must show you the *shunga* which Kenji brought back for us from London. Harumi, where did you put it?"

"I think it must be upstairs. I'll go and look."

"Perhaps you could get us some more *sake* as well . . ."

She got up and went inside.

"Does your wife's name mean Spring Beauty?" asked Boon.

"Yes, it does. So she's in season now." Ichimonji chuckled. "Flower-viewing in more senses than one. D'you know what *shunga* are?"

"Spring pictures, literally, so . . . erotic pictures, I could imagine."

"Very good. Japanese really isn't such a difficult language, you see. Here, take a look at this. Kenji picked it up in a second-hand bookshop."

Boon opened the folder that Ichimonji's wife handed him. The picture inside showed a young woman, sprawled over a man who lay half underneath her, apparently resisting his attempts to undress her. An old man, haggard and unshaven, was watching the couple through the open *fusuma* in the background.

"It's not original," said Ichimonji. "It's a copy of a much earlier print by Utamaro. Still, it's rather nice . . . by the standards of *shunga* it may seem a bit tame, but the point is that the couple in this picture are brother and sister."

"How can you tell that?"

"Because it says so in the legend."

Kenji leaned over his shoulder and pointed. Boon followed his finger down the inscription on the side of the page.

"*Ani-san, o-yoshi nasee . . .*"

"Elder brother, please stop . . ."

"To which he replies: '*kyodai wa tanin no hajimari to iu kara ii wa e—*'"

Boon smiled.

"The proverb says that strangers begin with one's own brothers and sisters, so don't worry. 'Strangers begin with one's own brothers and sisters' . . . I can't think of any English proverb to match that. What surprises me is this joke about incest. There's a sophisticated tone about it which seems to suggest that people at the time would have found such jokes quite acceptable."

"Well yes, I think they would," said the magazine publisher unexpectedly, leaning himself forward into the conversation, "judging by the fact that jokes about incest in texts accompanying *shunga* by Utamaro, Hishikawa Moronobu and many others were quite common throughout Edo. From time to time, when things began to get out of hand, the government would issue an edict and clamp down, but on the whole the artists were left to do more or less what they liked, so long as they avoided political subjects."

"It rather takes us back to what we were talking about this morning," said Kenji, turning to Boon. "At bottom the joke is a radical re-statement of the insider-outsider complex. Discrimination between insiders and outsiders being what it is in Japan, this is a deeply subversive, an anarchic joke. It shows yet again how deep-seated that *uchi* mentality is."

"And perhaps why we usually take care to enjoy ourselves only when we're well away from home – particularly enjoyment of a promiscuous nature," added the magazine publisher.

"I didn't quite follow that," said Boon.

Kenji explained in English.

"The *uchi* was traditionally very self-contained; perhaps people were aware of a risk of incest. One way of reducing that risk would be to discourage any kind of pleasure in the home. Drink, gambling, sex . . . anything that could be interpreted as *asobi*, or 'play', took place outside the home."

Nakao reached ceremoniously over the table and refilled Boon's cup.

"Bun-*san*, I was brought up in Tohoku. When I was a boy I often had to help in the rice fields with planting and harvesting. Hard work. It breaks your bones. Sometimes I would straighten up for a few minutes to rest my back, just stand, resting my back. And then the other villagers working in the fields would point at me and say *aitsu wa mata asonde 'ru yo!* You see, even standing there in the fields resting my back for a few minutes was thought of as *asobi*, as recreation, something done for my own pleasure and not for the benefit of others. Life for these small communities in the country has always been very hard. Have you read Endo Shusaku's *Chinmoku*?"

"No."

"Well, that gives a very clear impression of the distressing circumstances under which Japanese peasants used to live. Like animals. When someone left his village, for whatever reason, the main thing so far as the other villagers were concerned was that they now had one hand less to cope with the work. Absence from the village tended to be equated with recreation, doing something for oneself and not for the others. The idea of pleasure thus came to be associated with physical separation from the *uchi*, and this way of thinking still holds good today."

The nameless designer, who had not put in a word since lunch, suddenly lurched into the conversation.

"Perhaps it's true that we Japanese prefer to go out on the town rather than entertain at home, but surely there's a very simple explanation for that. Our houses are too small. There just isn't the space. And then there's the question of the neighbours . . ."

"Ah," said Kenji, "that's the typical Japanese point of view. But that's too easy. When you draw comparisons with other cultures and look at the matter in a broader perspective . . ."

When his brother began to talk, Ichimonji got up leisurely and wandered into the garden, motioning to Boon to join him. On the veranda they had been sitting in the shade, and Boon was now surprised to find how hot it was in the mid-afternoon sun. The warm temperatures had drawn the cherry blossoms out of their green casing and the tree on the lawn was suddenly in full bloom. The light wind that ruffled the flowers had a different sound, fuller now, like the bloom.

"The sound changes hour by hour," said Boon, a negligent chronicler. "The tree has changed the sound of the wind."

"Ah . . ."

Kenji's voice ground away in the background, grinding the designer's objection to powder.

"I hope Kenji wasn't boring you this morning."

"Oh no, not at all."

"Well that's good. He talks a lot these days, and some people find him a bit of a trial. Three years away from home, you see. I daresay he'll need more time to adjust to Japanese ways. He always used to be rather a quiet boy. Would you like it, by the way?"

"Like what?"

Ichimonji's mind had made one of its leaps and Boon's had failed to follow.

"That *shunga* Kenji brought back from London . . . I don't think we'll hang it up, you see. And it would be rather a pity to leave it lying in a drawer."

While Boon was trying to work out all the subtleties that might be hidden in this unexpected offer, Ichimonji's wife reappeared on the veranda, having cleared the dishes and washed up inside, to announce that she was now going out.

"What for?"

"To fetch the children."

"Oh."

Ichimonji had evidently forgotten about the children. Dutifully he followed his wife inside to be briefed on the measures she had already taken to ward off possible catastrophe during her brief absence from the house. Boon re-assumed his cushion among the veranda group, which by depletion seemed also to have shrunk into silence, and launched a thought that Ichimonji's offer had set in motion.

"I found what Nakao-*san* said a little while ago about the idea of pleasure being associated with physical separation from the *uchi* rather interesting. And I wondered if that might have something to do with *omiyage*."

"*Omiyage*? You mean souvenirs?"

Boon watched Kenji draw the two characters meaning souvenir in the palm of his hand.

"Yes, that's right. All this buying of souvenirs . . . is it a passion? Is it a duty?"

"Isn't it perfectly natural to buy souvenirs?" asked the designer, "doesn't everybody buy souvenirs?"

"Not like they do here. The Japanese are in a class of their own It's a national sport."

Nakao laughed.

"He's quite right, you know. I think we buy *omiyage* to remind ourselves of home, and we take something back home less as a reminder of the place where it was bought than as proof we'd been thinking of home at the place we bought it . . . somehow we feel we have to make up, don't we?"

"Make up for what?"

"For having been away from home, living it up while the family's stuck at home. Even if we *don't* live it up, although I suppose it's usually true that when we leave the roost we like to spread our wings."

"Or when the wife does – "

Ichimonji sat down with a smirk, nursing a two-litre bottle of *shochu*.

"In a sense we Japanese never leave the roost, never get out of the *uchi* at all – "

"How's that?"

"We're like snails. We carry it around on our back."

"Snails don't have wings to spread," said the designer, whose fuse took a long time to ignite, but this promising remark was drowned by the deluge of *shochu* that vaulted out of the neck of Ichimonji's bottle right across the table into his lap.

"*Ara! Gomen! Gomen nasai!*"

Apologies from Ichimonji, reassurances from the designer, each capping the other's effusions: a by now familiar kind of pantomime ensued. All further conversation fell into disarray for the next quarter of an hour and was only revived after full reparation had been made to the designer's trousers and apologies and pardons had been mutually tendered and received.

Ichimonji poured five large measures and distributed the cups.

"Well . . ."

He raised his cup, inclined his head. A moment's silence, perhaps for the trousers. All five drank solemnly.

"Do you know," said Ichimonji, "that Bun-*san* reproved me the other night for peeing against a wall?"

Boon protested.

"Reproved? Hardly. I followed your example myself. But the Japanese do seem to be much more natural about relieving themselves in public – Japanese men, that is – than we are. Perhaps because they have a more natural relation to the human body and its functions . . ."

"Ah . . ."

"More natural, yes . . ."

There was a spontaneous wagging of heads, as if someone had pulled an invisible string. Only Kenji's head remained unwagging.

"A more natural relation to the body? Perhaps. But then, doesn't this naturalness," he added slyly in English, "have something to do with there being no public to pee in?"

"*Nani o . . . ?*"

"Pee in? *Nani 'tte 'ru!*"

At this point the flower-viewing party began to get out of hand. Kenji was called upon to explain himself in Japanese, but his attempt to do so, entailing a summary of the thesis he had already imparted to Boon that morning, seemed only to deepen their mystification. Kenji cast around for fresh material, stoking the main body of his argument with matter pillaged from the footnotes.

Boon's conscious participation in this closely-reasoned argument benefited from his foresight in having brought along a tape recorder, which allowed him to reconstruct later what his *shochu*-addled mind could not follow at the time. Kenji argued that the lack of squares in Japan's cities was evidence of a lack of public consciousness generally, but his progress was stalled by frequent interruptions, some of them rebellious, and was more seriously impaired by someone's inadvertent attempt to pour *shochu* into the microphone, which in the fading light and with fading powers of judgement he had apparently mistaken for a glass. Soggy voices began to wrangle, background noise took over and the remainder of Kenji's thesis sank without trace. Boon recorded a lucid interval of silence, then amplified an already considerable sneeze, which only after it had been drawn out into a nasal keening sound, much too long for a sneeze, could tentatively be identified as the first note of a song.

Tschiii – !

The magazine publisher was keening the sounds of his country Tohoku, the song of his forefathers, farmer-fishermen on a distant shore. Peace settled on the garden with the dark. Nakao's voice fluted, arched, gently ebbed, recalling the sound of the waves in the song that he was singing. Looking into a garden larger now, the borders submerged in shadow, Boon imagined for a moment that he could hear the sea, and for a moment he thought he could understand a remark he had read somewhere about the Japanese garden being a paradigm of the sea. Nakao finished his song and began another. A train passed by, coming from Keihin, Tohoku-bound, reminding Boon that he had a train to catch at Ueno station in thirty minutes.

He stood up.

"I'm afraid I'll have to be getting on my way . . ."

His voice was lost in the chorus of Nakao's song. Ichimonji meanwhile, no longer too steady on his feet, was trying to sing and clap his hands and dance on tip-toe round his cherry tree all at the same time, giving a very passable imitation of the kind of middle-aged man he had warned Boon he would find at *hanami* in the local parks.

Ichimonji-*sensei*. Boon smiled.

A faint breeze stirred the garden and a cherry blossom sank, very slowly, to the ground.

Mariko. Boon experienced two springs that year. Spring in Tokyo came in passing, a casual affair. The air grew milder, parks he had never noticed before sprang up magically, like a splayed fan; and already the days were broadening into summer. Unlike this easy urban greening, spring in the country along the coast of the Sea of Japan came as a violent upheaval. After a long winter the entrenched ice cracked and split, rivers shook, the moist earth gaped and steamed. Boon travelled back and forth a great deal at this time between the two countries without ever quite being in either. According to whether he travelled north or south, with the change in climate the turning season was unnaturally arrested or advanced. He lost a sense of rhythm. The white plum-tree blossoms which he and Mariko saw in the hills behind Kanazawa at the beginning of May had flowered in Tokyo two weeks earlier.

Mariko worked in a bar in Toyama patronised by Sugama and a group of his friends. They had been at school together and all had left home for universities and jobs in Tokyo at about the same time. For the first few years after leaving home, ties within the group remained very close. Some of them attended the same university and shared rooms. They lived like expatriates, drinking together, playing mahjongg and baseball together, kept afloat in the vastness of the capital by a shared nostalgia for a common home. Gradually this changed. Old loyalties were overlaid by new. The companies they entered brought other opportunities, duties, colleagues, friends; the needs of companionship after working hours were absorbed by wives and families. After five or six years, home in the province had become remote. Most of them reckoned they would return one day, perhaps covered in glory, as the proverb said, but meanwhile they had put down their roots elsewhere.

The ties within this Toyama group were just beginning to dissolve when Boon arrived in Japan. Friends from a common background seldom lost contact entirely, however, because even after they had gone their own ways they were likely to meet during the new year and summer festivals, which were an occasion for nearly all Japanese to return to their native homes. It was thus no coincidence, although no arrangements had been made, that on the evening in late December when Boon first accompanied Sugama to the bar in Toyama where Mariko worked he found a number of people there whom he already knew from Tokyo.

It was a sophisticated bar, complete with fin-de-siècle decor, expensive liqueurs and a smooth proprietor in white tie who would have looked equally at home anywhere else in the world. For a dull provincial town the atmosphere of the establishment seemed pretentious and even bizarre. These qualities were probably its selling point. The place shrewdly catered for the dreams of patrons susceptible to international flair, who for a brief space of time and without forgoing the safety of familiar surroundings could imagine themselves elevated to bar-stools in Biarritz or the Bahamas. Sugama's closest friend, Ohashi, had first discovered the bar and he initiated the others. For the past two or three years it had become established as an informal meeting-place for members of the group on their occasional visits home.

Mariko's name had already cropped up in conversation in Tokyo. By all accounts she was an attractive woman. Boon learned many of the words detailing the stylish and erotic qualities of women without having set eyes on the person to whom they were applied. He was intrigued. His own impression from what he casually heard was that Mariko seemed able to deter men in the same measure that she attracted them. For some time Ohashi had considered making her a proposal, but in the end he had changed his mind and married someone else. According to Sugama, who was his confidant, Ohashi had withdrawn because a girl from the water trade would not have been considered a socially acceptable choice. No such reasons held back another member of Sugama's group; he had duly applied and been rejected. These offers or near-offers of marriage had been made to Mariko a couple of years ago. In the meantime all her previous suitors had either settled down into marriage or were about to do so. Mariko stayed alone. She was twenty-eight.

There was so much noise in the bar that evening, so many old friends, all with their own claims on Mariko's attention, that she and Boon exchanged no more than a few words. Boon was recovering from flu and still felt feverish. His perception of what was going on around him, of sounds and movements, light and shadow, even the passage of time, had the unpleasant quality of hallucination.

The following day he and Sugama made a trip to a resort in the mountains. They travelled for hours in a cold bus to a village at the foot of the slopes. Sugama knew someone there who ran a hotel. Apparently Boon had either already met this person or was due to meet him in the near future, he could not remember which. It didn't matter, because he wasn't there in any case. They were shown into a private room. A serving girl lit the stove and woke them half an hour later with enormous plates of steak and beans. Boon sat by the window looking vacantly at the icicles hanging from the eaves. The icicles and the shutters on the windows of a building opposite reminded him of the previous new year he had spent in the Alps.

In the afternoon Sugama went off to make enquiries about hiring skis. Boon waited at the entrance in hotel slippers several sizes too small for him, watching the guests pass in and out. The guests' outdoor shoes were arranged neatly at the entrance, toes facing out, in a line several yards long. Boon counted thirty-two pairs. Among them were his own boots, conspicuous by their size and shabbiness. He found the sight of them depressing. Somehow they didn't belong to the other shoes, which all seemed so sure of their place in the queue.

After a long wait Sugama reappeared triumphantly brandishing a pair of skis. They trudged up the slopes and to Boon's astonishment arrived at a plateau overlooking the coast. Beyond the tips of fragile hoar-shrouded trees he watched the leaden swell of the

Sea of Japan break white on a snowy shore. It was a miraculous sight. At a distance there no longer appeared to be any boundary between land and sea.

Boon gave an account of their expedition to the mountains in the bar the next evening.

"I've never seen anything like it," he said, and for Mariko's benefit Sugama did his best to translate Boon's description into Japanese. It was their last evening in Toyama. For the most part the conversation had been in English, with Sugama acting as interlocutor between Mariko and Boon. Oddly enough, it appeared that as Boon's health deteriorated, so correspondingly did his command of Japanese, by no means robust even at the best of times.

"What time are you leaving tomorrow?" Mariko asked, glancing at Boon.

"About ten. Why don't you come and see us off?"

"At ten? Usually I'm not up at that time . . ."

"What time d'you get home at night?"

"Not much before two, and often much later. Three, four . . . it gets very late at weekends."

It was already two o'clock when they left, and they were not the last customers. Mariko accompanied them to the door. It was still snowing.

"Shall I call a taxi?"

"It's all right. We'll walk a bit."

"Take care!"

Boon shook her hand.

"You take care too. It's cold outside."

"Goodbye. Perhaps if I wake up in time I'll come to the station and see you off. But don't wait for me!"

The snowflakes were turning into powder crystals and after a while it stopped snowing altogether. The stars came out. It was a brilliant night. They decided to walk home.

There was no sign of Mariko at the station that morning. Boon stood on the platform making small talk with Sugama's parents. The sky was overcast.

"Snow clouds," he said, glancing up.

"Yes, there's a lot more snow to come."

As he raised his head and looked up Boon caught sight of Mariko out of the corner of his eye, walking down the platform very fast. She was wearing a white coat and carried a parcel in her hand. He detached himself from Sugama and his parents and slowly went to meet her.

"Five minutes to spare. I didn't think I'd make it. There was so much traffic . . ."

"Thank you for taking the trouble to come," he murmured.

"Did you get the tickets all right?"

Mariko lifted her hair out of her collar and shook it out. There were shadows under her eyes. In daylight her face had a strange transparency through which Boon could see the shape of her skull.

"Sugama bought them three days ago."

He introduced her to Sugama's parents.

"Mariko," he said simply.

Mariko wished them good morning. They stood a couple of yards apart.

When Boon got into the train she handed him the parcel. Sugama's parents stood on the platform and waved as the train began to pull out, but Mariko immediately turned and walked away.

Boon opened the parcel a few minutes later. It was a book of poems. He treasured the gift, although it was many months before he was able to read any of the poems.

He wrote her a letter in clumsy Japanese thanking her for the present. The letter took a long time, and he practised the address several times on scrap paper before finally copying it onto the envelope. Mariko had been reluctant to tell him her private address.

"Surely it's not necessary," she said. Boon thought it an odd word to use. He thought it odd that she should be cagey about telling him her address one day and give him a book of poems the next.

A couple of weeks after he had posted this letter a postcard arrived from somewhere near Karuizawa. Mariko and her colleagues had gone on an outing to a local resort. It was cold; they had seen a film and fed swans by the lake; she hoped he'd call up some time. On the other side of the card was a picture of trees in winter. Looking at this picture he found himself wondering if the proprietor in white tie had also been feeding swans. The man was simply known as "boss". Mariko sometimes called him "master". Boon never found out his name.

Then another card arrived. It was an *ukiyoe* print, portrait of a woman. Something which Boon had resisted began to stir in him, just a trickle. He put the card in his bookshelf, took it out again, hesitated and at last replaced it, without knowing what he had been looking for. The next day he tidied out the cupboard in his room and found an old writing-case he had almost never used. He tucked the *ukiyoe* card into the lining of the case and zipped it up. None of this made any difference. He wrote a second letter, and a third. The trickle turned into a spate, a flood so deep and mysterious in its origins that not until he had been writing to Mariko almost daily for several weeks did he begin to grasp even dimly the full force of the feelings which had swept him so quickly so far.

The letters never seemed to travel fast enough. He wanted his feelings to be with her instantly. He sent the letters express, adding postscripts by telephone. He was out for most of the day, and she for most of the night. He sat up until the early hours of the morning, listening to the phone ringing endlessly in her empty apartment. Often she did not get in before five, and then so tired she had little to say. That didn't matter to Boon; he waited for her to speak, grateful even for her silences, upon which he could put his own constructions. Perhaps nothing Mariko could have said would have answered what he was waiting for.

In February he paid a telephone bill of thirty thousand yen, almost half his monthly allowance. It was a salutary shock, a reminder from the real world of which he had lost sight that for all things, and for none more than passion, one had to pay a price. Ruefully he told Mariko that in future he must call less often. In secret they were both relieved by the enforced respite, giving pause for him to sift his feelings and for Mariko to discover hers, but it was none the less a bitter disappointment when a week after he had last called her there was still no call from Mariko either.

His approaches were so reckless and imperious that they obliterated their object. It was less a courtship than an assault. Yet when Mariko remarked in one of her letters that she felt herself spiritually raped she was not registering a complaint; it was in the nature of Mariko's consent, as it was of her entire self, to appear as something taken rather than given, a submission rather than acquiescence. Boon was the predator and she his victim. This was not what she thought but what was thought in her, a conclusion that followed naturally from an irreducible fatalism lodged at the core of her soul. What Boon came to regard as the unbalance in their relationship she accepted without question as the complement of their different natures; at base, of their different sexes.

The abruptness of his intrusion into her personal life never troubled Mariko as it did Boon. It seemed it didn't even surprise her. The impact caused her to respond, no less, no more; a chord had been struck that agitated out of her passive expectancy a vibrant sound, at first audible only to herself, later to him. He was the agency of an effect in her, with her response they were complete.

For him the matter was different. The emotions released in him by Mariko were so powerful and sudden that they appeared suspect; not in themselves, but because he could trace nothing in the two brief encounters with Mariko sufficient to account for their intensity. He went over those meetings many times in his mind, searching for what was missing. He had seen her the moment he and Sugama entered; in fact, without having any idea what she looked like, he had *recognised* her. The sense of familiarity he had experienced when he first saw Mariko had given him a shock. Naturally it was not Mariko herself that was familiar but whoever or whatever she resembled. Boon had no idea. This was exactly what was missing.

If the sense of familiarity lay in some resemblance, the resemblance in turn lay in a common feeling that was clear to him even though its source was not. The feeling Mariko had about her was one that he already knew; and it was native to her, of this he felt certain, not something he had superimposed. It was native to her, it was quite her own, but deprived of the resemblance it would have been imperceptible: this ambiguity fascinated him, for the original of the likeness always remained absent. Accordingly it was in the nature of Mariko's attraction for Boon that it was accompanied by a sense of loss, of something that had been withheld at the same moment it was offered.

By degrees this notion of Mariko's likeness to anything other than herself faded, displaced in his imagination by the sensual correspondence of a feeling to a body; hips, arms, shoulders and at last the face. Mariko became a likeness to herself. Out of the obscure turmoil of such thoughts and sensations this was how Mariko emerged for Boon, just as he had imagined her to be, when she unexpectedly came up behind him among the Sunday crowds at Toyama station and called out to catch his attention. Nearly three months had passed.

"We never seem to get out of the station."

Mariko smiled. She looked just as tired as on the day he had left.

"When did you arrive?"

"This morning. At six o'clock. We came on the overnight train."

"Did you get any sleep?"

"A couple of hours. Well . . ."

Mariko was already turning, wanting to go on. Boon put his hand on her shoulder and looked at her. She was wearing a white trouser suit with a pink scarf; no coat, although it was cold. Vanity had decided against the coat. The pink and white set off her glossy dark head; her hair lay heavily in a coil on her shoulders. She looked beautiful.

"I thought you might like to go to Kanazawa – you've not been there, have you? It's worth a visit, not far from here but really quite different, as you'll see. What's the time? We'll have to hurry if we want to catch the train – you must be sick of trains. I hope you don't mind. Really not? There's so little to do here in any case . . ."

She drew ahead of him, and he realised that she was hurrying not towards something but away from something, away from the station, away from the town where people who knew her might see her with him.

In Kanazawa it was raining steadily. Neither of them was in the mood for sightseeing so they drove out to a hotel on the outskirts of the town. Once in the privacy of the car Mariko began to relax. On the train she had sat tight and unapproachable, hardly listening to Boon; he spoke softly, aware of the other passengers sitting there silently. Their silence had about it a quality that seemed to isolate himself and Mariko. Perhaps she had felt it too.

They reached a large white house on the spur of a hill. In the valley below them, grey with wind and rain, lay the washed-out roofs of Kanazawa. Mariko ducked her head and stumbled across the wet gravel while he was paying off the driver. A man in a black suit and bow tie waited under the awning at the entrance to usher him inside, apologising for the rain as if it were his personal responsibility. Boon followed him into the dining hall. The weak afternoon light was already beginning to fade. He joined Mariko at a table with a window overlooking the valley. Apart from themselves the place was deserted.

They ordered coffee.

"What made you choose this particular place?" he asked.

"Oh, well. I've been coming here for years. Don't you like it?"

"It's a bit gloomy."

"Gloomy? D'you think so?"

"Rain, nobody here, waiter in black. It's like a very private funeral. Who do you usually come here with?"

"Oh, various friends."

She rearranged the cutlery on the table and looked out of the window. He could feel her slipping away.

"How do you usually spend Sundays?"

"At home, usually. Sometimes I go out. Sometimes I visit my brother. He's my only family, so he feels responsible for me."

"When did your parents die?"

"My father when I was still very small. I hardly remember him. My mother died when I was twelve."

"D'you miss them?"

She sighed.

"Not my father. My mother, yes. At least I used to miss her; perhaps not any more. I suppose what I still miss is not having any family. There's my brother, of course, but . . . life in Japan isn't easy without family. I mean, not to live with, but just . . . in the background."

"I can understand that. So who brought you up?"

"My grandfather. When my mother died I went to live with my grandfather. Until then the three of us had lived together – my brother, myself and my mother. It was a happy time; at least in my memory it is. My mother was very gentle, very gentle . . . I used to sleep in one bed with her and I can still remember clearly the scent of her body. A beautiful scent, not something she used, just the natural scent of her body. When she died and I moved to grandfather's everything changed. My brother was also there for the first couple of years, but still. It was, I don't know . . . a dark house, somehow. He was a stern old man. I never played much as a child. I was glad to get out."

Boon tried to imagine to himself Mariko's mother and the scent of her body. She spoke matter-of-factly, but in the subtle texture of her voice there were resonances conveying something different from what her actual words were saying.

"How old were you then?"

"Nineteen."

"And what did you do? Did you get a job right away?"

"No. I had a little money from my grandfather. My brother helped too. I went to college for three years. I was taught the usual things suitable for young women: the tea ceremony, *ikebana*, dress-making and design. That was fun. What I enjoyed most of all was being with people my own age. I missed that at grandfather's. I started working part-time in a ladies' fashion shop, and after I left college I worked there for several months. That was before I took up my present job."

"How old were you when you started at the bar?"

"Twenty-two."

"So you've been there six years."

"Seven. I was twenty-nine in February."

"What made you switch there from the shop?"

Mariko glanced at her hands and then back to the window.

"I suppose it was money."

Okane desho. Her voice left soft, questioning echoes in the air.

Boon touched her hands and she placed them in his. On the inside of the index and middle fingers he noticed sores where she must have scratched the skin with the corners of her fingernails. Unexpectedly she laughed and leaning forward over the table kissed him lightly on the lips.

"It's still raining," she said.

He turned to look out, but it was already dark. The valley had disappeared and he could see nothing but their own reflection against a tracery of raindrops on the far side of the window.

Somebody must have come into the room to turn on the lights. He had not noticed it at the time.

The rain continued throughout the night and for most of the next three days. It was still raining in Kanazawa when they arrived there for the second time. Mariko bought a pink umbrella in a souvenir shop outside the castle. She was wearing the same trouser-suit, but had exchanged the pink necktie for a yellow blouse. She also carried a black bag. Boon didn't like the bag; it was out of place. But they wandered round the castle, peering at restored walls and illegible stone tablets, and he was happy in the knowledge that she was walking there beside him.

They left the castle and after a while found themselves in a wide green-bordered street with the scent of flowers and damp leaves. Crowds of flower-viewers, leisurely with children and umbrellas, picked their way under the dripping trees. From time to time they stopped, slanted their umbrellas and looked up, pointed, talked, passed on. Plum blossoms were bursting from pale green sheaths, here and there a spray of white. Mariko and Boon were drawn into the flocking holiday crowds and drifted separately to an exit on the far side of the park. There were too many people. They took a cab and drove up into the hills beyond the town.

In the hills it was just as crowded; lines of cars on the roadside with closed windows, hot-dog stands, immaculate hikers. Mariko wanted to sit down. There wasn't a bench in sight. They set off hopefully down a grass track leading away from the town into the valley. There were still no benches. Finally the track petered out on a knoll sheltered by a huge pine tree, with a view for miles over the tops of steeply-raked conifers into the smoky hills beyond.

"We're standing on somebody's grave."

Mariko crouched down by a stone under the pine tree and tried to make out the inscription. The stone faced the distant hills, exposed to wind and rain and listing badly; whatever memorial it once bore had long since been obliterated. Boon leaned against the tree with his hands in his pockets, looking for the waterfall he could hear faintly in the distance. The knoll on which they were standing reminded him of the magical hanging scenery in Hokusai's picture of the waterfall of Amida; the same quiet lay over the landscape in front of him like a glaze.

"Aren't you getting wet?"

"I'm all right."

Mariko stood up and drew him to her under the shelter of her umbrella. He folded his arms round her waist and kissed her cheek, resting against the tree. They stood together for a long time, their bodies gradually warming until they seemed to have softened into one mould. He closed his eyes. From the movement of her cheek against his lips he knew when she turned her head. The corner of her mouth, dryness first and then moisture, a slight shock: her lips were cooler than her cheek. A flurry of raindrops overhead caused him to open his eyes. A little beyond her eyelashes and the darker webbing of her hair the pink haze of her umbrella spanned his vision like a tent; almost, it seemed for a moment, like the interior of his own eyelids. Her mouth softened against his and he sank deep into her. He shut his eyes again. There was almost no change. This was how it might look from inside her, in a warm light filtered through the transparency of her skin. He was peaceful there, free of all desire.

He squatted in front of her and ran his fingertips up her spine. She shivered.

"Are you cold?"

"No. I'm not cold."

"It'll be dark soon."

"Soon. There's still time."

The bones under the skin of her back felt fragile. He could almost span her waist with his hands. There was a little slackness in her belly. He drew aside a corner of her blouse and kissed the smooth white fold of skin. The fleshed roundedness of her belly was unexpected; the skin so soft, fuller than elsewhere on her body, and somehow more vulnerable. He uncovered her hips and belly and stroked her with the palms of his hands, palming the flesh of her belly outwards and wringing it at her hips. The whiteness of her body started out against the dark encircling trees, banked green, the rusty bark of pines. The cool air pricked her skin, bared from the breasts to the pit of her belly. Excited by his hands, aware of her white naked belly, not resisting her pleasure, she shuddered and moaned. He laid his head against her and waited until she was quiet.

Later, with flushed cheeks and dancing eyes, Mariko sat in the lounge of the hotel where they had spent a wet afternoon the week before. Boon was astonished at the change in her. When her face shed its tiredness she became truly beautiful. In her manner towards him there was at times something tender. He had never yet seen her tender. For the first time in her company he had the feeling she wanted to be closer to him than to anyone else who happened to be around them. He had embraced her under the pine tree in the valley; they shared a secret now.

Mariko drank campari and talked fluently about herself.

"I was already twenty-two when I had my first lover. I started rather late, I suppose. I don't know why. Anyway, that's how it was. It didn't work out too well, but I didn't really love him so there wasn't a big disappointment."

"What became of him?"

"Oh, he's in Yokohama or somewhere," said Mariko casually. She screwed up a piece of paper and put it into the ash-tray. "There's another man now . . . I don't think I told you."

"You hinted at it in a letter, to try to dissuade me from coming."

"Your coming here makes everything so complicated," she said impatiently. "In a way I wanted you to come, and in a way I didn't. After all, I've got to live here. It's a small town."

"And life becomes difficult if people get to know you're meeting me?"

"Well, some people know already, and they don't like it."

"It's none of their business how you spend your weekends."

"No, of course not . . . still, it makes things difficult. This man, for instance, he doesn't like me seeing you."

"Who is this man?"

"He's an old friend. I've known him for several years. He's well-known in town, quite an important man, so we have to meet in secret. He's quite a bit older than I am. And he's married, of course, with children."

"How often d'you meet?"

"Once a week. I enjoy his company. He's intelligent, knows a lot, and I can learn a lot from him. I wouldn't say I love him. I'm fond of him and I admire him."

"But you don't meet in secret once a week just to talk, do you?"

"No, not just to talk. He's a gentle man, really, he is. We have a good relationship in all ways. Usually he encourages me to go out with young people, he likes me to have friends. But not in your case. He warned me about you."

"I warned you myself. I shall only be in this country for a limited time and at the moment I have no idea what'll happen afterwards."

"Well, and that's just the trouble. It would be different if I could say that we . . . if I knew that you had serious intentions."

"You do know that. My intentions are serious. But just consider how much time we've actually spent together. It amounts to no more than a couple of days in all. And most of that time is spent at stations, in parks and hotel restaurants. We've never been together privately once. You don't drag me off to Kanazawa in order to look at the scenery but in order to lessen the risk of us being seen together. All the time you are thinking of the best way of keeping me hidden. Our meetings are furtive and ashamed. It's not your fault and I don't blame you. But don't blame me either for being unable to make up my mind. You don't want me to stay with you when I come up for the weekend. I accept that. But you won't even consider inviting me home, you won't even let me through the front door of your house. You could hardly discourage me more effectively. D'you really find it so surprising then if I have doubts about our future?"

"I understand that," said Mariko sadly.

Boon had said enough and should have left it at that, but he was nettled by what she had said.

"Of course your friend doesn't approve of me. He's jealous. The deep sexual resentment of all Japanese men whenever they see a foreigner going with their women. Well, let me warn you about him. He can afford to be big-hearted only so long as he's not threatened. So you have the occasional date at the weekend – fine, why not? Go out my dear and have fun, he says. It doesn't hurt him; in fact it suits him rather well. He must spend Sunday with his family in any case. But he gives you to understand there are limits beyond which he'd prefer you not to go. And you don't, because you'd feel guilty if you abused his disinterested kindness. That's how he manipulates you. With this show of tolerance he actually keeps you tied to him most effectively. What vigorous middle-aged man would not be envious of the arrangement? Nice young girl once a week, nice fresh meat, no strings attached. Of course it must be done in secret – he's married, his other life must go on. Smart fellow. Best of both worlds. Does he at least give you money?"

Mariko shook her head and burst into tears.

"No," said Boon mercilessly, "his interest doesn't reach as far as that. What does he do for you then?"

"He gives me a feeling of security. He makes me feel secure. Simply his living in the same town means a sort of home for me . . . can you offer that? Can you give me that kind of feeling?"

He said nothing. He had been cruel to Mariko and now he felt bad about it. None of these things was her fault. And still – he listened to her sobbing with a kind of bleak satisfaction.

An hour later they left. He no longer had enough money to pay the bill and had to borrow a thousand yen from Mariko. She also paid the train fare back.

He felt remorse. He was gentle with her, trying to make amends, but already she did not need his remorse. He watched with sinking heart how quickly she recovered her composure. Secretly he had hoped that this first quarrel would somehow change things between them and bring a new outlook; but it hadn't. Mariko wanted nothing other than to be restored to the safety of the commonplace which Boon's presence somehow always managed to subvert. That was her reconciliation: just to get it behind her, look neither back nor forward, put on a bright face. The more cheerful Mariko became, the gloomier Boon. On the journey back it was just as it had been a few days before. As they approached her home town she seemed to become increasingly remote from him. They boarded the train in Kanazawa as lovers and got off it in Toyama as strangers.

The next afternoon he returned to Tokyo. She said she wanted to see him off, so they arranged to meet in a café an hour before the train left. He was not surprised that she came sixteen minutes late; he was surprised that she turned up at all. Meeting Boon at the station was becoming more and more of an ordeal for Mariko.

*

In April he took up teaching English part-time at a couple of private schools, one in downtown Tokyo and one out in the country. He was used to being short of money, but now, all of a sudden, he found himself considerably in debt. The expensive trips up north had to be discontinued. There was no question of Mariko coming to Tokyo either, because she seldom had more than one day off at a time. Since January he had been trying to arrange short weekends at some place half way, but for one reason or another she always turned down these suggestions. Now there was no money anyway.

Mariko best loved Boon at a distance. Although she always told him how much she was longing to see him when he called her up in the early hours of the morning, their enforced separation suited her temperament rather well. She wrote him letters that read like dreams. They were beautiful letters, but the woman who wrote them was never quite accessible. He pored over them for hours. The letters were addressed to him, very often they were about him, and yet in the end he had always somehow been excluded from them. Boon found that he was competing against a ghostly idealisation of himself who could pass in and out of Mariko's apartment as effortlessly as she could think of him, unseen, unheard and leaving no trace. Gradually he began to resent this privileged likeness of himself whom Mariko loved.

He told her he had applied for transfer to a university in the Toyama area where he hoped to be able to resume his studies in the autumn; whatever difficulties lay between them were due entirely to their separation; even if they could not live together, and that was not something he expected of her, merely the fact of coming closer and being able to see each other more often would allow them to make the decision that under present circumstances was impossible. Mariko agreed that this was the best solution. When his application was finally turned down she regretted the outcome much more fervently than she had hoped for its success while the matter was still open. So the plan had come to nothing. She consoled him on the telephone. And again the way was free for Boon's likeness in her imagination to usurp the place he had left vacant.

Mariko was an enigma. The ambiguity about Mariko, the ambiguity that Mariko herself was, began to torment him. She had come to the station sixteen minutes late the day he left, although she knew they would only have an hour together. Ten minutes, a plausible margin, or twenty minutes, because something had gone wrong: either more or less would not have bothered him. Instead she came exactly sixteen minutes late.

"Something hold you up?"

"Oh no, nothing in particular ... I'm just late," said Mariko airily, and handed him her coat.

He told himself that she was late because in her heart she was anxious not to be seen with him. The trouble was, he knew that Mariko would never tell him anything like that, even if it were true and she felt an urge to tell him. That wasn't how she set about things.

He would have liked to believe this had been the reason, but he was nagged by a much simpler explanation: that she was just late, as she herself said, for no particular reason. But how was it possible for her to be *just* late, wondered Boon. How did her heart measure their precious time? Did it have so little value for her?

What a fuss about sixteen minutes – he felt he was being very mean-spirited. How mean he could be in his suspicions! He told himself to forget it. He was grateful when Mariko told him on the telephone how much she was missing him.

These were the things that would pass through Boon's mind when he stood in the classroom of Maruta's private school, where he taught an occasional class. He would look absently out of the window, forgetting the children, for minutes at a time. They were either very obedient or very wise, for they never disturbed Boon when his attention wandered. After a while he would pull up with a start and turn back to the rows of shining faces watching him curiously.

"Have you all finished the exercise?"

"*Hai!*"

He would ask this question a dozen times an hour, just for the pleasure of hearing them all shout *hai!* It was his favourite word in Japanese, and perhaps the best word for Yes in any language: it had such an open sound. The children seemed to enjoy the drill too. It was an easy response and they always knew it was right, even if they'd got the exercise wrong.

The children chirped away, the director of the school was satisfied. Privately Boon doubted if any progress was being made. So long as he stuck to the routine the results looked impressive, but if he wandered so much as an inch from the beaten track there was immediate disaster. When the children trooped into class one day he turned to them and enquired in his greeting voice

"Have you all finished the exercise!"

"Good afternoon, Mr Boon!" came the predictable chorus.

Modern *juku* like Maruta's establishment in the heart of downtown Tokyo were not really schools but crammers. In recent years, as the school curriculum became more and more demanding, *juku* began springing up all over the country. Afternoon and weekend classes were geared to help thousands of struggling children to keep up with the exacting requirements of day-to-day work at school, to prepare kindergarten graduates for the competitive entrance exams to good primary schools, primary school children for a better intermediate school, and so on, through a frightening treadmill that ideally ended with graduation from one of the best high schools and a place at a distinguished university.

The *juku* no longer catered just for backward or difficult children. They were private institutions, and attendance (for a reasonable fee) was supposed to be optional, but in practice it seemed that the majority of children had as little chance of getting round extra tuition as of avoiding school proper. School effectively went on all day, the only difference being that in the morning it was free whereas in the afternoon it had to be paid for. The children likewise had two sets of homework, a morning homework that cost nothing and an afternoon homework which their parents paid to have corrected. Children did their homework in the evening when they returned from the *juku*. They led busy lives.

Some of Boon's children were genuinely obedient, but many were just apathetic. He had three classes – about fifty children in all, whose ages ranged from seven to thirteen. The signs of strain were different at different ages. The movements of very young children were often unnaturally slow, as if they needed to conserve their energy. They toiled over mountainous letters in empty copybooks with aching slowness, lifting their heads and gazing into space with a kind of wonder-eyed numbness, grateful when Boon released them from their tasks. Older children, who had lost the gloss of childlikeness, appeared cramped and sullen.

For the first couple of weeks they were a bit frightened of him. They shrank into their desks and inspected him warily from behind an armoury of books. After the second week Boon summarily removed these defences by announcing that in his classes they would not be using any books. They would make drawings instead. Listless faces at the back cheered up. Drawings of what? Of me, said Boon. Make a drawing of my face. What? A drawing of Boon Teacher? Initial glee was followed by creeping doubts. For it turned out that they didn't know Boon Teacher's face as well as they thought. They had never looked at it closely enough to be able to make a drawing. Apart from that, would he like the drawing?

From the moment the children made their drawings of Boon Teacher's face they began to conquer a deep-seated inhibition and became less shy of him. For Boon the exercise also turned up some interesting results. The way boys saw him was clearly different from the way girls saw him. The boys worked quickly and decisively, drawing him with firm, aggressive lines which they didn't bother to rub out if they happened to go wrong. The girls set about the task much more cautiously. After a long time and a great deal of rubbing out they produced a careful, finely-drawn outline of a face which in some cases remained incomplete. There was nothing inside the outline – no eyes, nose or mouth. The face was simply left blank.

"Have you all finished the exercise?"

"*Hai!*"

The wail of tiny voices rose like a swarm of flies.

Maruta-*san* was well-suited to be the director of a *juku*: a hard-headed businessman who could talk like a philanthropic educationist when the occasion required, dispensing pep-talks and brisk doses of corporal punishment with the same vigorous enthusiasm. He was a born pragmatist, with a great respect for principle so long as it squared the account books. He furthered the educational standards of the nation: he made money: no room for the slightest doubt on either score. He was one of the most complacent men Boon had ever met.

"What I want," Maruta-*san* explained, "is to provide an opportunity for contact between Japanese children and foreigners. I want them to become accustomed to foreigners, to learn from personal experience that they are not really any different from the Japanese. Maybe in the process they'll also pick up some English. That would be nice, of course – English is important. But at the moment I don't see that as the main point."

So English lessons with Boon Teacher were easy; the children could do more or less what they liked. Otherwise they never had an idle moment. Classes went at a cracking pace, in an atmosphere more reminiscent of a parade ground than a classroom. Concentration was most sharp and discipline most stern in the large, old-fashioned schoolroom downstairs where Maruta-*san*'s father taught his pupils the use of the *soroban*, or abacus. Boon sometimes slipped in to watch from the back of the room. It was a chilling spectacle, and quite irresistible.

The gaunt, dour-faced old man was a master of the recitative style employed by instructors of the *soroban*. To Boon's ears it had much in common with the incantation of Buddhist liturgy. Impassive, priestlike, he lifted his head and began to declaim the columns of figures on the paper held up to his eyes as if he were reading a score; sums of addition, subtraction, multiplication and division which his pupils instantly translated into the movements of their fingers and the urgent clatter of abacus beads. His voice pitched out over the rows of bowed heads and fell in monotonous cadence, a tedious chant without interruption or respite, insistent, monosyllabic. At last he reached an end. A flurry of clicks, hands shot up. The solution was given and at once the dirge of the *soroban* master resumed.

Every other Saturday Boon travelled out on the Keihin Tohoku line to Omiya, where he boarded another train which, if he was lucky, stopped at a small station out in the country, where he had been asked to take on kindergarten classes. The kindergarten was a depressing place. Straggling, meagre huts had been assembled in a barren compound surrounded by marsh and paddy fields stretching as far as the horizon, as if the builder had ditched them there, out of spite.

On his first day the secretary directed Boon to Hut 1. About fifty children were assembled in the enormous classroom he entered, singing obediently to the accompaniment of an antique piano. Sounds emerged from this instrument sporadically and with the utmost reluctance; the pianist had to pounce on the keyboard to get anything out at all. Boon waited in the doorway until the notes of the final chord had been ambushed and rounded up. The woman who had been playing the piano closed the lid reverently and turned to the class.

"Stand up, children!"

All the children stood up, with the curious effect that they seemed to diminish rather than grow in stature. Many of them were not more than about four, and they appeared more considerable when sitting than when standing. Boon looked at this little army with dismay.

"Let's greet the teacher!"

"*O-hayo gozaimasu!*"

"Good morning!" replied Boon.

The woman bowed and softly withdrew, leaving Boon alone in the centre of the room. He asked the children to sit down.

'Hallo!" he said with a nod and smile.

"Harrow!"

"No, not Harrow. That's in London. Listen carefully and try again. Hallo!"

"Harrow!"

He demonstratively rolled his tongue and stuck it out. The children laughed.

"Put the tip of your tongue behind your teeth, like this. Low!"

"Low!"

"Very good. Hallo!"

"Harlow!"

Once a fortnight he travelled out to this remote kindergarten among the paddy fields to play greeting games with the children and teach them their letters. Spring passed, summer came; the children and the list of letters they could write grew steadily before his eyes. By the time the school was closed for the summer holidays they had negotiated the worst of the alphabet without loss or serious hardship, and by Christmas there was a good chance of their literacy having advanced far enough to incorporate X in their seasonal greetings. When the sun shone through the east window of Hut 1 they wished him Good Morning, when through the west window Good Afternoon, sometimes unhesitatingly, sometimes in doubt, waiting to see whether he would move towards the blackboard window or the window by the piano. They enquired how he was, expressed their pleasure when he was feeling fine and occasionally when he was not, repeatedly told him their names, asked him his, shouted Harrow and Goodbye with equal enthusiasm.

On his deaf days, when his hearing was bad, all these greetings and enquiries had to be submitted on paper, a great labour for many of the children and for some of them a hopeless one. Boon wandered round the room sampling their efforts. God MNIG. Dak. HarROw. Runic marks, not identifiable as letters, but evidence of an abandoned intention, seeking refuge in the corner of a page. There were children who produced nothing at all and scrupulously rubbed it out again. He encouraged all efforts, letting each child get on in its own way as best it could. He didn't count in any case. He appeared and disappeared, something altogether too improbable for the children really to believe. With the return of the woman accompanist into the classroom at the end of each lesson they were reclaimed by the reality they knew. She played, they sang, stood up, were dismissed. Rain or shine, in identical smocks, boots and plastic hats they trundled across the compound and out into the dusty road, tethered in a long orderly line to the familiar figure in wide blue pantaloons and spotted scarf who went out in front. Life was already drill. The discipline in groups seemed to come so naturally that Boon wondered if it had ever needed to be learned.

By early summer his finances had been sufficiently repaired for the journeys to Toyama to be resumed. It occurred to him that teaching ought equally well to be able to support a longer stay there during the summer vacation. Sugama explored his local connections and eventually found two companies where Boon could be engaged on alternate evenings teaching English to the employees. He would take up his duties in late July and return to Tokyo when the university term opened in September.

Meanwhile he travelled up regularly on the overnight train after he had finished teaching at Maruta's *juku*. The journey took six or seven hours and frequently he had to stand. Long-distance trains were always full, whatever their destination and at whatever time of year. He soon learned that if he wanted to be sure of a seat on a train it was necessary to be waiting at the booking office of his local station by the time it opened at eight in the morning, not on the day of departure, but a week in advance.

Mariko took all these arrangements, the time, money and trouble involved, entirely for granted. She booked him into a hotel within walking distance of her apartment. Boon usually arrived in town just after dawn, at about the time Mariko got home from work and went to bed. She was never up before noon. He whiled away the morning in his hotel room, drinking coffee and writing letters. His heart ached. He knew that just a couple of hundred yards away from him Mariko was lying in bed asleep. He didn't mind staying in a hotel if that saved her unpleasantness, but her refusal to allow him into her apartment at all was something he could not understand.

"Is it really necessary?" she asked him on the telephone, a few days before he arrived.

"Necessary? What does that mean? Is it some sort of *effort* for you if I come and visit you at home?"

Mariko sighed.

"It's not my apartment, you know."

"No I didn't. Whose is it then?"

"It belongs to the boss. I rent it from him. The thing is, he's forbidden me to let you come here, and he'd prefer me not to see you at all. He advised me against it. If he found out that I'd let you come here there would be consequences . . ."

"What sort of consequences?"

"I might even lose my job."

"This is ridiculous. It just can't be true!" said Boon angrily.

He didn't know what to believe. Sugama thought it unlikely, but in the provinces this kind of thing was still possible; perhaps Mariko was telling the truth.

Piecing all this information together, Boon gradually became aware of a suspicion that had hung at the back of his mind from the very beginning: that Mariko and her boss were secretly lovers. He went a step further. It was conceivable that the boss and the middle-aged man whom she met each week were one and the same person. Boon's imagination began to embroider this unexpected thought, solicited by a jealous sexual passion that had drowsed in him for the past months. He was quartered by doubts. Mariko brushed them aside with a laugh. In the end he believed her, though without conviction; he was afraid of the consequences of not believing her.

When he saw her, however, when she was actually there beside him, all his doubts instantly vanished. Her presence was like a spell. They changed trains at a country station and waited on the platform in sunlight, watching a man hose down cars in a siding. It was almost summer. Mariko was wearing a dress for the first time. There was a sweet breath on the wind, a scent it had brought down from the mountains, sweet and clear. Boon's mind idled. He watched the man hose down the cars and thought of Mariko's bare arms. A single shining track narrowed at the end of the platform and ran swift and straight across the plain.

An old locomotive lurched out of a siding and pulled up along-side the platform. The cars must have been built between the wars. They were furnished in brass, mahogany and blue felt. Nobody else was in the car. Boon whooped. Mariko kicked off her shoes and sank low into the sprung cushion, her skirt peeling back over her thighs.

At a store outside the station where they got off Mariko bought some rice balls, a bar of chocolate and an orange. She asked the woman in the store to cut a strip of peel from the top of the orange so that it would be easier for him to eat. The woman put the things in a plastic bag, but he kept the orange in his pocket. It was the first time ever that Mariko had done something for him like that.

She had suggested a picnic in the amusement park up on the hill, but when they reached the entrance and saw the crowds that were trekking up the slopes they changed their minds and turned back.

They left the village and followed the road down to the river. A long narrow bridge spanned the river. On the far side the roof of a shrine was just visible among the trees. The sea is in that direction, said Mariko, and pointed. They set out across the bridge. The river broadened into an estuary at this point, but he could see nothing beyond the mudflats about a mile off. Light rebounded from the surface of the water and settled in a brilliant haze. It was windless. The white road shimmered ahead. No one else was crossing at the time. It was as if the bridge had been made just for them.

The shrine was set in a park, shaded by huge trees, cedar and pine. They heard voices but saw no one. Mariko scooped water from a trough with a wooden ladle, sprinkled her hands and drank from the spring. It is sacred water that purifies, she said, filling a cup for him to drink. He went over with her to the shrine. The sound of gravel rolling under her sandals detailed her footsteps, made him more closely attentive to the way she walked. Under the eaves of the shrine, where the shade was even deeper, he leaned against a bolted door and watched her pray in a shaft of sunlight. She flung a coin into the votive box, clapped her hands and closed her eyes. The ritual meant nothing to her. She was like a child playing a solemn game. She smiled at him and stretched out her hand. He had the impression he had once seen her like this in a dream.

They left the shrine and walked down a lane by the river, past overgrown gardens running wild and large houses that were apparently deserted. Mariko strayed into the thickets by the roadside to pick flowers and discovered a flight of steps, almost hidden by the weeds, descending to the river's edge. She sat on the bank sunning herself, while Boon took off his clothes and swam across the icy channel to a shoal in the middle of the stream where he warmed himself on the pebbles. Several hundred yards upstream a fisherman was casting his net. The net flew up and spread out of his hands like a bird opening its wings.

He swam back to the shore, dried in the sun and got dressed. While they had lunch he asked her about the curious monolith marooned on an island close to the shore. It was shaped like a phallus, tall and smooth and with a colour like tar. Apparently these stones were the relics of some fertility cult; he had often come across them in the neighbourhood of shrines. But she knew nothing about the stones. They were just there, she said; they would always be there. She peeled the rind of the orange into the plastic bag and wiped her fingers on the grass. Boon lit a cigarette. He was waiting for the fisherman to pass.

The fisherman had slowly worked his way downstream and now Boon could see him clearly on the opposite shore. He was an old man. He didn't seem to have caught anything, but he worked patiently and without hurry. It took a long time to draw in, untwist and fold the net; casting the net took a few seconds. Boon watched it leap out and billow, the four corners stretched and the centre slack, like an awning suspended in mid-air. It seemed to hang there a long time. The fisherman barely glanced at the net when he pulled it in. Perhaps he was less interested in catching fish than in the exercise of his mastery, in feeling his heart leap out when he made those marvellous bird-like casts.

A cloud passed between them and the sun. Mariko felt the sudden coolness and opened her eyes. Boon lay resting his head on his arms. She leaned over and kissed him, unbuttoned his shirt, explored his chest with her fingertips. He felt her hand travel down over his stomach. Unexpectedly she opened his trousers and began to fondle him. The sun came out again. He shaded his eyes and lay motionless, listening to the shallow patter of the stream. He felt the coarse tips of her hair tickle his belly as she lowered her head, and the sudden warm moisture of her mouth. In the way she touched him he sensed not only gentleness but also curiosity; when she withdrew her hand she looked at him and said softly *gomen nasai*. He wondered why she asked his pardon.

The moment he sat up he became aware of something in the landscape that had changed: on the bridge they had crossed earlier in the afternoon, about sixty yards downstream, a figure was silhouetted against the sky. At that distance Boon could clearly make out the figure as a man. He was leaning against the rail watching them. He must have been watching them for some time.

Later, in the evening, when Mariko had come back with him to his hotel room, the telephone unexpectedly rang. A voice at the end of the line asked him if he had a visitor with him.

"What business is that of yours? Who are you, anyway?"

"Hotel guests are not permitted to have visitors in their rooms. Please ask the lady to leave immediately."

Boon said nothing and hung up.

Mariko came out of the bathroom wearing his *yukata*. She drew the curtains and stretched out on the bed beside him.

"Who was that?"

"Just a man."

"What sort of man?"

"Probably someone at the reception. He said you weren't allowed to be in my room."

He opened the *yukata* and looked at her naked body.

In late July Boon arrived back in Toyama to take up his teaching job. Mariko hadn't really believed that he would come. She panicked. For the first week she refused to see him at all.

With the help of the Sugama family he had been able to rent a small apartment in the backstreets of the town which by chance was only ten minutes' walk from the Spring of Seven Waters where Mariko lived. He passed the house often. The paper address he had written to was very different from the reality he now visited: a dingy two-storey building with a corrugated iron roof and an iron-plated outside staircase which gave access to the rooms on the first floor. First-floor tenants aired their bedding on the corridor railing outside their front doors. When they walked up and down the staircase it produced a toneless metallic resonance, like the striking of a gong.

Boon lived in a long low room opening at one end onto a courtyard. There was only one window, screened with *shoji* and netted with gauze to keep out the mosquitoes; even when he removed the *shoji* altogether the room remained half-dark. Unless he pressed his face up against the gauze it was impossible to tell whether the sky was grey or blue. At eleven o'clock in the morning a shaft of sunlight burned through the gauze and penetrated about a yard into the room, briefly lighting up the interior before it retreated and passed on.

There was nothing in the room at all. He borrowed a roll of bedding from Sugama and slept on the *tatami* under the window. In the cupboard where he stored his bedding during the day he found a board. He propped the board on his suitcase and upended typewriter cover to make a kind of desk; the wall of the room served as a back-rest. He laid his Japanese texts out on the board and sat down to his studies every morning. He could forget the bleakness of the room, the straggling, mournful light, but the humidity was intolerable. There was no ventilation at all. The air hung in the room and never moved, for days at a time, making concentration difficult and sleep almost impossible.

Through the paper-thin walls and the courtyard window voices reached him from everywhere. With the exception of his landlady he never saw the people to whom these voices belonged, but on the evidence of his ears he could in time make up a picture of the families living round the courtyard. One family, in particular, he got to know quite well. The wife was young, probably about thirty. She had three children, two boys and a baby girl. There must have been a grandmother too; the children often called for her. He only heard the husband a couple of times, as he usually came home at about the time Boon went out. The sound of his voice was rather hard, a dissonance in the accustomed daytime harmony. The daytime was unmistakably a woman's world, full of soft sounds, slow and peaceful.

On the day of Boon's arrival his landlady brought him a melon, on the next day a glass of cold tea. When her curiosity was satisfied her hospitality also ceased and thereafter he hardly ever saw her. It only became clear to him that he did not much like her when day after day he heard her laugh on the other side of the wall. She was a corpulent woman and had an unexpectedly brittle, flaky laugh, which curiously reminded him of grated cheese. There must have been someone else in the landlady's house, perhaps another lodger. This person never spoke, at least not audibly, and it was only as the object of his landlady's constant nagging that Boon had any evidence of his or her existence. On the floor upstairs there was also someone with a piano who played the instrument as if it were a typewriter. Voices called, *fusuma* doors slid to and fro. All these neighbourhood sounds reached their peak around midday and then, like the light, began to fade into the afternoon.

At the beginning of his second week he persuaded Mariko to meet him for lunch. She described the way to a temple about five minutes from the house and asked him to wait for her there at one o'clock. She arrived late and seemed nervous. "This way," she said, turning back quickly in the direction from which she had come. He followed her into a labyrinth of narrow cinderpaths that ran along the backs of houses and enabled them to cover the whole distance without once crossing a street. From the pace at which she was walking it was clear that she was anxious not to be seen. He followed her in silence. At last the path opened into a street and she ducked abruptly under the awning of a noodle shop just round the corner. Once she was inside she seemed to relax.

"It really is unbearably hot," she said, slipping off her sandals. "What'll you have?"

"Anything."

She ordered cold noodles with spice.

"There was no need to walk so fast."

"Did I really walk so fast? I'm sorry. I didn't notice."

"It won't do, you know," he said. "You're making me feel like a criminal. If we're always going to have to be as secretive about it as this then I'd prefer not to see you at all."

She said nothing for a while. Then she reached out and touched his hand. "Please, you know it's difficult for me. They put a lot of pressure on me. Be patient. I'll do my best."

She kissed him so affectionately that he relented and promised to say nothing more on the subject. After that they chatted happily like old friends.

And things really did seem to get better. Every morning for the rest of that week they went to the public swimming baths and afterwards ate cold noodles at the little noodle shop just round the corner from where Mariko lived. She never invited him to her place and he never asked her. But the sight of her soft body when she sunned herself beside the pool each morning began to stir him. The way she lay in the sun, stroking her belly and arms and smiling at him, was as ambiguous as everything else about her. She liked her own body and it was natural for her to touch herself. At the same time she was aware that it excited Boon. She, too, wanted him; but what she wanted even more was his desire. And when on their way back from the pool one day they passed his room and he asked her inside of course she said No, it was out of the question, people would immediately get to know.

On the last day of that week, instead of parting as they usually did after lunch at the noodle shop, they set off at random and after a long walk found themselves in an outlying district of the town. A dusty red track leading over a strip of wasteland between the buildings gave an unexpected view of fields brimming with flowers and the shadow of the mountains beyond. He instinctively turned off from the road and followed this track.

"Where are you going?"

He said nothing and she followed him. As they walked down the track a building which had been hidden from the main road gradually emerged between the trees. At the entrance to the building a deep thicket crowded the borders of the drive, forming a natural tunnel. They passed through this tunnel and came out into a grassy sunlit yard. On one side was a ruined outhouse. Weeds had sprung up and almost covered the piles of rubble, rusty iron and shattered glass. Doors had been taken from their hinges. The building was deserted.

He faced her in the middle of the yard and unbuttoned the top of her frock. She looked over each shoulder and whispered something he couldn't understand. He unbuttoned her frock down to the waist. The sun burned down steadily into the yard; the crickets trilled and rasped. He slipped the frock over her shoulders and arms. It dropped to her hips. She shook her head and looked anxiously towards the thickets. She put her hands on his shoulders. Her breasts lifted and swung. He rubbed the nipples with his thumbs and kissed her throat. No, she said, but she did not move. She kept her eyes on the thickets. He kissed her breasts and put his hands under her buttocks. No, she said again, and this time she pulled away. She stood a couple of yards from him and turned towards the distant field. A tractor was coming towards them. She slipped her hands into the sleeves of her frock and drew it back up over her shoulders.

He took her hand and led her into the building. On one side a wall was missing, the room was open to the courtyard. It's not safe here, she said, what if someone comes. No one will come, he said. He leaned on a ledge by the wall and drew her to him, neither willing nor resisting. Someone might come, she murmured, putting her arms around his neck and kissing him. The noise of the tractor in the field approached and died away. He reached under her frock and slipped her pants down her thighs. But you mustn't do that, she said, not here. He put his hands between her legs and pressed his fingertips into the small of her back; he felt her moist and bushy against the inside of his arm. She rode up and down on his arm, arching her crotch and pressing down into his cupped hand. He opened his trousers and reared up at her, impaled her, snatched up her legs and lifted her whimpering. Her buttocks sagged, her calves curled more tightly round his hips and she cried out no, even as he was flooding into her.

Afterwards she wiped herself with his handkerchief, clean and catlike, got dressed and walked home with him as if nothing had happened. She did not seem surprised, showed neither irritation nor pleasure. When they parted at the corner of her block there was nothing in her manner betraying the slightest change.

Two or three times during the next few weeks they made love in the deserted building on the outskirts of the town, always with the same brutish desire on his part, the same reluctance, abortive sexual passion and, when the coupling was over, negligence on hers. He took her like an animal, against the wall or on the floor or in the grass outside, neither with nor against her will. And each time she would crouch on the floor, cleaning herself in her quick, catlike way and glancing out of the corners of her eyes at the dark tunnel that led out onto the road. Her aloofness from her own body and the desires her body had, the sensuality her body claimed and the gratification it was not allowed, the spirit of the woman always as remote from him as her prickling flesh was close: never able to have her entirely he was driven wild. The warm, wet, matted midsummer heat got into his blood, dulled his mind and breached his senses; his desires lay in the surface of his skin like open wounds, chafed and inflamed at the slightest touch. And somehow she was infected with the same recklessness that was in his blood. At noon they met behind the temple in the shade of its dipping eaves, backs to the fence, half naked, groping and şhuddering in silence as an endless stream of homecoming children crowded the path on the other side. At night they met there too, in pitch dark or broad moonlight, when the temple was deserted. He sweltered in his room, he could get no air. It was like a coffin. He ran out down the cinderpath and breathed the cloying summer night. Sometimes she came, sometimes not. She appeared almost without a sound, an indistinct moving whiteness, very faint, like an echo of the daytime thrown back at him out of the dark. They sat on the stone steps whispering while he fondled her breasts and stroked her hair. She could easily have come to his room or taken him to hers. There would have been less risk there than in meeting him furtively in the open. But she remained implacable. Denying him access to her room was no longer a precaution but the last privilege she had to withhold herself from him. What else remained? Her room was her retreat, her sanctum, her self. And she would not let him come in there, never.

The morning visits to the public swimming baths ended after a week. Mariko gave no explanation; she simply could no longer go there with him, she said. Boon kept his promise and did not press her. He knew without asking that someone must have seen them there together and that Mariko had again been warned. Late one evening he turned up drunk at the bar where she worked, had a row with the proprietor and made a fool of himself. Although Mariko's name was not mentioned, both men knew that it was her they were quarrelling about. Their dislike of one another had come out into the open now.

"Something's going to happen," he told her gloomily the next day. "The fuse is already burning."

She begged him not to come to the bar again.

It was not just two or three people, not just a private feud. Boon knew that he was up against the inveterate hostility of a provincial town towards the stranger and that he could not win. He felt himself changing for the worse. Invitations to people's homes, acquaintances that in Tokyo were made so easily on the streets or in bars were denied him here, and he was aware that it was partly his own fault. It was not his fault that he was a white man, a European. In Tokyo, where the sight of a European was not uncommon, that did not matter; but in a provincial town whose population was entirely Japanese he was always conspicuous, something different, something apart. He carried this sense of difference around with him wherever he went, and there were even days when he felt ashamed to go out.

In Mariko's company it was far worse. But for her, in fact, the uneasy awareness of his difference would not have been so humiliatingly brought home to him. Sometimes when they appeared together in public the hostility towards himself was as unmistakable as the contempt for her. Japanese women who went with foreigners were liable to be openly despised, but their escorts seldom knew the language well enough to understand the casual abuse spoken in an undertone by passers-by, and the women would not tell them, because they felt ashamed or had become resigned.

For Boon a disenchantment with Japanese life began to set in during those summer months. The tact and gentleness of the Japanese, qualities which he admired in their dealings with one another and of which, as it were in his official capacity, as a foreign student who was the guest of the state, he had himself enjoyed the benefit, gradually came to be overshadowed by the very different experiences he was gathering in his private life. At the prestigious local firms where he held English classes every evening he was again the beneficiary of the civility and respect accorded any *sensei*, even a *sensei* as humble as Boon. Here, being official, he was treated with official kindness: dinners, flattering speeches, convivial evenings and solemn pledges. But he no longer took pleasure in any of this. He felt it was hollow, a masquerade. Some of his companions, generous as they could afford to be with sentiments that cost them nothing and which in practice they need never honour, were also, under different circumstances, just as capable of hissing sly abuse in the street and would do so without being troubled by any sense of discrepancy.

Among his students there was one man, a man of about his own age, with whom relations were friendly and unstrained. What he had in common with this man was that they were both outsiders. Unlike all his colleagues, Tani-*san* did not come from Toyama; he had been transferred there by head office in Tokyo for a period of three years. When Boon met him he had been living in his new surroundings for about six months.

He was a large, slow, amiable man. He too, although in a different way from Boon, had difficulties with the Japanese language. Frequently he found himself ensnared in labyrinthine sentences with no hope of getting out. His conversation was full of stops, gaps and fillers. *Yosuruni*, in short, the point is . . ., he would say for the tenth time, still inside the same sentence. Boon leaned forward attentively. Tani did not find it easy to make himself clear. He wore glasses. He was a bachelor.

Tani had fallen in love with the manageress of a restaurant-bar where he invested about a third of his income. He had his supper there almost every evening and politely declined all invitations to go elsewhere.

"I think I have prospects there," he confided to Boon, and asked him along for a second opinion.

It was a very ordinary place and the manageress seemed a very ordinary sort of woman. From what Tani had told him beforehand Boon gained the impression that his courtship of this woman had now entered a particularly subtle and delicate stage; so subtle, it turned out, that the manageress herself still remained unaware of it. She gave him exactly the same attention she gave to any other customer and Tani made no effort to attract more. He sat with his back to her eating nuts, as confident in his own mind that his suit would have a favourable outcome as it was clear to Boon that, so far as the manageress was concerned, there wasn't any suit at all. It was the same trouble he had with his sentences. Tani failed to make his point.

He was the dupe of his own feelings, his imagination and his boundless good faith; also, no doubt, of his loneliness. Absurd details acquired importance in the private scheme of his heart. Boon saw a vulgar, sleazy woman who dyed the curls on her forehead red. Tani described the same colour as maple tint. She brought him a chop and, forgetting the napkin, at once went back to fetch it. He was enchanted. Behind him Boon could hear her laugh at the wisecracks and coarse banter of the drinkers lounging over the bar, men who treated her with the familiarity to which she was accustomed. Tani had no inkling of this. It merely proved her desirability and confirmed his own good taste. The sight of a man so obviously in love and at the same time so completely out of touch with the reality of what he loved made Boon uneasily aware of what else they might have in common. Mariko, too, stood behind a bar night after night making conversation with all comers. She also, if more discreetly, dyed her hair. For a long time he had not noticed it.

Towards the end of August Sugama arrived in Toyama for a few days. He showed up in the street outside Boon's apartment one morning on a bicycle, wearing Bermuda shorts and a baseball cap. He got off his bicycle reluctantly, as if to do so would somehow interrupt his holiday, and came inside for a couple of minutes. He could see that Boon was in low spirits.

"Tomorrow's Sunday. Why don't you come out and spend the night with us? It would do you good to get out of this hole for a while."

"Yuzo stuck it out here for several years, you know."

"Poor Yuzo."

Boon was pleased to see Sugama. He had missed him. He realised for the first time that he would be glad to get back to Tokyo. This admission took him by surprise.

Sugama noticed the books on the board in the corner of the room.

"You seem to be living here like a monk."

"In some respects, yes."

"How are you getting on with the translations?"

"Slowly. The heat is as bad as you said it would be. Probably even worse in here."

"Ah, the heat. And Mariko?"

"Things are different from what I had imagined . . ."

He would have liked to say more, but he felt ashamed. Even as he spoke he was admitting in his heart that the relationship with Mariko had already failed. She and Sugama were old friends. Sugama had helped them both in many ways to a better mutual understanding and Boon now felt that he had somehow let him down.

It was an extremely sultry evening that Sunday and during the night there was thunder. No one could sleep. Boon, Sugama and his father sat in the *kyakuma* almost until dawn, waiting for rain. For about an hour before dawn it became a little cooler, but still the rain did not come. Sugama's father went upstairs to bed and Sugama fell asleep on the *tatami*. The sun rose, the cool passed. Boon sat on the steps outside the house, numb and exhausted and glazed with sweat, until the mosquitoes drove him inside. In the other half of the *kyakuma* grandfather lay under the mosquito netting that spanned the room like an enormous tent, breathing stertorously and turning in his sleep. The old man coughed and woke up. He crawled out of the netting, wiped his chest and arms with a towel and got to his feet. For a man over eighty he was amazingly agile. He wore nothing but a loincloth. His body was lean and straight. In the half-light it looked like the body of a young man.

All day, however, he lay in his tent and did not stir. The heat strained his heart. His granddaughter knelt by his pillow and spoke to him through the shadowy gauze, her blouse open and breast out, nursing her baby. In the afternoon the child was laid in the tent for his nap and he fell asleep in the crook of the old man's arm. Boon went back to his rooms in town in the afternoon. Sugama returned to Tokyo the next day.

The rain everyone was waiting for did not come. There wasn't a breath of wind. Boon no longer stowed away his bedding in the cupboard in his room; the doors and the wooden panelling inside had begun to sweat, and on the jacket which had hung there unused for a month mildew had already formed. Whatever he touched was moist. Books drew moisture like a sponge; the leaves stuck together, the covers glistened. His pillows, his sandals, the washing he took in from the yard, toilet paper, paper napkins in restaurants, even chalk and coins, everything was damp and stuck to his hands. Humidity changed the natural chemistry of things, turned all things porous, seemed able to draw water even from stone. It was like a curse.

In the dead days before the typhoon began to sweep inland from the sea during the first half of September the world seemed to have come to a standstill; the summer smelled foul and rotted like a corpse. Boon was not surprised to learn that this kind of weather was often accompanied by violence, particularly by sex crimes.

In the local newspaper he read several reports of rape in the course of a single week.

He and Mariko had a strange experience themselves at this time.

One Sunday, about ten days before his return to Tokyo, they made a trip out to the mountains. Both of them guessed that it might be their last journey together and they went further than they had ever been before, setting out at dawn and returning late at night.

They got off the train at a remote station in the foothills and began to walk. Up there, said Boon, pointing to the smooth top of a distant hill, let's go up there. He had a sudden urge to climb up to a high place from which he could see the landscape in its entirety. He let her pass and she went a few yards ahead.

The road twisted up the hillside like a coil, tight and steep. His spirits rose as they climbed up out of the valley. With every step the brackish valley air shrank and became lighter. The road turned into a track, red soil, the colour of rust. Mariko took off her shoes and hooked them over her thumb. She wore a white dress, knotted at the neck with a large bow. Her back was bare to the waist. From time to time she stopped, panted, went on. Her skin began to glisten.

For the last few hundred yards up to the summit the track narrowed to a path. The summit was as smooth and round as a dome, covered with supple, broad-bladed grass through which they waded up to the waist and which closed behind them after they passed, leaving no trace. On the far side of the plateau the ground once again curved down and fell away steeply into a wooded gorge. Boon squatted and flattened a patch of grass, making a window out onto the valley.

"Where are you?"

"Here. Come and sit down."

He heard Mariko giggle.

"Can't you stand up for a moment? I've lost sight of you."

She was only a few yards away, but she still couldn't see him.

"Just look at my sandals!" she said ruefully.

"It's the red clay up here. Why did you put them on again? Never mind, it'll wash off."

"I can't very well sit down here. I'll get this stuff all over my dress."

"Then take it off."

Mariko undid the bow at her neck and pulled the dress over her head. She looked around for somewhere to put it down.

"The ground's filthy."

"It's only mud."

"All very well for you sitting there in those dirty jeans. Suppose it were your white dress."

"Why don't you try spreading it over the top of the grass?"

But that didn't work either.

Boon said, "What we'll do is this: I'll take off my clothes and you can lay yours on top of them."

He took off his shirt and trousers and spread them out on the ground. Mariko folded her dress carefully and placed it on top. She started to sit down and then thought better of it.

"What about – ?"

"Yes. You might as well take off those too while you're about it."

"Beast!"

So Mariko's clothes were saved. They sat on top of the hill naked and admired the view. Down in the valley a motor started up with a whine. Boon shaded his eyes. He could make out someone on a motorcycle driving across the fields.

Mariko lay facing him with her head resting on her hand and her legs curled up. He pricked her navel gently with the tip of a stalk, drew it down through her maidenhair and stroked the insides of her thighs. He jousted with an ant in the crease of her groin, and losing sight of it on the far side of her hip leaned over in pursuit. The ant had disappeared. The imprint of the ground had left a dusty reddish film on the cheeks of her buttocks. He drew his finger over the soft skin and stroked away the dust. A painful tenderness for her stabbed his bowels and began to grope out of his heart, like daylight flooding through a drawn curtain. She turned and pressed him down onto her.

The whine of the motor which had started in the valley and then faded was again suddenly audible, clearer now and much closer. There could be no mistake: the motor-cyclist was on his way up the hill towards them. The noise regularly advanced and receded, following the bends in the road. But the road only goes up so far, thought Boon.

He lay inside Mariko and moved on her rhythm almost without effort. She stretched her arms behind her head and arched her back; her motions carried him and gave him a weightless sensation, as if he were swimming on her body. The shrill grinding of the motorcycle engine was very close now. The track must be behind him and he's already on the path, thought Boon, who the hell is this fool? He's coming to the top. Who'll get there first, he briefly wondered, just as he felt the sweet moisture begin to rise inside her and Mariko bound him to her with her legs and arms, smothering a cry of fear or pleasure against his shoulder.

The motorcyclist had ploughed through the grass and come to an abrupt halt when the engine stalled, not more than a dozen yards from them. He was close enough for them to hear the click of a lighter and the sound as he exhaled. Mariko caught her breath and gripped Boon tightly. For a few seconds there was absolute silence.

Then the man gave a tremendous shout.

"Bakayaro!"

The valley and the mountains trapped the echo and broke it up. *Bakaya akaka yaro kayaro yaro ro ro!* The echoes pitched and rolled the length of the valley as if they would never end.

After the echoes had finally died out there was an eerie silence which lasted for a long time. Occasionally there was the sound of the man exhaling and a sharp click, as if he were tapping his teeth with his fingernails. Boon and Mariko lay motionless in the grass, as still as the earth on which they lay, their naked bodies entwined. They lay like hunted animals hiding in a covert.

He knows we are here, thought Boon, he must know. And for a moment he was afraid; not of the man but that he might scent, like a hunter, that they were there. And then he thought: but he can't see us. He moved cautiously to take his weight off Mariko's body. They exchanged questions with their eyes. Her lips formed words.

Who was this man? Was he crazy? Why had he driven to the top of a hill and shouted "Fool!"? And who was the fool? Whom had he wanted to call a fool? Perhaps he was not the man Boon had seen driving across the fields in the valley. Perhaps he was someone else, who had seen them on their way up the hill and followed them. But who was the fool?

The man lit another cigarette, and then another. Apart from the hiss of his lighter and the sound of slow exhaling the man didn't make the slightest noise. He never moved. He was waiting. And he waited for nearly an hour.

At last he started his motorcycle and drove away. They heard the engine whine on the far side of the hill, grow distant, fade. Mariko sighed and Boon sat up. They were both dripping with sweat.

For the rest of the day they wondered about this strange incident. Mariko thought the man hadn't seen them and that it was only a coincidence they happened to be up there at the same time. Her explanation was that the man must have experienced some setback, probably in connection with his work, and had made his way up to a lonely spot where he could give vent to his frustration; the *bakayaro* was his boss of course. She could well imagine someone acting like that, for she heard the confidences of dissatisfied men every night at the bar. It was a plausible explanation, one that would never have occurred to Boon. But he couldn't believe it had been a coincidence.

At the beginning of September it began to rain. It was Boon's last Sunday, a couple of days before his departure. He was awoken early in the morning by a terrific thunderclap which seemed to shake the entire house. The thunder rumbled without interruption for a couple of hours.

At about ten o'clock the wind suddenly got up. He was sitting by the window where the air was cooler and he heard the leaves of the tree in the courtyard begin to rustle. Out of nowhere the big gust came. A door slammed shut. The branches shook, the leaves spun on their stems and tore loose, whirled in frantic gusts on the courtyard floor and hung flattened against the gauze screen in front of the window. The *fusuma* rattled, loose papers flew across the room. He closed the window and went out into the street. He could almost see the wind. It burst through the narrow gap between the buildings like a flood bounding from the mouth of a gorge, sweeping everything with it. The shopkeepers had already wound up their awnings and shut their doors. The street was deserted.

In the course of the afternoon the wind blew itself out. It began to rain.

At six o'clock he went to the streetcar terminal to meet Mariko, who had been out of town visiting her brother. She had asked Boon to go with her, but he refused. The visit had been planned weeks in advance, when she had already known that he would be returning to Tokyo two days later.

He stood in a doorway, soaked to the skin. It was a pleasant feeling. The air was fresh but the rain warm. At the end of the track there was a loop where the streetcar turned and waited for ten minutes before starting out on the journey back into town. Mariko would board the streetcar at the station and ride out to the terminal. From there it was only a few minutes' walk to her house.

She wasn't among the passengers on the first streetcar. He waited for the next one to arrive. She didn't come on that one either.

She came on foot from another direction. He saw her a hundred yards away under the light of a street-stand where she had stopped to buy something. It was a yellowish light, dimmed by the steam that rose off the wet pavement. When she stepped out of the light and walked on he lost sight of her for a few moments in the dark. It was as if she had vanished into thin air.

She crossed the street and he went up to her. Her hair was wet. Her face was white.

"Has something happened?"

"No. I got back earlier than expected and went home to change."

Mariko seemed very tense.

"I want you to come home with me."

Boon was so astonished he said nothing.

"That's what you want, isn't it? You've always wanted to come home with me, haven't you? Well, and now you shall!"

She turned and walked away very fast. He caught up with her.

"But do you want me to come?"

"There's no help for it, is there? You want to come, don't you? To my place. That's what you've always wanted, isn't it?"

She repeated the same words again and again, getting more and more excited. They turned into the street where she lived. The rain began to pour down. Mariko broke into a run.

She seemed close to hysteria. She ran all the way down the road, water spurting out from under her feet. Boon walked after her slowly, wondering if he should turn back. Mariko stood under the eaves of the house and called to him. A man came out of the house. She ran lightly up the iron staircase, her footsteps reverberating incongruously, like muffled gongs. Boon heard the sound forty yards down the street. He saw her open the first door on the dark landing upstairs and disappear inside. Her room lit up like an explosion. The light burst out of the frame of the door as if it had blown a hole.

The man who had come out of the house got into a car and switched on the headlights. Boon's heart beat faster. The man started the car. He opened the door towards the side of the road. A woman ran out of the house and got into the car. She almost ran into Boon. He stood aside to let her pass and went upstairs.

There was no sign of Mariko.

"Shall I close the door?"

"As you like."

Her voice came tonelessly from somewhere inside.

"You seem to be trying very hard to let everyone know I'm here."

"What does it matter."

He shut the door and looked round. He was in the kitchen. A curtain of beads hung in the doorway. He parted the curtain and went into the next room.

On one side was a rocking-chair facing a mirror; on the other side a dresser, shelves, a table and a couple of chairs. The *fusuma* opposite had been drawn back. Mariko knelt in the opening drying her hair.

"Where d'you sleep?"

"Where I am. There's a towel for you on the table. You might like to put on the bathrobe while your clothes are drying. It may be a bit small. It's my brother's."

He left his wet clothes in the bathroom. He put on the bathrobe and stretched out on the *tatami*. Mariko sat at a dressing-table brushing her hair. He watched her face in the mirror. Around the mirror there were photographs of young girls pinned on the wall; fey, virginal girls of not more than fourteen or fifteen, with slim hips, small breasts and wistful faces. He lit a cigarette. The rain drummed steadily on the roof.

"They're beautiful, aren't they," she said.

"The photos of the girls?"

"They're pure. Don't they look so pure?"

In the next room he sat at the table facing her in the rocking-chair.

"Here you are," she said, "you've come to my room for me."

He wondered quite what she meant.

"You're the only man to have come in here during the last seven years, you know."

"The only one?"

"Apart from my brother."

She began to talk, rocking gently in the chair. Sometimes the wind curled the rain under the eaves and a sharp gust slated the window. She sat in the chair looking straight ahead, seeing and hearing nothing as she rocked herself into a trance, hands in her lap, spinning dreams. She spoke his name but did not look at him. And with a start he realised that she was talking to her reflection in the mirror. It seemed that the mirror revived images of the past. She spoke now to herself as she once had been. Seven years had never passed. He called her name, softly, as if to wake her from a sleep.

She went into the kitchen and made supper. He could hear her humming to herself. She seemed happy.

Just after they had finished supper the doorbell rang. Mariko got up and said nervously

"That's probably the boss."

"The boss?"

He was taken aback. She went out into the kitchen. He heard her open the door and say "Good evening!" in a bright voice. It was the voice she used at the bar. Boon lit a cigarette and prepared himself for a scene.

But nothing of the kind happened. The conversation he over-heard at the door turned out to be completely different from what he had been expecting.

"He's here now," he heard her say. She used the word *honnin* when talking of him: the person in question. It sounded remote, formal, and under the circumstances it seemed an odd word to use: it meant that the boss must have known in advance that he would find Boon there.

He got up and stood behind the curtain. He couldn't see the boss and he could only understand him imperfectly, because he remained in the passage outside and there was a door between them; but he recognised the voice.

The boss said something in an undertone and Mariko laughed. Boon could see her hand on the inside of the door and sometimes, when she laughed, her face in profile. She seemed very relaxed.

They chatted about the weather. She told him she had been out to see her brother. No, she had gone alone. Perhaps that was just as well, said the boss in his smooth deep voice. And when was he leaving? Tomorrow? Ah, the day after. Mariko said she didn't want to talk about that now. There was a pause. A sudden shower of rain rippled along the passage floor, drowning their words. They began to talk of other things, business, stock he wanted her to purchase for the bar, the arrangements for the coming week. Their manner with each other was familiar, the tone of their voices confidential, at times almost intimate. Clearly they were the best of friends; perhaps more than friends. They shared a common life. She talked to him as she had never talked to Boon. He stood a couple of yards away from them behind the curtain and might have been in a different world. He was stunned.

They stood at the door talking for a quarter of an hour. There was no need for him to hear any more. He went into the back room and lay down. He felt nothing. His mind was blank.

He heard Mariko shut the front door and begin to clear the table in the next room. She carried the things into the kitchen and washed up. Then she sat down in the rocking-chair. For a long time he heard her rocking to and fro.

He listened to the wind and the rain and the sound of her rocking and imagined himself adrift in a boat on the open sea. She had loved him, she had loved other men, she had deceived him as she had deceived them, yet whatever she had said or done she still remained true to her own divided self and the complexity of her nature. She had not misled him, for she lacked any direction. She was simply opaque. He had not understood her at all.

She sat in the chair for hours, not moving.

"Are you really going away?"

She lay beside him in the dark and wept.

"Did you ever really come?"

She put out her hand and touched him. They lay awake until it grew light and slept until noon. She got up, went out to work, came back, lay down. He stayed in the room a day, a night and a day. The rain continued to fall without a break.

In the evening he caught the train back to Tokyo. He only met Mariko once more, the year after next, when he came up to Toyama for the funeral of Sugama's grandfather.

Of ethics and bamboo whisks. The summer in Toyama marked a watershed in Boon's journey from West to East. His confidence ebbed, his personality began to change. The process of change was involuntary and gradual; alterations, at first confined to his speech and certain characteristics of his outward behaviour, which later impinged on his self-understanding.

Eager to find acceptance with the Japanese by meeting them on their own terms Boon had consciously imitated their mannerisms, gesture and intonation, without realising the extent to which he implicitly began to share the attitudes underlying them. In the wake of surface changes of which he was aware, for example the pitch of his voice and even the way he walked, followed a corresponding shift of more subtle assumptions which he failed to register; only, at times, an uneasy sense of dissociation. He spoke words which were not his own and whose meaning he sometimes did not even understand, expressions of self-effacement, in particular, caution, superfluous agreement, solicitude and deference which he did not feel and for which his native language did not provide; in fact spoke Japanese much as an exercise, often divorced from what he felt at any one moment, while what he did feel, at first because he could not express it and afterwards because he did not wish to, in many cases remained unsaid. In time, however, habituation enforced a need, and these expressions, important less for their content than as rhetorical gestures, came naturally to him, and the sense of dissociation from what he was saying began to fade.

It seemed to Boon that in the process of undergoing this gradual change he aroused less attention, in public he somehow felt less conspicuous. Probably this impression was more correctly attributable to his own increasing sense of familiarity with his surroundings, but whether the effect was actual or imagined it betrayed a concern he was reluctant to acknowledge: a concern to merge with his surroundings as closely as possible. This in itself showed the extent of the Japanese influence, for willingness to conform was as self-evident to the Japanese as for Boon it was out of character, who on home ground believed in a measure of detachment as a guarantee of his individuality. Such a position no longer seemed tenable in Japan.

Perhaps Boon was unduly sensitive to an awareness of his changing because the life he had chosen to lead in Japan committed him unequivocally. He had become emotionally dependent on the Japanese. From the outset he had avoided contact with other foreigners as distractions liable to interfere with the immediacy of what he experienced; and beyond a certain point, he gradually found, his capacity to assimilate the new culture would depend on his willingness to sever, or at least temporarily suspend, the attachment to his own in a much deeper sense.

The relationship with Mariko made plain to Boon that this was a sacrifice he was not prepared to make. The differences between them had not merely been of a personal nature. In her background, her temperament, beliefs and expectations he recognised the influence of a view of life based on cultural premises very different from his own. The failure of their relationship therefore came as a double shock. Much of what he had learned and thought he had acquired from the Japanese character and way of life was only a precocious veneer, something on the surface which in his heart he did not share.

As if this insight had disqualified him in his own eyes Boon began to feel almost like an impostor among his Japanese friends. What were these things he could not share? Ruefully he had to admit he did not know. His claims to familiarity with Japanese culture were unfounded. During the following months he patiently set about acquiring the broader knowledge he lacked and which was indispensable to a deeper understanding.

In his book *Nihonjin no shinri* (The psychology of the Japanese), first published in 1953, the psychologist Minami Hiroshi remarked that there must be few countries with as advanced a civilisation as Japan's where the events of life and people's reactions to them so easily tended to be described in terms of providence or fate. Thirty years later Boon found this generalisation to be still broadly true. The belief in and readiness to submit to the caprice of fate possibly constituted the single most pervasive influence on the character of the Japanese.

The words in current use were *unmei* and *shukumei*. Under the auspices of *unmei* the course of events in life was regarded as being largely coincidental, while the view associated with *shukumei*, which incorporated Buddhist influences, was more deterministic, conceiving the individual span of life in terms of previous and subsequent incarnations. In popular usage, however, there was no clear distinction between the two.

The obsolete terms *tenmei* and *tendo*, the Way of Heaven, had been used loosely to include both meanings. These words had been used very frequently until the close of the Second World War, and perhaps as a result of their abuse in the service of the emperor cult they had been discredited and faded out of the popular idiom, in exactly the same way that the analogous concept of *Vorsehung* had been eliminated from the German language. It was an instructive parallel, showing how absolute power availed itself of absolute concepts, the dazed servitude enforced by the appropriation of fate to serve political ends.

Theories of fate might by their nature be expected to resemble one another whatever their provenance, and to any such theory some notion of the individual's "lot" or personal fortune in life is indispensable. In Japanese this notion was represented by *bun*, "that which should naturally be so", and *mibun*, a person's station in life. The second word being a compound of the first it likewise bore the connotation of "that which should naturally be so".

The consequence of a belief in fate was the patient acceptance of whatever fate ordained, calling upon resources of stoicism and self-discipline that Japanese moralists enshrined in the quality of *akirame*, resignation without despair. In the spirit of *akirame* one could allow all events to take their course passively and without anxiety, recognising it as the way ordained by providence.

Recognition of fateful dispensation, however vague, as manifest in even the most arbitrary series of events, was instrumental in shaping a spirit of obedience which at times was indistinguishable from self-sacrifice. Naturally it was exploited by feudal rulers to reinforce the system that supported themselves, and in the twentieth century by Japan's military establishment in their conduct of the war. On the admission of many officers, continuation of a war which they knew had strategically already been lost was borne with this same belief in a providential turn of fate to Japan's advantage, and when defeat finally came it was likewise accepted in terms of *unmei*, in terms of a natural disaster rather than military inferiority.

If the retention of traditional concepts in the modern Japanese language could serve as an index of accompanying attitudes, then an outsider like Boon might feel entitled to assume that Japanese susceptibility to a belief in fatalism was still very much in evidence. Common references to fate (*un*) and expressions of resignation (*shikata ga nai*) on the one hand were complemented by exhortations to persevere (*ganbaru*) and to endure (*gaman suru*) on the others. Candidates who sat entrance examinations in the spring of each year, perhaps the single most important occasion in their lives, were notified of their success or failure by at least one famous university in the Delphic phrase "the cherry blossom is in flower" or "the blossom falls". Among those for whom the blossom had fallen cases of suicide were by no means rare. The childlike curiosity with which visitors examined the prefabricated horoscopes available at most Shinto shrines, the more earnest attention they gave to pavement fortune-tellers in the stylish surroundings of central Tokyo where one would have least suspected evidence of popular superstition, all this was a matter of course in everyday Japanese life. Oracles still did good business because they obviously catered for an undiminished need.

Fatalism and its accompanying attitudes of passive expectancy and serene despair in the face of things to come could only have been cultivated on the assumption that the things to come would always be of a bad rather than a good kind. If the Japanese had learned from experience always to expect the worst, their pessimism was elsewhere endorsed by a moral doctrine that canonised unhappiness as a form of spiritual discipline, as something desirable, then, even as something beautiful. In this derivation of "beauty" from unhappiness, the experience of self-reproach as something pleasurable, Minami Hiroshi found evidence of masochistic leanings in the Japanese temperament.

The comprehensive vocabulary available in Japanese to register the shade and degree of feelings of unhappiness contrasted strikingly with the paucity of words for happiness. Probably this unbalance reflected the fact that happiness had not been the concern of traditional moral teaching. As if mesmerised by the lure of inveterate pessimism, the attention of moral apologists invariably confined itself to the edification that could be achieved through acceptance of unhappiness. The subject of happiness never benefited from comparable analysis, for until very recently it had not been considered a worthy aim in life.

This espousal of unhappiness as a moral premise had a sombre resonance in classical aesthetics, notably in the concept of *fusoku-shugi* associated with the name of Kenko, a poet-essayist of the fourteenth century whose writings were still on the curriculum of Japanese schools over six hundred years later.

Fusoku-shugi was a theory of insufficiency-incompleteness which identified the most profound aesthetic experience as lying in precisely that which had been withheld and left unsaid. The power of what is absent to reverberate in what is present, contraction with the purpose of expansion, abstention for the sake of implicit suggestion: in Boon's opinion it was largely the operation of this principle which still accounted for the distinctive quality of whatever was excellent throughout Japanese culture, in life as in art.

The ideal of *fusoku-shugi* prescribing the restraint of emotions in art applied analogously to their regulation in life. The love that is endured without hope of fulfilment or even expression, however intensely it may be felt, supplied one of the classic themes of Japanese literature. Love was idealised as unconditional service, as self-sacrifice. The service of a warrior was considered then exemplary when the feudal lord to whom it was dedicated remained unaware that it had been performed.

Altruism had its price; namely, the influence and even the power it conferred on the benefactor over the beneficiary. The position of women was accordingly much stronger than their traditional subordination in Japanese society might have led one to suppose. As wives and mothers the greater part of their lives was spent in a paradoxical spiral of self-effacement and self-advancement. Persons in authority exercised the same kind of power, if for different reasons. Their power derived not from undertaking sacrifice for others but from extending patronage, thus putting their dependents under an obligation.

Among the many formal sentiments voiced daily in Japanese life those concerned with gratitude and apology were probably the ones Boon heard most frequently. He noted with interest that expressions of gratitude often tended to follow the wording of an apology. Almost no area of the modern Japanese language was more elaborately structured or handled with more circumspection than the phrasing of regret for inconvenience caused and of thanks for services rendered. In very few of these cases, however, had anything actually been done to occasion an apology.

The asking of a favour was approached with as much reluctance as an obligation incurred involuntarily was acknowledged with discomfort, and the same phrases, *sumimasen*, *mooshiwakenai*, doubled as both preface and epilogue. It seemed to Boon that the great frequency of such expressions, regardless of whether there was any justification for them or not, betrayed an underlying sensitivity of the Japanese to the fact that in relationships of any kind the pattern of beneficiary-benefactor was always implicit.

An obligation once incurred must be scrupulously honoured. Behind the ever-present reluctance of the Japanese to impose on other persons, the display of moderation in attitudes of *enryo* (often cited to Boon as proof of their delicacy of feeling), there was in fact a very lively awareness of the counter-obligation which imposing on others would incur. Conversely, acts of generosity or assistance would sometimes be deliberately omitted because the inconvenience-embarrassment thus enforced on the beneficiary was considered likely to outweigh the advantages. This way of thinking was characteristic of Japanese tact.

The common word for a favour was *on*, the requital of a favour *on-gaeshi*, part of that broader sense of duty and acknowledgement of obligation expressed by the concept *giri*. Boon once had to translate a television play whose story-line resulted entirely from the consequences implicit in this principle of requital of favours. A retired couple moved as paying guests into an apartment they shared with its owners, two young people who had overreached themselves financially and needed this extra income to pay off a mountainous debt. By charging only a modest rent, however, and by encouraging the old couple to use the apartment as if it were their own home, the young owners inadvertently caused them feelings of great unease. "One shouldn't impose on the kindness of strangers," the old man tells his wife, "we have nothing to give in return."

Two points about this play seemed to Boon to have a more general application. The first was the contrast in the attitudes of the older and the younger generation. For the older couple, conditioned by their "old-fashioned" education to honour the principle of paying back a favour at whatever personal cost, the acceptance of a kindness posed a genuine problem of which the younger couple, on the other hand, hardly seemed to be aware. The second point was the old man's significant qualification of the favour as the "kindness of *strangers*". Here, yet again, one crossed that invisible boundary between insiders and outsiders that one came up against everywhere in the discriminatory consciousness of the Japanese.

Why did acceptance of a stranger's kindness provoke such unease? In Boon's opinion because it might breach the integrity of the insider group and threaten its corporate sense of belonging (*ittaikan*). Receipt of a favour initiated an exchange of feelings (even if this exchange was often effected in the spirit of duty rather than fellowship) which should properly be reserved for those inside the *uchi* and not outside it. The acceptance of a favour from and therewith the incurrence of an obligation towards an outsider depleted the stock of collective feelings in which the *uchi* had its being.

Indispensable to an understanding of traditional Japanese ethics were the two concepts *giri* and *ninjo*, often regarded as complementary and treated as one, *giri-ninjo*. Kenkyusha's Japanese–English dictionary offered "justice; (a sense of) duty; obligation; a debt of gratitude; (a sense of) honour," and so on as translations of *giri*, and "human feelings; human nature; humanity; humaneness; sympathy; the heart," as translations of *ninjo*. This word was often interchangeable with *nasake*, meaning "empathy".

Even a cursory study of these terms made clear one extremely important point: every discussion proceeded unquestioningly from the assumption, not merely that there were naturally discrepancies between behaviour in public and behaviour in private, but that the entire structure of Japanese ethics was divided root and branch by the application of fundamentally divergent principles of conduct towards those who were members of the *uchi* and towards those who were not.

It was for this reason that the definition of *ninjo*, for example, as "human feelings" was apt to be misleading. In substance they undoubtedly were "human" feelings, but feelings that were forthcoming, at least as far as classical ethics were concerned, *only under certain conditions*. Neither humanity at large nor individual human beings would or could expect to be the recipient of feelings of *ninjo* from persons outside their own *uchi*. This was not to say that relations between outsiders (people from different *uchi*) were never characterised by such feelings, but that ethically there was no provision for this kind of relationship *in principle*.

The qualification of *giri* and *ninjo* in terms of insider morality and outsider morality was generally valid but still not sufficient. Where did "inside" end? Where did "outside" begin? A poll just after the Second World War gave one person's view of the outside world as consisting of "his two neighbours and the three households across the street". A politician, by contrast, regarded it as consisting of Japanese society as a whole. It was likely that the majority of the present generation would take the latter view; and a modern politician's awareness of the outside world would by now extend to the international community. The frame of reference was an important consideration, because recognition of where one's duty lay might range in meaning from "not causing offence to the neighbours" to "not getting a bad reputation" with people in general.

In *Giri to Ninjo* (1969), a study of the meanings of these terms in Japanese literature, Minamoto Ryoen suggested that *giri* constituted the moral code applicable in public (*ko*) which in private was represented by *ninjo*. In cases of personal attachment (i.e. between fellow insiders) one accordingly spoke of *giri-ninjo*, because the sense of duty was here infused with and thus reinforced by feelings of empathy. Where personal commitment was lacking (i.e. between outsiders) the precepts of *giri* subsisted without empathy, *giri* was the performance of "mere" duty.

Minami Hiroshi regarded *giri* as the antithesis of *ninjo* "The most common form of resistance to *giri* is expressed by the word *ninjo*, representing a need for humaneness and fellow-feeling. For a long time the two have been coupled as *giri-ninjo*, as though the one were somehow unthinkable without the other, but although this has become customary it none the less remains a fact that *giri* constitutes an obligation to which feelings of *ninjo* must be subordinated. It would accordingly be more correct to speak of them as being in opposition, as posing a dilemma which has cast its shadow on the Japanese mentality . . . the insolubility of situations characterised by the deadlock of *giri* versus *ninjo* is the essence of Japanese tragedy."

If this dilemma were still present in the consciousness of Japanese living today, the shadow it cast had perceptibly begun to recede Sugama, for example, was undoubtedly in a dilemma of this kind, caught between the conflicting demands of *giri* towards his parents and *ninjo* towards his future wife, but it was no more than a dilemma. It was no longer the stuff of tragedy.

Despite subtle shifts of emphasis and corresponding differences in interpretation the general drift of the argument was clear. Relations between insiders were characterised by duty infused with love (empathy), relations to outsiders by acknowledgement of duty alone. What was not clear to Boon, however, was *the specific nature* of this duty towards outsiders from which fellow-feeling, the feeling based in one's common humanity, had expressly been excluded.

There appeared to be nothing in Japanese ethics corresponding to the injunction "Thou shalt love thy neighbour as thyself" which was at the root of Christian morality. In the Japanese version of the bible Boon discovered that "neighbour" was translated as *rinjin*, a word not in common use and meaning no more than "the person next door". It was not surprising if the translation of the biblical commandment as *jibun o aisuru yo ni, anata no rinjin o aiseyo* failed to cut much ice; it had very much the air of appropriation from some remote language. In fact, what was intended with the word "neighbour" could only have been effectively conveyed in Japanese by translating it as "outsider" (*tanin*). A translation along the lines of "Thou shalt love the outsider as thy fellow insider" would without exaggeration be an astonishing, a revolutionary concept in Japanese ethics.

In modern Japan the precise connotations of *giri*, the instant recognition of one's duty that was once guaranteed by feudal values, had long since been extinguished, but apparently no attempt had yet been made to compensate for that loss by infusing *giri* with new meaning, notably by extending the restricted concept of *ninjo* to embrace relations with outsiders as well. In practice this process had already begun, making the discrepancies of ethical theory still more obvious, its exposition anachronistic. *Giri-ninjo* was an institution; it ran the risk of becoming a museum.

The lack of adequate content which Boon felt in all descriptions of *giri*-towards-strangers became somewhat easier to understand if one momentarily allowed the concept of "duty" to recede and make way for the concept of "honour". Minami Hiroshi saw the object of *giri* as "avoidance of getting a bad name"; Minamoto

Ryoen called it "preservation of one's integrity and honour". One's *giri*, therefore, was seen as a reflection on oneself and, more importantly, on the group with which one was associated. In the Japanese understanding of *giri* there was a tendency, perhaps, to consider the consequences of a breach of honour more in terms of how they would affect the offending than the offended party. Expressed in rather drastic terms, awareness of having done something wrong resided not so much in remorse of conscience for the person harmed as in feelings of shame for having compromised the group to which the wrong-doer belonged.

Doi Takeo, for example, discussed shame in terms which for most Japanese would have been self-evident, but which for Boon were by no means so familiar. "Towards those belonging to one's immediate family (*uchiwa*) feelings of guilt and shame are rare. Towards the complete stranger (*tanin*) such feelings are likewise rare Where shame and guilt are most often experienced is with reference to the wider group (e.g. village community, school or firm) to which one belongs." (*Amae no kozo*, 1971)

There appeared to be many situations that caused the Japanese genuine embarrassment where Europeans, on the whole, would probably have felt none, or, if they did, would certainly not have confessed to it. By far the most common cause of embarrassment, in Boon's experience, was not the fact that the person concerned had committed a faux pas or made a fool of himself but simply the fact that for a moment he had been *conspicuous*.

Proneness to embarrassment only became evident outside the protective insider circle. The psychology of embarrassment was understood and accepted by the Japanese, who recognised in adults the survival of psychological patterns originating in infancy. Thus the word *hitomishiri*, first applied to the tearful reactions of very young children at the sight of an unfamiliar face, was also used to describe the behaviour of adults who continued to feel ill at ease among outsiders later in life. Such insights and the language in which they found expression were not confined to the arcane repertoire of professional psychologists; this was how ordinary people thought and talked.

Thus Okonogi Keigo, discussing embarrassment in his book *Moratorium ningen no jidai* (1977), merely articulated thoughts with which all Japanese were perfectly familiar. "(The child's fear of strangers that is the original meaning of) *hitomishiri* is primarily a conscious acknowledgement of the fact that there is a boundary between that intimate circle where one's 'being known' does not matter and outsiders who cannot share this intimacy. Embarrassment arises when something otherwise kept concealed is exposed, and it is one aspect of Japanese family feeling that although one accepts being known by other insiders, when it comes to outsiders one wants to keep such knowledge of oneself concealed."

It was important to understand that the statement "embarrassment arises when something otherwise kept concealed is exposed" did not mean the public airing of skeletons in family cupboards, but the mere disclosure to outsiders of family matters *as such*. This alone was sufficient to cause embarrassment. In a letter that Sugama wrote to Boon a year or so after he had left the country, Sugama concluded a harmless account of himself and his family with the following remarkable admission. "Japanese men actually consider it something of an embarrassment [*haji*, literally "shame"] to talk to outsiders about family affairs. I share that feeling myself, so when I write about these things it's only because I make an exception in your case. Even to such a close friend as Yoshida I could never bring myself to speak of the love I feel for my new daughter, I would never say anything like 'I could put her into my eye and it would not hurt!' "

Boon was grateful for this privileged treatment. Even as a temporary insider with limited access he benefited from all those advantages conferred by *uchi* membership which foreigners were seldom in a position to enjoy. With the trust that accompanied his acceptance, the openness, generosity, loyalty and affection of his fellow insiders were also forthcoming. Unfortunately, this side of the Japanese was rarely seen outside the intimacy of the *uchi* even on home ground, and never when they went abroad.

Boon's survey of traditional Japanese ethical concepts brought home to him yet again the central importance of the insider-outsider issue. It seemed to him that the widespread acceptance among foreigners of the image of Japan as a society whose chief characteristic lay in a formal hierarchy vertically structured was much in need of revision. Certainly the *tate-shakai* existed and it was more pronounced than in Western European or American society. However, probably very few people by comparison were aware that the horizontal insider-outsider axis also constituted a line of demarcation in the Japanese consciousness with consequences that were quite as far-reaching as those arising from the view of Japanese society as structured vertically.

In a famous comparison of "octopus-pot" and "bamboo-whisk" types of social structure the political philosopher Maruyama Masao drew the attention of the Japanese public to the fragmentation resulting from the self-sufficient *uchi* mentality in their own society (octopus-pot type), contrasting it with societies which could afford to be pluralist in character by virtue of their common base (bamboo-whisk type – the prongs of the whisk are cut from a single piece of bamboo, to which they remain attached). Christianity supplied one obvious example of such a base; the democratic traditions guaranteed by respect for an unwritten English constitution, the vague but none the less meaningful appeal to an *abendländisches Kulturgut* as understood in central European countries, might be cited as further examples.

Rather surprisingly, perhaps, for those who observed the serried ranks of Japanese society only at a distance, Maruyama argued that in his own country it was precisely this base of the bamboo whisk that was lacking. Religious, social, educational and political traditions had all failed to create, in the Johnsonian phrase, "a community of mind".

Boon entirely agreed with the spirit of this critique, although he had his doubts about what conclusions should be drawn. Maruyma's thesis would have sounded more persuasive had Boon been able to look around and find Japanese society seriously in disarray; but no, on the contrary, it seemed to be doing rather well. Reading Maruyama, he could not entirely exclude the impression of a man continuing to belabour an obstinate donkey long after it had obliged by getting up and going its way.

Still more cohesion, even better organisation? A formidable thought. Paradoxically enough, perhaps the notion of the *uchi* itself provided the base for a very serviceable bamboo whisk.

*T*he water trade. "What then," enquired Okonogi Keigo, "does 'self-expression' mean for the Japanese? It is not something that can be realised in public discussion but in the kind of communication that takes place after hours ... in the evenings, in an atmosphere of companionship fortified by alcohol, the Japanese will open up, speak of their dissatisfaction and show their real feelings ..."

In other words, this was the world of the water trade.

Perhaps because of its connotations of loose morals and low life the word *mizu-shobai* was openly disparaged, but without the commodity it supplied, Japanese civilisation, past and present, would be hardly conceivable. Tens of thousands of bars, snacks, cabarets and clubs, ranging from a minimum capacity of five or six, like the Sign of the Crane where Boon gave his début, to pleasure palaces around the Ginza and Nihonbashi with a capacity of several hundred, opened their doors and catered every evening for hundreds of thousands of eager customers.

The water trade was a valve. This was where the strain of Japanese society was borne, more or less everything found a reflection or an echo here. For a student of Japanese affairs like Boon study of the water trade was a duty as rewarding as it was congenial. Knowledge acquired in more conventional ways was also necessary, but without the attuned, receptive ear schooled in the forum of the water trade a library of books would have been of limited use to an understanding of the Japanese. The transition from spoken to written Japanese not merely brought a loss in immediacy; it also evinced a change in character. Distaste for the written memorandum, the preference whenever possible for the physical presence of one's interlocutor, made evident a reliance on the spoken word for which it would be difficult to find parallels in any modern society as sophisticated and complex as Japan's.

What the water trade reflected was not the "true" side, perhaps not even a different side of the Japanese. The significance of what they did and said inside the refuge of the water trade could only be understood with reference to their behaviour outside, and vice versa. Each culture assumed the existence of the other, neither could have taken the form it did without the other. *Basho-gara*, behaviour in keeping with the circumstances, applied inside the water trade just as it did outside, paradoxical though that might sound. Frivolity, frankness, promiscuity and drunkenness constituted appropriateness in the world of the water trade just as their opposites did out of it. Excess was obviously not an obligation, there was not a premium on lechery or drunkenness as outside there was on propriety and temperance, but neither were they frowned upon; behaviour which in similar establishments – not joints but normal drinking places – in Europe or America would have been inadmissible was condoned in Japan. A customer who did not stint his drinks and let his hair down with the others demonstrated good fellowship; this much, at least, in many circumstances did constitute an obligation. The rules were waived in the case of people whose intake of alcohol was limited for medical reasons, but the Japanese teetotaller was an unhappy man who would self-consciously warn his companions in advance; alcohol intolerance was not a minor inconvenience but a biggish social handicap.

Within the water trade images of Japan's past were revived more vividly before Boon's eyes than anywhere outside it, even on historical locations in Nara or Kyoto. In the bustle and colour of a few water-trade quarters in Tokyo one could still, for a brief moment, enjoy the illusion of standing on a street in Edo. The atmosphere in certain bars might sustain this illusion further. The *mama-san*, or proprietress, typically a woman in late middle age, and the *kanban-musume*, a younger woman whose attractions had always to be on display to lure customers, often wore *kimono*. A good *mama* needed to have a discreet but firm hand when dealing with her clients, good humour, lusty lungs, a shrewd knowledge of human nature and an indestructible liver. Being able to play an instrument was a bonus, to draw on a very wide repertoire of traditional folk songs indispensable, for what her customers wanted above all was to sing, and to sing their own songs, the songs of the region from which they came. The water trade lived by song and provided a living for those who could sing. *Nagashi*, or wandering folk singers and musicians, "borne on the waters of the trade", drifted from bar to bar and played and sang whatever the company called for. Confessions, boasts, proverbs, puns, risqué jokes and sustained banter across the bar, the nice art of the *double entendre*, a tradition of wit and a use of language which seemed to have disappeared from Japanese life resurfaced and found an outlet in the racy currents of the water trade.

With its casual working hours and liberal morals, chronic deficits and overnight closures, its survival sometimes inexplicable, its operations inscrutable, the abrupt appearance and disappearance of its personnel unexplained, but always, so long as it was there, extending to its patrons an unqualified welcome, the water trade showed that there could be constancy despite change, permanence despite the vicissitudes of individual fate. Its existence was rooted in ambiguity: a bright surface spanning a sombre background. Customers slipped away from their settled lives to catch a glimpse and sniff the air of this floating world which was the evocation of an authentic Japanese spirit.

In the noble cause of learning Boon now took upon himself a life of studious dissipation. He launched his new career with the purchase of two pairs of laceless shoes to facilitate the swift entrances and, above all, exits he anticipated, and a dozen cartons of Nishin Instant Noodles for consumption on return home in the small, hungry hours of the morning. His meagre nightly budget covered beverages but not food; he became a great eater of pickled radish and green peas, supplied free of charge with the drinks in all establishments and without limitation in some. Boon was unwilling to go through the night without something solid in his stomach, so those places where stupendous portions of *tsumami* could be had for the asking quickly secured his approval and loyalty. His life came to resemble a scenario from commedia dell'arte, improbably produced in Japanese surroundings. Overtaken by a flurry of faces, places and events, plunged into a world of mistaken identities, vanishing wallets, mislaid keys and shameful entry via neighbours' balconies, Boon's sense of reality for a long time deserted him, suspended somewhere between his laceless shoes and a nebula of green peas.

He bought these shoes in Kita-senju, one of the best cut-price shoe markets in Tokyo. The market was five minutes' walk from the school where he taught English on Saturday afternoons. On his way back from the school to the station he passed through one of those bustling quarters crowded with restaurants, bars and cheap cabarets, that were so characteristic of downtown Tokyo. It was only a matter of time before he picked himself a drinking shop here and was established as a regular customer. The more acquaintances he made and the further afield he went in pursuit of casual jobs, the more scattered became the locales of drinking shops where he held informal membership and was treated with the hospitable familiarity typical of *akachochin*, or red-light bars. In the course of a year Boon became a customer of the house in more than a dozen drinking shops in Oji, Ikebukuro, Ueno, Koenji, Takadanobaba, Toranomon, Shinbashi, Nihonbashi, Akihabara, Shibuya and Shinjuku where he was fed pickled vegetables once or twice a month, but it was in a bar in Kita-senju that he was put through his basic training and for which he always reserved a very special affection.

It must have been one of the scruffiest bars in town. The glass panels of the doors were never cleaned, photographs on the walls had acquired a second frame of dust, the counter was only wiped with the effect of superimposing a new smear on a layer of others, the ceiling sweated and smelled offensive, the floor was unswept and the bar-stools, like the ancient proprietress, were slowly but surely falling apart.

Mama kept her age a secret, but she must have been close on seventy. On his first few visits Boon saw a frail old lady officiating among indescribably filthy pots and pans with compensatory old-world charm, a woman of the past, a widow who had fallen on hard times; she aroused his sympathy. This impression was correct so far as it went, because *mama* never touched a drink before nine o'clock. After nine o'clock, he soon discovered, this dear old lady could talk like a brothel-keeper and drink like a horse.

The better he got to know her, the fainter that first impression became. In its place emerged a less flattering picture of a sly, cantankerous, miserly old woman. She had a soft spot for Boon because he reminded her of one of her past lovers, an American she had known during the occupation after the war. She was always talking about this man and repeatedly asked Boon if he was not an American after all. But no, to her chagrin he was a mere Englishman. On bad evenings, when she had a hangover from the day before and was in a particularly spiteful mood, she relieved her bile by taking him to task for his inadequate nationality. Her personal reasons apart, *mama* belonged to that generation for whom all foreigners were Americans. Boon let her have her way. After nine o'clock the present receded, her journey into the past began, and by the end of the evening Boon had invariably become an American citizen.

He liked *mama* none the less, and not merely because she only charged him two hundred yen for a flask of *sake*. Her girlish, mischievous spirit had probably not changed much in the course of half a century, and physically she was as tough as an old boot. Her body seemed able to withstand the nightly onslaught of tobacco and liquor without ill effect, but how her business survived neglect of custom remained a mystery to Boon.

Sometimes she sat perched on her umpire's stool behind the bar and saw a whole evening pass with only three or four customers. The attractions of the bar were not conspicuous. *Mama* herself had little to offer. She couldn't even sing. Once customers were there, even if only by mistake, they would usually draw others. There were men who came in evidently believing that there must be more than was on show, that the old crone was keeping a sharp number out of sight behind a curtain. In principle this kind of double-think was justified, but in *mama*'s case it was wrong: there were no surprise numbers. No matter, once customers were inside they started the ball rolling. But an empty bar discouraged even these crafty optimists. It was shunned like a house with plague.

For several months *mama* employed an attractive young assistant called Fumiko. Fumiko was good for business, but business was unfortunately not good for Fumiko. Although fifty years younger than *mama*, Fumiko lacked her iron constitution and within a short space of time had been worn down to a shadow. She became seriously ill. After a long absence she appeared again for a couple of weeks and gave the water trade a second try, but finding it didn't agree with her was forced to seek a living elsewhere. Boon missed Fumiko's youthful presence, her artless personality and her beautiful long hair, but he was glad for her sake that she went. The water trade would have ruined her.

In the critical months of Fumiko's illness and again after her final departure *mama*'s colleagues from drinking shops down the road rallied round the old lady and kept her foundering bar afloat. It came to resemble a sort of green-room, convenient for professional hostesses to rest, gossip and restore their make-up between takes in the rowdy sweltering dens where they were employed. There were four or five of them who regularly came and they all had a preference for *kimono* in sombre colours – dark green, navy blue and black. They were immense, formidable women. They sat in *mama*'s parlour with a funereal air, like crows waiting for a scavenging.

They took their turns behind the bar and, more importantly, in front. Here they sat, with the unshakeable dignity that accompanies greatness of flesh, were fêted, coaxed, petted and squeezed by clients half their size. Body and soul they were built like fortresses, well stocked and redoubtably armed, able to resist the longest siege. They overwhelmed by the superiority of their mass, disposing of importunate clients by drinking until they were no longer fit to contest the issue, not just now and then, but two or three customers a night, between one and two dozen a week, making a total of over five hundred in the course of a single year.

Unengaged hostesses, once called *ocha-hiki*, because geisha in want of custom had nothing better to do than attend to the drawing of tea, sat imperturbably on the little *tatami* dais at the back of *mama*'s shop, apparently seeing and hearing nothing, but actually keeping a watchful eye on the street. Men roamed up and down outside like stray dogs, passed, came back, peered in, went on. The women had a sharp instinct for undecided customers and how they could be lured inside. They got up and waddled to the door, often even out into the street, calling *shacho! shacho-san!* Promoting clients to the rank of company director or conferring the flattering title of *sensei* belonged to the conventions of the water trade, and those who resisted flattery usually succumbed to main force. A sleeve, an arm, a little calculated pressure of bosom and belly, and the prey was theirs.

The *akachochin*, or red-light bars, in cheap areas of downtown Tokyo like Kita-senju, were the gutters of the water trade and by the laws of social gravity drew their own kind of human sediment. Real company directors were not among their clientele; they sported and frolicked elsewhere, in the more spacious, elegant conduits of the Ginza and Nihonbashi, where they were less likely to be reminded of their eminence because it was in order to forget their eminence that they were there. The elevation of their humbler colleagues in humbler bars, at almost exactly the same time of day, to those positions which they voluntarily resigned, was the inverse proposition of a basic water trade rule testifying to its democratic spirit. Customers most easily escaped from one reality by substitution of another, and if this reality were to be desirable it must be recognisable, it must seem, at least, to be authentic. What was most authentic about the world of the honorary directors in *mama*'s bar was the price tag on the slip of paper discreetly pushed over the counter at the end of the evening.

It was a shrewd and, in Boon's opinion, a fair ploy. The water trade had no fixed tariffs and traditionally enjoyed the privilege of presenting bills as a total sum, not itemized and not calculable other than by rule of thumb. *Mamas* varied, and so did thumbs. How much was a squeeze worth, a groping in laps, a handling of breasts? How choice were the breasts that had been handled? How had they been handled? Was the handler an eligible customer, did one wish to see him again? Any *mama* who knew her business had to have sharp eyes in her head; she kept the score like a judge in a ringside seat, awarding points for clean body checks and heavily penalising moves below the belt-line. She would also take into account the rates she had to pay, margins of profit, a bullish market or a depressed economy. But above all it was her personal assessment of the customer that counted. No wonder, then, that these magical slips of paper, little anatomies of the state of the nation and masterpieces of character analysis, were handed out with the same authority as a verdict passed by a court of law. Few customers appealed, none failed to pay up.

According to this way of thinking, the vanity of a customer was a need like thirst or the hankering to fondle women, and satisfaction of his vanity by appropriate flattery as tangible a commodity as a glass of whisky or a female companion; for whatever the establishment supplied it was perfectly entitled to charge. On the whole it was probably true that the kind of client who assented to his promotion as company director was also the kind of man who derived pleasure from forking out disproportionately large sums of money, because an extravagant action was a display of power; the soothing of flawed self-confidence was his ultimate personal benefit. So long as Boon sat tight in *mama*'s bar he could afford to take a philosophical view.

His drinking habits were unorthodox. He ranged far and wide, following his nose, and at least for the first few months he usually went alone. Most Japanese wisely remained with the bars where they were already known or became acquainted with new places in the company of friends who were regular customers there. This was the best guarantee against being conned, or "downed in one go", as the water trade idiom appropriately had it. A cosy evening among fellow insiders was also more enjoyable. On his forays into new territory Boon always ran the risk of being bilked, and occasionally he was.

In a very ordinary bar in Shinbashi (high rates), for example, after consumption of a glass of beer and a few slices of salami, and without so much as a squeeze or nudge, he was presented with a crippling bill which put him out of action for an entire month. He once fell into the company of small-time gangsters in a very low bar near Ueno station who wanted to procure him a woman and, not succeeding, at least managed to drink a bottle of whisky at his expense and for good measure relieved him of his watch, as he discovered on his way home. These were minor details which did nothing to alter Boon's impression that on the whole people in the water trade were surprisingly honest, and that Tokyo could well claim to be the safest city in the world.

All of these tens of thousands of nondescript bars astonishingly managed to preserve their own distinctive personality and flair. Unfortunately Boon could not vouch for them all, but in the course of a year he sampled over a hundred and found that each was always different from the last.

Bars were people, an extension of the personality of the *mama-san* who ran them. In a typical *akachochin*, where there were not more than a dozen customers at any one time, *mama-san* could make her presence felt and it was to glean something from her presence that customers came. In establishments with a capacity much larger than this the effect of even a very forceful personality was dissipated, the place lacked character and accordingly became anonymous. In the higher echelons of the water trade, Boon later discovered, the bars might be more sophisticated, the women younger and prettier, the bills a reflection of more lavish entertainment, but in shutting out the vulgarity of the common *akachochin* they also forfeited its warm familiarity. They had a discreet, clinical air, like the waiting-rooms of fashionable consultants.

Boon's choice of bar varied with his mood. In Oji, for example, where his evening always ended, he had a choice of three. In the improbably named Willow Lane, hard by the paper processing factory in a rustic bar where the glasses trembled on the counter whenever a train passed by, he spent many an evening fencing with a nimble, dapper soubrette whose age was as uncertain as the colour of her hair. She was not the *mama* but her adjutant; *mama* herself was an ogre, and in order not to scare away customers usually kept out of sight. There was something about this adjutant, or a number of things, her spotless apron, her subtle wit, her unobtrusive catlike sensuality, the challenging modesty of her smile, which Boon found irresistible.

Kimiko came from Sendai. She was reserved, as women from north Japan so often were. Astute, capable, self-possessed, she gave away nothing. Boon never learned a single thing about her private life, and Kimiko enquired only desultorily about his. What interested her was here and now. Her opinion of Boon was formed entirely by what she saw and heard over the counter, and the counter was always between them, as Kimiko never ventured out in front. She wasn't that kind. She came round the counter in other ways.

Her preference was for allusion, nuance, veiled suggestion, and the style of her talk reflected her character. The inclinations of her temperament went one way, her judgement another, no doubt from experience. Like many women who are not obviously attractive, nature had compensated her with the kind of appeal that made her the more exciting to men the less they were able to give it a name. Boon would have been hard put to say what made Kimiko erotic. He delighted in her plump white fingers, her puckered throat, the retreat of her sleeves up her arms when she took a glass down from the shelf and placed *sake* on the counter. One moment she was round and snug and seemed willing to make her snugness available, the next demure and schoolmarmish, questionably snug, categorically not available. Boon was both foiled and disarmed.

After this had gone on for several months he invited her out to dinner. She accepted. If it was a major concession it still brought no perceptible change; his line had drawn a little closer, but she behind hers remained entrenched as ever. The dinner was a success. Kimiko brought along her counter, none the less solid for being invisible. However, she allowed Boon to infer that if he made a reasonable suggestion it would be given due consideration. He made various suggestions, she had various considerations. Eventually they arranged to spend a couple of days at a hot spring, but at this very promising stage of their relations Boon ran out of money, and worse, out of time. Not long afterwards he left the country and did not visit Willow Lane again for three years. Kimiko had vanished without trace.

A stone's throw from Willow Lane, he frequently resorted to *Yoshimi* for the good-fellowship it advertised in its name. It was run by a classic *mizu-shobai* mother-and-daughter team as generous with their information as Kimiko was reticent, which must have had something to do with the climate, as both women, unlike Kimiko, were natives of the warmer and more exuberant south. Boon came across this difference between northern and southern temperaments too often for it to be a coincidence; just as the difference from Sapporo to Kagoshima was roughly equivalent to the distance between Copenhagen and Madrid, so also was the change of temperament that corresponded to the respective change in latitude.

Yoshie was the name of the "daughter"; Boon never enquired the name of the "mother", because there was no need. She was the archetypal, nameless *mama-san*, one of those women whose job it was to cook fish and heat *sake* every night for a meagre wage, but whose function, unacknowledged and priceless, was as a pillar of the Japanese establishment.

Mama was a large, frank-faced woman of about fifty, a widow and mother of three grown-up children. She was as deft with an accordion as with a frying-pan and had memorised songs from almost every region of Japan. Her advice was wise, her consolation reassuring; both were often required. In the warm glow of the first few jars of *sake* customers wanted to sing and in the later hours of the evening, when they were maudlin, many of them also felt an urge to confess.

Mama well understood why this was so. She was herself a sentimental woman. When she laid aside her accordion and opened her heart it proved to be just as capacious, able to accommodate as many tunes. "You are all really like children," she once said to Boon, her gesture embracing not merely the row of men perched on stools in front of her, but all those who had already been there or were yet to come. Tears were occasionally shed in *Yoshimi*, the making of resolutions was a nightly event. Errant husbands did not go home reformed characters but they left with the warmest intentions, which accompanied them at least as far as the next station.

Yoshie in her own way was as typical a daughter of the water trade as *mama* was a mother. Twenty-eight years old, divorced, one child. It was a piquant fact of the *mizu-shobai* world that many of the girls who spent their evenings entertaining male customers did not really like men. Some bore lovers and husbands a personal grievance which they transferred to men in general; others harboured a less definite resentment because in the course of their work they were required to behave in ways which went against their true nature. A streak of masochism, an involuntary self-humiliation borne almost as a kind of penance, was unmistakable in Yoshie's case.

She alternately flirted and froze, offered and withheld herself, was forthcoming or coldly aloof. Like many girls in her trade she had a preference for older men and it was in their company that her personality seemed most stable. She was an attractive girl, both in temperament and physique. She treated Boon with the wariness she showed all younger men, but they might have become good friends had her sexuality not been so overpowering and Boon not made the inevitable advances. It was a bad mistake made worse by the fact that she had gradually begun to trust him. Boon felt obliged to stay away from Good-fellowship for almost two months as a result. On his return, *mama* made no enquiries about the absence of one of her most loyal customers; she knew the reason and approved his tact. Thereafter it was *mama* whom he went to visit in *Yoshimi*, not Yoshie.

Following Ichimonji's instructions Boon later discovered the nefarious hovel under the bridge on the far side of the railway, his third and definitely last resort when drinking in Oji, last both in its abysmal quality and the lateness of its opening hours, usually about two o'clock in the morning. It was a descent in every respect. The two or three shacks there had gathered like the silt of the sewer that crept under Oji bridge, encrustations of a slow brown effluence which leaked out of the guts of the city. Nothing could be seen of these hovels from the bridge. One had to go down to find them.

The company was mixed. There were itinerant construction workers from the country, in dusty moccasins and with cloths knotted round their foreheads. Raucous, drunk, reasonably warm, these men found it cheaper or preferable to stay up drinking until the morning than to get themselves a bed for the night. Others, in crumpled suit and tie, remained incommunicatively in corners. Perhaps, like Boon, they had lost their keys and locked themselves out, or were ruminating on the depths to which they had sunk. It was a place entirely suited to self-castigation, about as cosy as a dungeon.

One of these men, in need of company, once took Boon into his confidence. Amiable, if rather incoherent, he seemed to have two worries on his mind: lack of money and a pregnant wife. He fetched out a piece of paper and performed dizzy calculations, not for Boon's benefit but for his own, itemising the costs of a son and daughter respectively over a period of twenty years. The daughter came out a little cheaper, but in either case it was an immense sum.

"As you see," he concluded in the manner of an accountant, "the second problem aggravates the first."

Boon commiserated. There was not much he could do except buy his companion a drink and regale him with tales of foreign parts. Whether, as a result, the man felt himself in some way indebted or wanted to give a spontaneous token of friendship, was unclear, but he suddenly invited Boon to accompany him home. Boon demurred. The man insisted. Boon pointed out that it was now three o'clock in the morning, rather late to be intruding on a pregnant wife. But the man wouldn't hear any excuses and forcibly bundled him outside.

It was bitterly cold and not a taxi in sight. They walked briskly for twenty minutes, while the man talked in detail about his job. At last they reached a dingy, barrack-like three-storey building which Boon at once recognised as the kind of accommodation with which many companies provided their employees in compensation for a smaller disposable income. He had been wondering on the way if the evening might yet end unexpectedly with high jinks, but as they groped up the dark stairs he buried all hope. The man took a key out of his pocket and pushed open a door.

"This is my home," he announced grimly, without any attempt at pride, "typical salaryman's *uchi*. Please come in."

Boon slipped off laceless shoes and followed his host into the well-appointed sitting-room of a typical salaryman's home. The man's wife must have fallen asleep while watching television; she lay reclined on the sofa in the shadow of a thriving rubber plant. When they came in she awoke, opened her eyes and looked at Boon without any indication of surprise.

The man introduced his second problem, she mumbled a greeting. From the casual way this took place Boon assumed she must have grown accustomed to visitors in the middle of the night. Her husband asked for food and drink. In silence she got up and complied, a drab, whey-faced woman, carrying her stomach like an injury, big with child, into the kitchen out of sight.

The man said nothing, as if infected by the reproachful silence of his wife. Confronted by the material evidence of a burden which at least on paper he had attempted to cope with, his accountancy no longer seemed able to help him and he shrank under its weight. It was evidently the couple's first child. Boon felt like a comedian hired for a wedding and arriving at a funeral. Jokes were discouraged, conversation was minimal. The wife spread out her hospitality and retired. At half-past four Boon took her place on the sofa and for a couple of hours escaped in sleep.

Although Boon was sure he had done nothing to cause offence, the attitude of his host at breakfast the next morning had completely changed. Sober now, restored to the real world, he probably felt ashamed. He had been exposed in his intimacy, seduced by one of those heady impulses of friendship which were peculiar to the water trade and which snuffed out as quickly as they caught fire. They ate breakfast hastily and Boon accompanied him to the station, where they parted, once again total strangers. From the opposite platform Boon saw him briefly, uniform in dark blue suit and striped tie, barely distinguishable from the endless crowd into which a few seconds later he for ever flowed. An image remained with Boon which quickly lost all contours of individuality. He had never even learned his companion's name. He had met Everyman.

The part of Tokyo with the biggest human turnover was Shinjuku. It was a world in itself, but although Boon had circumnavigated it early on in his career he had unfortunately happened to set foot in two establishments where the natives were very unfriendly to strangers, and for a long time this hostile reception he had been given deterred him from undertaking any further landings. Later he returned in the company of guides, who secured him an unequivocal welcome. Somewhere in Shinjuku there was probably something for everyone, if not among the bright lights then in the intriguing, less frequented backstreets. It was a microcosm of Tokyo, an encyclopaedia of venal delights.

With a homosexual friend he toured the buzzing, febrile haunts of the city's gay legions, where the conversation was sharp and witty and the customers sometimes of a marvellous beauty which

Boon never saw outside on the streets. They were treasured creatures, whose owners kept them jealously to themselves. Homosexuals were more discreet than transvestites, who dressed magnificently and touted openly on certain streets. Some of them could afford to be so bold because even at close quarters they were indistinguishable from women. Boon was one of their dupes. Lured into a sleazy transvestite bar he enjoyed an hour of intimate conversation, complete with squeeze and nudge, before becoming aware of the true sex of his companion.

Japanese transvestites undoubtedly had more scope to celebrate femininity than their colleagues in Europe. The softer vowels and more graceful intonation of women's speech was one resource which they exploited to the full. Elsewhere, of course, in the theatre, the art of portraying women was cultivated as a great male actors' tradition. Boon's most memorable experience of this kind was not, however, at the Kabuki-za, but the performance of Lady Macbeth by a celebrated *onnagata*. In a generally dismal production her mere presence on stage had been spellbinding.

Some of these bars housed considerable talents that were quite unknown outside the bounds of Shinjuku Ward. On the fourth floor of a dreary building Boon often went to listen to the bawdy recitals of a small neat *mama-san* whose voice had unexpected resonance and power. Always in *kimono*, with rich shining hair traditionally coiffeured, making her head seem somehow much too large for her body, this proper-looking lady punched out songs of inspired obscenity. She composed her own songs and accompanied herself on the guitar. Often funny, always superbly delivered, the texts of her songs combined the traditional sexual allusions of Japanese folk songs – shells, the sea and so on – with a more direct and racy modern idiom. These songs were one example of the possibilities of a synthesis that Boon looked for and usually missed in contemporary Japanese culture.

It was in Shinjuku that Boon first got to know about bars in the style of *akachochin* which catered for men and women on an equal footing. Unaccompanied women who were not professionals in the water trade never visited *akachochin*; even when with an escort they were very rarely seen. There were host clubs that supplied housewives with the same kind of entertainment their husbands sought in cabarets, but they were not otherwise comparable. Young single girls mostly frequented coffee houses. There were also harmless, large-scale bars where in the safety of the crowd they could drink alone or accompany their boyfriends. In discotheques it was currently fashionable to dance not with a partner but with one's own reflection in the mirrors; no problem for single girls. But bars with the characteristic flavour of *akachochin*, cheap, casual and intimate, where male and female customers were equally welcome to talk, sing or explore the venues of sexual contact, seemed to be few and far between.

There were probably more such bars in Shinjuku than elsewhere in town. Typically they were run by amateurs, often by people who would have had difficulties in making a living in any other way – drop-outs, young men and women who had got into trouble with the law. Their clients, likewise, were less conventional than the average Japanese.

Visiting these bars was not unlike dropping in at a private house, with the difference that one would be required to pay for one's drinks when one left. The easy contact such bars made possible between men and women whose only point in common was that they were all customers introduced an almost European atmosphere. The clientele was generally young. As it was unlikely that newcomers would find such places unless brought along by an initiate there was little danger of the peace of their select communities being disturbed. Even here, however, *mama-san* ruled supreme and the vocabulary of the water trade went unchallenged.

Inevitably the customers who patronised a particular bar became cliqueish; the ineradicable root of the *uchi* blossomed in unexpected places. One bar no bigger than a cupboard which Boon sometimes visited rattled with the skeletons of political outcasts. The owner of the cupboard was a man known as Butch, who had done time for his part in an explosion which had demolished a police box and, unfortunately, its occupants.

Butch swore by all that he hated that he was an innocent man who had been framed by the police. Quite possibly he was. Boon liked him and considered he was honest. None the less, some odd types hung out in his bar and occasionally there were nasty scenes. The friend who had first smuggled Boon into Butch's cupboard was beaten up by the customers one evening because they took exception to his suit and tie, the bourgeois stigma of a man who had gone over to the other side. No serious injury was done. He was just given the vigorous collegial drubbing meted out to fellow conspirators who hadn't quite toed the line. Boon did not know the ins and outs of their quarrel, and he did not ask. Political in-fighting ended violently, sometimes in death. He knew a friend of Sugama's, for example, who had been involved in radical activities at university and never been able to escape his political past. Whether he was paranoid or genuinely had reason to fear for his life was impossible to judge, but he changed his address several times a year and lived on the run. Boon's curiosity was quite satisfied on this score.

There was no better example of the *uchi* mentality that sometimes took over a water trade establishment than in those bars frequented by fellow countrymen – not as Japanese, of course, but as men from the same region of Japan.

Boon had his attention drawn to this kind of bar by Sugama, who took him along to a place in Shibuya patronised for the most part by men from his native Toyama. The very personable *mama-san* was herself a co-regionalist; she and Sugama had been to school together. The bar was naturally open to all comers, but the word soon got around and within a short space of time such places became informal clubs. Consulting his old-boy network, Sugama was able to report to Boon that there were at least half a dozen other Toyama bars in Tokyo alone, and what was true of his own prefecture presumably applied to others. All companies, needless to say, had their own bars for the more or less voluntary imbibing of a spirit of communal fellowship during prolonged sessions after office hours.

A nice illustration of how the presence of a House Spirit could bring harmony to sectarian interests was carried to Boon's ears by a professor of anatomy at Kyoto University. The House Spirit of the bar where he and his scientific colleagues were regular customers was charmingly impersonated by a *mama-san* of such fascinating character and physique that for the first time ever concerted interdisciplinary action was agreed by an academic community which otherwise preferred to cherish its squabbles.

From faculties far and wide they came in droves, the natural scientists, the men of letters, linguists and philosophers. The bar became a talking shop. Common problems were ventilated through different pipes, the results pooled, sifted, unanticipated insights gained. These heady free-thinking days were followed by catastrophe: *mama* announced her engagement to the treacherous reader in particle physics. She resigned her function as their unifying spirit and the academic men duly went their separate ways.

In whatever form of bar, catering for whatever kind of client, the *mama* was irreplaceable. She need not be an attractive woman, although in the majority of cases it turned out that somehow she was, for her heart was no less important than her figure or her face. In the few hard-bitten cases, where even the best intentions were of no avail, she delegated grace or sensual bloom to a more youthful assistant; either she did that or didn't run a bar at all.

Boon was an unashamed sensualist who paid attention to this bloom. There were other men who went to bars with other motives, but for him at least it was always there: a suspenseful prickling in the air, intimations of the void space shrinking between himself and the women who leaned over the counter. Sex was always there somewhere, between the *mamas* or their daughters and those hopeful doggy men who sat with cocked ears, but just how, and where – this was a vexed question.

Straight sex could be had instantly, on demand, for cash and by the hour, at any respectable Turkish baths. Boon was genuinely not interested in a commodity so easily available, and he was too poor in any case. Certainty of pleasure intimidated him. He preferred it to steal up on him unawares.

Second only to the Turkish baths were the so-called Pink Cabarets, where delivery was as prompt if not as complete. These places resembled the *séparées* of cheap hostess bars in Europe. Boon went along once in the company of a group of colleagues shortly before he left the country.

With echoes of the former pleasure quarters in Yoshiwara, pink cabarets tended to be confined to a few parts of the city where they came not singly but by the street. The Japanese were enthusiasts who did not do things by halves, least of all in their pursuit of pleasure. The house touts who vied belligerently outside the dark entrances gave such explicit and graphic accounts of what awaited the customer inside that for Boon's taste, at least, the entertainment was over before it had begun. He would have found it very difficult to decide whose recommendation to follow, but fortunately his companions knew exactly where to go.

Entrance was by flashlight, the five of them treading cautiously in Indian file, with one hand on the shoulder of the man in front. Submissive and slightly anxious, they were herded in more like prisoners than customers, thus making it a lot easier for the cashier inside the door to extract considerable sums of money from each man as he passed without inconvenience of protest. Singly or in pairs they were shown to tables which Boon heard the sleek usher in the dark behind him refer to by numbers. Boon was Six, his friends, from whom he had been separated, Nine and Ten. The numbers travelled like a password back into the gloomy interior and elicited whispering female echoes. Five minutes passed, and Boon began to wonder if rather than pay he should not have been paid to sit there alone in the dark. At last more whispering. Two or three rustles approached.

Someone wearing a *kimono* sat down beside him.

"*Konban wa.*"

"Hello, are you number six?"

"What? Oh, yes . . ."

Laughter.

"Six is my table. My name's Michiko."

Common enough name. Boon wondered what her real name was. He thought about the five minutes he had been kept waiting and hazarded a guess.

"I suppose you'd gone to the toilet . . ."

Michiko gasped.

"How d'you know that!"

"My name is Sherlock Holmes," replied Boon in impeccable Japanese.

Rustling consternation in the dark. Michiko got down to business.

"Aren't you going to give me a kiss?"

"Where are you?"

"Here."

Boon aimed his head. The first part of him that struck Michiko's face must have been his beard, which after a couple of years of unimpeded growth was approaching biblical dimensions. Michiko gave a squeak of astonishment.

"What are you doing?"

"I was hoping to kiss you," replied Boon abashed.

"But what's that?"

"My beard."

"Beard? Is it real?"

"Of course it's real."

But Michiko's suspicions were now thoroughly aroused. In the reddish glow of a flashlight she held inside her sleeve she briefly inspected Boon's face.

"But you're not Japanese."

"I never said I was."

"Are you a half?"

"Certainly not. I'm whole. I'm English."

The furtive show of light at table number six elicited jubilant, bawdy comment from tables nine and ten. Gales of laughter. Boon spoke out firmly in the dark to quash base imputations. Michiko took his hand and inserted it encouragingly between her breasts. He fondled her, she gave an audible sigh of relief to find that her client, though not Japanese, was normal, and deftly began to open his trousers. Not entirely at his ease, Boon was in favour of making a private arrangement and pursuing the matter after business hours, but Michiko rejected this suggestion as improper.

At this delicate moment the usher's bodiless voice oozed out of the dark and substantiated a request for eight thousand yen. Boon said no. The request was repeated at tables nine and ten, where the absolute silence was momentarily broken by the thick crackle of ten-thousand yen notes. He wondered without envy what they were getting for their money. "Whatever you like," he heard them gleefully urge him, but Boon's knees were wedged under the impossibly small table, and even had he felt carnal he was not an acrobat.

Back in the street, where they were deposited after quarter of an hour, there was a great deal of hitching up of trousers and conspiratorial merriment. His friends were entirely relaxed and unselfconscious. An experience which in Europe would have been shabby in Japan did not seem so, redeemed by a naturalness which Boon, though he came close to it, could never quite share. He went away with other things on his mind: pounds of flesh turned over per night, manhandling, womanhandling: how did the girls do it? Well, a lot of them no doubt welcomed the opportunity of a living made possible by pink cabarets, where they remained nameless, unseen and, however impersonally, desired. Michiko had seen Boon's face, but he also had seen hers: she was an extremely ugly girl.

In the straight cabarets she would not have been employed. It did not matter if the girls in straight cabarets were stupid, indeed, it was an advantage, but they had to pass a minimum standard of attractiveness. The prettiest girls naturally made the most money, and they graduated from school to establishments on the Ginza as unquestioningly as the cleverest students were dispatched to Tokyo University. The also-ran were distributed more or less evenly over the rest of Tokyo.

Boon's own preferences would have led him to give cabarets a wide berth, because they were usually rip-offs and rather soulless, but in the interests of completeness a knowledge of cabarets was indispensable to his studies, and so he sampled quite a few. Rather tiresomely, the less he wanted to visit them the more the opportunities seemed to be thrown at him. His reluctant career was eventually crowned by the paradox of being *commissioned* by a Tokyo radio station to do a report on cabarets, actually paid to endure an enforced pleasure. If the things he wanted in Japan had come to him as effortlessly as those he did not Boon would have been a very happy man.

The first visit to a cabaret was in the company of Sugama and co-regional friends. In his early innocence, the invitation to a cabaret had aroused in Boon visions of the plangent Liza Minelli, pneumatic girls and acerbic political wit; he was quickly undeceived. Between the bosoms of the entertainers and those they entertained there was no such thing as a stage, in fact not any distance at all. In cabarets one practised the art of the clinch, either in cubbies with motionless feet, or in a lumbering shuffle over the dance floor.

Under discreet but all-revealing purple lights hands were allowed in laps when stationary, when active with wilful intent they were not. On the six inches of stockinged flesh between hemline and knee more assiduous clients could span a hand and grope for chords, but these efforts were misplaced. In cabarets it was not the knee or thigh that came into its own, but the breast.

Boon, an ardent if still bashful student, watched with astonishment how Sugama's friends sat down with the hostesses they had been assigned and almost at once reached out for their breasts as nonchalantly as they helped themselves to the fruit on the table. Sugama was not much of a fruit eater himself, so he was willing to handle Boon's questions instead. Boon admitted cautious surprise: were then these vegetarian devotions the dietary concomitants of some religion hitherto unknown to him? Religion, answered Sugama, in the conventional sense, no; an archaic instinct of adoration, yes. Witness his friend Kato to Boon's left. Married, with three children, he had long since vacated the suckling place who was himself most sorely in need of maternal nourishment. Boon looked to his left. The hands of the meagre Kato were cupped like a chalice. With greedy reverence he squeezed, snuffed and pawed his companion in search of a surrogate fuel, not actual, but also not fruitless. Still, persisted Boon, again facing Sugama, the promptness with which his friends fastened themselves to the breasts of strange women had rather taken him aback. Sugama told him to look more closely. Did Kato's actions display sexual intent? Were his gropings lecherous? Were they not rather the gropings of a spent animal towards a haven of safety? Boon granted that the latter seemed to be the case. Quite so, said Sugama, and that was why they caused no offence, however forward, however importunate their behaviour might seem to Boon. The women might be strangers, but their breasts, ah! – their breasts were familiar. For the breast was the sacred if unacknowledged fount of all the nutritious gentleness that flowed through Japanese life.

Consider, said Sugama, getting into his stride, the word *chichi*. – He and Boon leaned forward over the table, inadvertently drawing into the conversation their two hostesses, who for better or worse remained firmly attached. – It means "father", said Boon. Sugama chided his fatuity and the two girls laughed, pointing at each other's vacant breasts. It is an androgynous word, ventured Boon. No, said Sugama, a homonym: *chichi* could mean either breast or father, and when it referred to breast the word was written with a Chinese character meaning milk. The breast was milk or the vessel of milk, not primarily sensual or even aesthetic, but utilitarian – his friend Kato's behaviour was the best example. Nowadays they were concerned not just with size but with bare adequacy of supply; there were not enough breasts to go round. To satisfy demand on the home market reinforcements had to be imported from foreign parts. Boon's girl was Taiwanese, his own from Korea. The two hostesses became uneasy at this turn to the conversation, for although their breasts were welcome as tourist attractions their misappropriation for any professional purpose had not been sanctioned by the director of immigrations. The upshot of Sugama's breast theory, Boon concluded facetiously, was that the term *mizu-shobai* was a patent misnomer. And they drank a toast to the water trade, which all agreed should thereafter be known as the milk trade.

Boon now turned to his Taiwanese girl and things started to come on very nicely. He was just wondering how an evening that had begun without preliminaries could appropriately end, when Sugama and his friends got up as one man and headed for the door. They will have arranged a party, he surmised gratefully, picked up his coat and followed them outside. But no, suddenly the evening seemed to be over. Hurriedly they took leave of one another, climbed one by one into separate taxis and drove straight home to their waiting wives. Boon couldn't understand this at all.

It was the rule, however. The fruit sampled in cabarets was merely an *hors-d'oeuvre*, by and large the water trade as a whole supplied appetizers but not the full course. Dinners warmed by professional caterers were usually eaten in the privacy of the home. This was not just the practice of raffish individuals but of millions of ordinary married men. Boon's evidence for this after exhaustive field studies was irrefutable. At last the time came for him to write up his findings and draw a few conclusions.

His first conclusion was that the licence of the water trade and the stability of marriage were not unconnected. He did not read any statistics, but comparing the marriages of dozens of Japanese acquaintances with those of European friends he found there was an unmistakable tendency. In European marriages both wives and husbands shed their partners with an ease which in Japan was unimaginable. Withdrawing from an embrace with another woman, even men who were egoists and frank sensualists gave voice to sentiments about their wives and marriages which in Europe would have been dismissed as rank hypocrisy. Coming from Japanese mouths such claims of loyalty were quite true. The integrity of marriage, the form of marriage if not the content, was unshakeable. Men who no longer loved their wives sought their pleasure outside marriage but continued to honour their duties inside it. Of course there were cases of men ditching wives and women husbands, though from his own experience Boon personally knew of none. In cases of divorce, rather than desertion, Boon knew only of separations taking place after children had passed the age of parental responsibility. The exception was in the water trade, where there were quite a few young women who had divorced or parted from their husbands; that was the reason why they had taken up their trade. It provided a refuge for all kinds of outsiders.

This stability had its price. Over the question of form as opposed to content of marriage Japanese and European attitudes were clearly divided. Perhaps the difference which became evident here was a more general, a fundamental one. Both the social mores and the underlying morality of Japanese life everywhere stressed the importance of preserving the form. A bad marriage was still better than none. Wife and children constituted an *uchi* that was second to none and which was not easily separable from the professional *uchi* in which domestic stability was firmly anchored. For a man to catapult himself voluntarily out of either was to enter limbo and a free-falling void. To relinquish the one or resign from the other might entail disaster and not just change. When he stuck to the rules his house was cast iron, but when he tried to revise them his world came down like a pack of cards.

Men and women in Europe, by contrast, could afford to put personal relations before the marriage that symbolised them because they lived in a society with more scope for alternatives. For them a bad marriage was not better than none. As a matter of course they would look around for another partnership. There were no comparable repercussions. A man's place of work had nothing to do with his private life, and he could change his job as easily as his shirt. His decision to do so was typically not subject to moral constraints but to supply and demand on the labour market. For the average European a job was an income, for the average Japanese it was a home.

The average European was not a member of a Bunny Club. When wives and husbands pursued intimate relationships outside their marriage it was usually at parties or at a private rendezvous, not necessarily secret, with their intimate friend; and if they showed interest in the *hors-d'oeuvre* they were as likely as not to demand the full course. Dinners were cooked and eaten by the same persons.

Women in Europe could play the same games as their husbands because they were less dependent on them than Japanese wives. Conversely, women in Japan were prepared to stay at home while their husbands were entertained by professional alternatives because they were not their rivals and their own security was never in doubt. They knew that the water trade, in the majority of cases, supplied no more than harmless titillation. As Boon saw it, however, the blunt truth of the matter was that when those husbands at last returned home their wives became the dubious beneficiaries of appetites which had been whetted on other women. This view was cruel, but he believed it was the truth.

Boon personally would have felt this as a humiliation, but as an impartial observer his personal opinions were neither here nor there. What did Japanese women think? The justification they might have offered in defence of their remarkable docility was already clear. Without recourse to the water trade their husbands would in the long run probably have found it difficult to guarantee the inviolability of marriage, so the wives tolerated the escapades of their spouses in exchange for domestic security. For women without alternatives there was indeed not much choice.

But if security was agreeable it could also be rather dull. The mothers of the young women whom Boon knew well enough to sound their views would have sung, darned socks and hushed babies night after night and been reasonably content, but with their married daughters this equanimity could no longer be taken for granted. There were signs that they were beginning to find the long evenings at home a bit boring. They were becoming restive and wanted to get out.

Japanese men, even those with more flexible attitudes, were very sensitive when approached on this subject. They knew they were onto a good thing, and they didn't want to change it. They knew better than their wives and spoke for them as a matter of course. Discussions hardly ever got off the ground, remaining clogged in vapid, sententious utterances. And behind that protective attitude which husbands sometimes liked to assume towards wives nothing was better protected than the male interest.

Boon's studies in the water trade did not end here, however. There were other conclusions to be drawn, of a different nature and for him at least of wider interest.

What began as a mistake with the androgynous word *chichi*, which in fact was a homonym, either breast or father but not both at the same time, opened a line of enquiry into the water trade that nourished Boon's desultory imagination as satisfyingly as the paps of a hundred *mama-san* stilled his restless thirst. For here, amid the pragmatic, no-nonsense values of glass and steel and international corporations, existed an ancient model of a matriarchal state, perfectly intact.

The water trade was *mama*'s domain. She was absolute and un-challengeable. She had handmaidens, nominally her daughters, whom the men awaiting judgement at the bar convention required to call *o-neesan*, or elder sister. Sister handmaidens, but not sons; only, on rare occasions, a menial handyman. But *papa* was not there. He hadn't been forgotten. In the water trade he just didn't exist. Either breast or father, but not both at the same time. During festivals outside it was the phallus that was borne in triumph through the streets, but one step across curtained thresholds into water trade territory and the prerogative of male succession was instantly cut off. No symbols were erected here; one was clasped at once to its bodily presence: not martial but meek, shaken by no more than the snoring exhalations of its own reassuring, constant bulk, the safe, round, warm, soft, adipose breast.

Not all customers, however, were as undernourished as Suga-ma's friend Kato; they did not all apply to the water trade for the comfort of a wet nurse. The illicit point of their interest was smuggled inside and kept under the counter, concealed in their trousers. This interest was not one that could be openly declared to *mamas* and elder sisters, but by custom it was tacitly acknowledged and remained, though itself unspeaking, a potent source of suggestion. Unseen, unheard, it none the less piped a melody which irresistibly set in motion the steps of a ritual dance. Boon was as fascinated by this dance as by the circumstances under which it took place. For although the partners belonged to different kinship groups, by the nomenclature of the water trade they were all members of the same family. *Mama's* drinking shop was analogous to an *uchi*, which she ran as if it were her own household.

With half-closed eyes and instinct wide awake under the dome of his imagination Boon allowed himself to plummet deep into the primeval twilight of the water trade. A myth as old as humanity was being enacted here on the borders of dream and truth. The desire for mothers and sisters, real enough but unafraid of censure, defied taboo under the veil of symbol. The partners of desire were mothers and sisters in no more than name; it was only play. In this watery mythological landscape there was no Laius, and hence no Oedipus. Sage *mamas* prevented sons from putting out their eyes by keeping fathers eternally out of sight. The heroines cooked fish while mermaids played the *shamisen*. It was a gentler scenario, and Boon much preferred it.

The cactus eater's family. In May of his second year, about eighteen months after arriving in Japan, Boon moved out to a village near Hiratsuka to live as a paying guest in the house of a bicycle dealer.

Neither the bicycle dealer himself nor the locality of his home held any particular attractions for Boon, but this was the only family which had offered to take him in. Although he advertised in a weekly circular that was distributed to all the housing estates in the Metropolitan area and must accordingly have had a readership of at least several hundred thousand, only one family responded. For a stranger to penetrate the privacy of a Japanese home was always a delicate problem, in the case of a foreigner even more so, but probably the main reason why Boon's advertisement provoked such a meagre response was because housing estate families had no room to spare.

The bicycle dealer could accommodate Boon because he lived in his own house. The old man himself, however, would never have dreamed of inviting anyone to come and live in his home. The negotiations were conducted secretly by his daughter-in-law, whose mother lived on a housing estate where Boon's advertisement had done the rounds; she passed it on to her daughter, for reasons which did not become clear to Boon until after he had moved in. Officially he was invited to come and teach the family English, but this was only a ruse to smuggle him in against the wishes of the older residents. Once he was installed they would have other uses for him.

On Boon's behalf Sugama had long telephone conversations with the daughter-in-law, supplied character references, sketched Boon's academic background and expounded his family antecedents for the past three generations. Boon wondered whether all this information could be of the slightest interest to a bicycle dealer living out near Hiratsuka. Sugama assured him it was.

"Because to a certain extent, you see, you'll become a member of the family yourself. So naturally she wants to know all about you."

"What about her?" asked Boon.

"Yes. She has a very nice voice indeed – really a very nice voice."

"I don't mean her voice. Her family."

"Her family doesn't matter. Now she's married and moved to her husband's home it's the bicycle dealer's family that matters. You'll meet them all on Sunday in any case. There seem to be rather a lot of them. Four generations."

The following weekend they duly trekked out to the village where the bicycle dealer lived and at a formal lunch in the spacious *kyakuma* met representatives of four generations of his prolific family, ranging in age from one to eighty-six and all somehow living under the same roof. Boon was approved and invited to come and stay for a trial period of six months.

By chance the household he now moved into supplied an example of family life that was much more typical of past than present Japan. At least in urban areas, cohabitation of successive generations living as one family under the same roof had been superseded by the "nuclear family" pattern. Grown-up children no longer lived with their parents or felt obliged to support them. It would not have been possible anyhow. They lived separately with their own families.

With the Ohashi clan matters were different. On the surface, at least, they followed that traditional large-scale pattern of family life to which many Japanese, secretly glad to be rid of their parents, still occasionally felt bound to pay lip-service. Experienced from the inside, however, life in the Ohashi household made very clear to Boon why the large-scale family pattern was no longer feasible in modern Japan. Space limitation might be given as a convenient excuse, but the real difficulties were of a psychological kind.

Downstairs in the large two-storey house (recently built to accommodate the third-generation Ohashi family) lived great-grandmother, her eldest son and her daughter-in-law. Great-grandmother slept in an all-purpose *tatami* room leading off the *kyakuma*, where during the day she sat and sewed, hushed the youngest child, served tea and gossiped with customers when their business was concluded in the shop. Born in the Meiji era, she was a contemporary of Sugama's grandfather. Her husband had died about a decade before. Boon often came down to listen to her talk about her life. As a young woman, in the 1920s, she had served in the residence of the Foreign Minister; later, after marrying and moving out into the country, she had spent decades working in the paddy fields. Like many people who had done this kind of work for any length of time great-grandmother suffered badly from rheumatism. Her body was bent double at the waist and she could hardly walk at all. She was a calm, cheerful soul, however, and Boon never once heard her complain.

Her grandson, his wife and their two small children had the floor upstairs to themselves. They shared the bathroom downstairs with the older generation but in all other respects led an independent life – that at least was the idea.

Boon was established in a nondescript room where the husband stored his books and the housewife her linen; previously it had been their sitting-room. Husband, wife and their two children aged one and three were left with two small rooms in which to live, eat and sleep. Although he paid generously, Boon felt uncomfortable about taking up so much of their space. He was assured it was not a sacrifice; the family seldom had visitors and preferred to sleep together in one room in any case.

At first he was enthusiastic about his new home. He seemed to become one of the family at once. When he got tired of his studies he wandered downstairs and chatted with the old folk. Great-grandmother had an art of spreading out hospitality on a spot no bigger than a handkerchief, conjuring tea, sweet cake and rice crackers from behind her back before Boon had even sat down. Something festive in her manner made the simplest gifts seem lavish. Boon accompanied the younger daughter-in-law when she walked with the children through the paddy fields behind the house, sat idly in a corner of the shop listening to talk with the customers, played games or watched television with the family, free to come and go as he pleased and privy to all their conversations. For the first time in months Boon got up in the mornings with a light heart. From his balcony he could see Fuji soaring up out of the huddled plain; white-capped and braceleted with cloud, the summit floated in the middle of the sky.

In the other direction lay the sea. He often cycled down the river path to swim at Oezu beach, where the fetid waves swilled over sand the colour of cinders, not dirt but volcanic dust. Dutifully, with distaste, Boon exercised in the murky water, practised dives from a rock, flexed his muscles and was photographed with girls on the pier. After his swim he would go and visit an Ohashi relative, a fisherman who lived in the village.

He was intrigued by the fisherman's family. They had a frugal

Japanese house, built in the old style, about a hundred yards from the shore. Everything was neat and clean. Boon always doused himself under the pump in the yard when he arrived, to avoid bringing volcanic dust into the house. The fisherman immensely enjoyed these antics under the pump. He sat on the veranda gripping his knees and grinning from ear to ear. His wife hung Boon's trunks up to dry on a washing-line as high as the house. She fetched the bamboo rod down with a pronged pole about five yards long.

Cross-legged he sat on the veranda and chatted with his host. The fisherman's white vest shone against his burned skin like something luminous in the dark.

Friendly but shy, fortunately unaware of his luminosity, the fisherman was afflicted with a terrible stammer. He relied on those listening to him to supply his cues for him, but Boon's Japanese wasn't always up to this task. Through the mouth of his wife the fisherman said that he didn't much like the sea and couldn't swim. Boon wondered vaguely what difference it might make to his stammer if the fisherman got a job on land.

His wife fetched a bottle of beer and slices of horse-mackerel, shooing the cat energetically out of Boon's lap. A daughter in school uniform with a portentous black satchel, a stifled greeting barely escaping her lips, flitted across the yard and disappeared into the house. Her appearance was incongruous in these surroundings. The girl was rather shy, explained the fisherman's wife. Boon thought it quite likely that the white-vested father made the girl self-conscious. He noticed her pale skin and fashionable curls. Her attention was claimed by another world.

The wife made up a bundle of fish for Boon to carry inland to the people back home. Fresh horse-mackerel from that morning's catch hung in a basket from the eaves. The basket was well within the jump of the cat and so Boon asked how come the fish hadn't been touched. The fisherman grinned and pointed to the row of cactus plants directly underneath the basket. Ouch! They all laughed.

Cactus plants and nervous ailments were points of interest the fisherman had in common with the bicycle dealer who was his cousin; in direct association in his case, for he used the first to cure the second. In the house of the inland Ohashis cactus plants did not occasion any hilarity, far from it. Almost in a spirit of totemism they were solemnly revered. The bicycle dealer ate them, root, spike and branch.

He was a spiky old fellow himself, if not by nature then by metastasis, in the course of long cactus-eating years. Sometimes he lapsed into warmth, almost as into an error, for at once he would correct himself, brace his shoulders again and bare his teeth. Boon learned from his wife about the tyrant who had been his father and his terrible experiences in the war. The military manner was an enduring scar. He bore a certain resemblance to Onoda, the soldier who had emerged from the Philippine jungle after thirty years in hiding. Ohashi had been there too.

There was something chronically wrong with his stomach. Nobody knew quite what. He also suffered from nerves – *shinkeishitsu*, as it was known in common Japanese parlance. A remarkable number of Japanese appeared to suffer from this complaint. Ohashi's wife grasped the obvious question and put it to Boon succinctly: was her husband nervous because of his stomach or did he have his stomach condition because of his nerves?

Ohashi himself had no time for subtleties of this kind. Ever since his stupendous discovery some years previously he had become a blind apostle of the cactus cure, nerves, stomach or whatever: his patent cordial did the job. It was an extraordinary medicine.

For a long while he held out on Boon, wary of taking him into his trust, until one day Boon recounted the miracles of an Austrian herbalist who had helped to relieve his catarrh. Ohashi must have considered this admission as qualifying Boon, as placing him squarely inside the same faith-healing pale, for there and then he touched him on the shoulder and motioned him into the kitchen.

Squatting on the floor he laid out his instruments, wheezed, gave garbled instructions. A ripe cactus was shredded like a carrot, spikes and all. Cactus. The task was best performed with a gloved hand. Glove. Ohashi put on the glove and shredded the cactus. Next came a mortar and pestle. Grind the shredded cactus to a paste and tip the paste into any suitable container. Personally he used a jam jar. Ohashi held out a sample jam jar for Boon to examine. Add garlic and honey to the cactus paste, stir thoroughly

– thoroughly! – and dilute with hot water to taste. That was it. Ohashi's patent ulcer cure. Ugh!

Two things about Ohashi's cordial particularly intrigued Boon. Just how had he ever come to make this fantastic stuff? And if his stomach condition was as bad as ever, which – not surprisingly, considering the demands he made of it – appeared to be the case, why did he bother to go on drinking it? Ohashi was impenetrable on the first point. And as for the second, well, there was no doubt in his own mind that if he hadn't drunk it daily he would have died long ago.

And drink it daily he did. He kept a flask on his work-bench, a toddy by his pillow. Boon underwent a tasting once but declined regular doses. After all, there was nothing wrong with his stomach.

Boon's abstention from the cactus cure was quite acceptable to Ohashi, but he could not for the life of him understand why his son would have nothing to do with it. Naoharu had inherited his father's nerves and stomach, yet he firmly rejected the magic draught. He trampled his own salvation underfoot and spurned it with his heel. Sheer folly. That was how young people were these days.

Naoharu was a computer engineer. Soft-skinned, soft-mannered, body and mind he was as pure a man as Boon had ever met, transparent as glass, and as fragile: Naoharu's brittleness was his one failing.

Tetchy father and timid son, both the senior son, had inherited a birthright they could not stomach. Sound nerves and a good digestive system seemed to be the prerogative of their younger brothers and sisters. Naoharu and Naohiru, whose names differed by only a vowel, were separated by a tradition. Naohiru lived in a shed in the garden beneath his elder brother's windows, claiming no rights and claimed by no responsibilities, robust, carefree, poor, squandering instead the almost insolent vitality he had inherited from his mother.

The computer engineer left the house early and returned late. The small firm that employed him was currently in difficulties. He worked overtime in the evenings and on Saturdays, without extra pay. He was the bacon-bringer, the man on whom they were all counting, his firm and his family alike. Sometimes he worked on Sundays too. He made desperate efforts, as if by force of will he could expand the week and gain non-existent days. His wife washed and ironed his white coat, packed his lunch, and stood drowsily each morning at the top of the stairs in a quilted dressing-gown.

Throughout the long days the house was left to the women, children and Boon, so he saw much more of Chieko than did her husband.

The struggle between mother and daughter-in-law for power over the son was just beginning to break surface when Boon moved into the house. The billeting of Boon in the upstairs sitting-room was itself part of that struggle, a declaration of hostilities, a masterly pre-emptive stroke in the incipient household war. Chieko was a natural tactician, she intrigued in her sleep. What she needed was an ally in the house, and time; time to ween the vacillating Naoharu from the still powerful influence of his mother. Isolated among strangers, her position apparently hopeless, Chieko had come up with a brilliant solution in the unexpected person of Boon.

The downstairs people were stumped. They had already encroached up the stairs, the landing was almost within their grasp, when Boon's appearance forced a retreat and banned further advances.

For a short period after their marriage Naoharu and Chieko had lived independently in a room of their own. At that time the Ohashis didn't have enough space. However, the feeling that the senior son ought to be living with his parents must have been very strong, strong enough to build an entire new house at great expense that fulfilled the condition on which Chieko agreed to return – a separate apartment for Naoharu and herself and now, three years later, their children.

Although Boon was a complete stranger, the intensity of the feelings aroused by this issue was so great that both women were unable to contain themselves and before long approached him in private to air their grievances. Chieko hated the house that had tricked her into consent, her mother-in-law bitterly felt the separation of families for which it had been designed to be an enduring disgrace.

Boon had seldom seen a woman so angry. There the house stood, divided, literally a monument to her defeat, and there she had to live. She writhed. Long before her language became explicit her gestures made plain her contempt. Hands staunch on her hips, she pulled back the corners of her mouth, lowered her eye-lids and tossed her head in scorn. *Tschk!* She hissed and recoiled, snake-like. Hate made her sensuous. Boon didn't think the right of the argument was on her side, but he liked and admired her.

She had a devastating euphemism for her daughter-in-law. She called her Upstairs.

"Don't you think Upstairs is rather odd? Don't you think Upstairs' behaviour is unnatural?"

What she deplored as most unnatural was the fact that the families took their meals separately. She had an archaic, almost super-stititious belief in the shared meal as forging a common bond. Apart from that, she doubted her daughter-in-law's competence. How thin her son was! And Boon, who paid good money: was Upstairs giving him enough to eat? Whenever he wandered down into her part of the house she secretly fattened him up in the kitchen.

Chieko, meanwhile, less dramatic than her mother-in-law but just as reluctant to take the enemy's name into her mouth, apostrophized her as "she". How each woman chose to refer to her rival illuminated their different characters. Anyone who happened to be eavesdropping would immediately know who was meant by Upstairs, but the neutral pronoun "she", in the best tradition of *aimai*, the vague language of the Japanese, left room for equivocation. Mother-in-law had the courage of her convictions and couldn't care less if she were overheard, whereas Chieko, the intriguer, was circumstantial in her malice.

Reluctantly Boon supported her cause – reluctant because he liked the enemy and disliked Chieko. Still, her husband, her children, her upstairs meals and the general running of her household were definitely her own affair and none of mother-in-law's business. The problem was exacerbated by Chieko's character. Despite their utterly opposed views the two women might yet have been reconciled had Chieko not been thwarted by her vanity and her cherished social pretensions.

Her own family, the one that didn't count, was the dreariest Boon had ever met. Her father, a harmless drudge, had been prematurely retired; in the interests of the corporation rather than in his own, according to malicious gossip. Still, he had been an official of sorts. The father of Chieko's husband was a bicycle dealer; the family had traditionally been shopkeepers. Generally there was little evidence of class snobbery in Japan, but in the fight for recognition of Chieko's rights it came to the fore.

Chieko's high-nosed mother was the villain of the piece. Nothing was too good for her daughters; for herself, actually. Her life with the encrusted official husband appeared to have been more shabby than genteel. Sour, spiteful, she lived vicariously through her daughters, into whom she breathed a vengeful spirit. The elder had already triumphed. Her husband owned a factory, consorted with politicians, drove splendid cars. But what had Chieko acquired through her marriage? A father-in-law who got oil on his hands when he ran them through his hair.

So the young bride moved to the bicycle dealer's home with her trousseau and a bundle of her mother's prejudices. She was not entirely without originality herself. To the faults she had learned from her mother she added her own considerable personal vanity. Boon, the young foreigner who sat upstairs while her husband was out, was in some sense a luxury that flattered her vanity, like a tropical aquarium or an exotic dog.

Naoharu was too trusting, perhaps too unimaginative a man to respond to the kind of innuendo of which Chieko would undoubtedly have been capable. Boon, otherwise not fastidious, never gave the slightest cause for jealousy, either in his actions or his thoughts, as long as he lived under Naoharu's roof. Accordingly he was very interested to learn afterwards, in a roundabout manner but from a reliable source, that during those months Chieko claimed she had lived in constant fear of being assaulted by Boon.

Was this how the afterthought worded the desire? It didn't matter, but with hindsight it became easier to understand the abrupt decampment of the upstairs people and Boon's subsequent expulsion, clearing the ground, like a purge, for the family's return and a brave new beginning at the turn of the year.

In August Naoharu took his summer holiday – five days. His company couldn't spare him for longer. It had been decided to spend the holiday with Chieko's sister, who lived a couple of hours' drive northwest of Tokyo. Naoharu was as excited as if he were setting off on a trip round the world. A few days before their departure his father's stomach condition got worse, and in a mood of prescient sentimentality the relations between Chieko and mother-in-law briefly improved. Rather to his surprise, Boon found that he had been invited along too.

After a tedious journey along congested roads (roads in Japan were never anything other than congested) he was delighted by the house at which they arrived late one Saturday afternoon. He liked the sweeping roof with its knobbly ridge-end tiles, the wooden veranda skirting the house, the long corridors smelling of waxed pine, the spacious, airy rooms. They were furnished in a style of softened austerity, allowing an ornament here, a low table there, just enough to rest the eye and leave spaces for the imagination. The owner of so much space in a country that had so little must evidently be a wealthy man.

Chieko's brother-in-law was not there when they arrived. The tawdry relatives from Hiratsuka squatted in his house and waited an hour for him to come.

Fujiwara Jusaburo was a man worth waiting for. He staged his entrance from the pine corridor, visible through glass panels, somehow conveying the impression of a man who has come from very far. He was a big, burly man who wore his Japanese robe lightly, with an air of casual magnificence. The Hiratsuka clan rose eagerly like a band of petitioners. With a grunt and a terse broad-handed gesture he bade them welcome. His jowls shook, his eyes narrowed in the creases of a fleshy, expansive smile. Punctuality was clearly not part of this man's style. He would not be held accountable for his use of money, space or time; he needed a surplus in which to manoeuvre.

Just as Boon noted his impressions of Jusaburo, so Jusaburo was making a note of Boon. Evidently accustomed to making quick judgements of people, he looked Boon cursorily up and down and then, unexpectedly, seemed to falter, as if his instinct had let him down.

There was something about Jusaburo that put Boon on his guard. Perhaps it was his power, and perhaps confidence in this power encouraged him to force the issue, to demand simple distinctions between friend and foe, between who was the stronger and who the weaker. But Boon was merely his guest, and beyond that did not want to be drawn out of a neutrality which suited his temperament. The relationship between the two men remained ambiguous.

Naoharu was very much in awe of Jusaburo. He called him *o-niisan* (elder brother), as if to use his name might have been an affront, as if at least by nominal association with the Fujiwara family he could glean something of their health and prosperity.

The three men sat in the *kyakuma* eating *sushi* and drinking beer. It was a sultry evening. Jusaburo drew a fan out of his girdle, extended it fully with a flick of his wrist and leisurely fanned his chest and throat.

"*O-niisan* is only a couple of years older than us," said Naoharu, "but look at the difference! He's quite a bigshot in this area, you know. Plays golf with all the party bosses, manages their campaigns, and on top of that he's a first-class businessman. Did you know that he's got his own factory? And then the house – imagine owning a house like this! At thirty! And the car! You must see his car!"

Naoharu prattled on. Jusaburo fanned himself and smiled indulgently, as if listening to a child.

At Naoharu's insistence they all got up and went outside to see the car. A bright yellow Cadillac was parked in the yard at the back of the house. Jusaburo had bought it only last week.

Naoharu whistled.

"That must have cost a packet!"

He and Boon inspected the car.

"My goodness, this must have set you back a bit, *o-niisan*."

And finally, after another pause,

"What did it cost, I wonder . . ."

Jusaburo said he wasn't sure how much it had cost, he hadn't been sent the bill yet.

"Not sure how much it cost!" echoed Naoharu admiringly, giving Boon a nudge. "What a fellow, eh? What he's got standing out here in the yard is worth more than I earn in a year, I'll bet you that."

Jusaburo asked them to come and have a look at the factory, which stood fifty yards from the house. Nothing on the grand scale, he said, addressing himself to Boon, but even so, he was one of the main suppliers in the area. Yes, bricks. Modest but steady trade. He pointed and explained. Boon listened, his eyes following the movements of a small, dingy man who was loading a pallet in a corner of the building. Jusaburo mistook his attentiveness for interest, but Boon was actually much less interested in what he was saying than in the sound of his voice. It was a hoarse, rasping voice pitched uneasily between a bark and a whisper, a voice that the more corpulent politicians had in common with wrestlers. Tanaka for one, Ohira for another. Boon decided that this must be the effect of obesity encroaching on the vocal glands.

For the next couple of days he didn't see his host at all, but even in his absence Boon found that he was continually learning more about him. He was a big man and he cast a long shadow.

Jusaburo and his wife slept in different rooms, and early each morning Chieko would visit her elder sister in the privacy of her bedroom. The room was just across the passage from the *kyakuma* where Boon had been accommodated. By reaching out and drawing open the *fusuma* behind his head he was able to follow the intimate conversations between the two sisters as easily as if he had been sitting in the same room. As a keen student of Japanese affairs Boon had no compunction about eavesdropping, which was, after all, a national pastime.

He listened to an endless complaint. Jusaburo had come in late again last night. Again? Chieko low-voiced at first, cautious until she had warmed to her theme. Of course. The elder sister gave a snort. It had been going on like this for months. Off every night with his cronies, not here, in the next town. Nothing but his own pleasure, all the time. Liquor and women. Women? Chieko's naivety made her elder sister impatient. She should count her blessings, she said, with a man like Naoharu as her husband. At least he didn't go dancing off and leave his wife alone in bed. Pause for Chieko to digest this startling counsel. Still, she said at last, Elder Sister could live in style. The house. The money. The marvellous car. Leisure to do as she liked. Leisure? Didn't Chieko understand what it meant to be married to a factory owner who was out to make a political career? The constant guests, the never ending flow of hospitality, all the organisation involved. It was hard work running a household like that. But Chieko wasn't prepared to relinquish her dreams, and so the two sisters continued to haggle over their miseries, bemoaning the iniquity of their respective fates and capping each other's claims for sympathy.

From Jusaburo's younger sister, Haruko, Boon heard a different story. Born twenty years ago on the first of May she had been given the name Spring Child; appropriately, for the girl was as fresh as her name. In the room upstairs where he helped her with her English homework he stood at her shoulder and noted with approval the smooth white buds already ripe under her summer frock. Haruko studied in Tokyo and had come home for the summer vacation. In long parentheses lacking any connection with the matter in hand she freely discussed her family's affairs.

Haruko liked her sister-in-law as a person but had a low opinion of her competence as a housewife. No, it wasn't she who really ran the household; she was much too lazy for that. The household pillar and drudge was unquestionably her mother. Boon narrowly escaped embarrassment here, for until this moment he had mistaken Haruko's mother for a servant. At the time they arrived she hadn't been there, and on the two or three occasions he had seen her since she had either been in the kitchen or cleaning the house, always wearing a white apron. This misunderstanding rather made Haruko's point for her.

The warm respect which Haruko felt for her mother was nourished by pity and consolidated by the emotional estrangement from her father. She dismissed him matter-of-factly as a rake, who for years had neglected his responsibilities to the family. Even during her childhood he had often absented himself from the house for days at a time, ignoring the needs of his wife and children, his duties at the factory which he had inherited. He went fishing and amused himself with his mistress, whom he kept openly at the family's expense. Naturally Haruko's mother was embittered.

Boon did not know all these details at the time. Haruko's father appeared only once during his stay. Boon found him sunning himself in the passage one morning, sipping cold tea through a straw. He seemed a pleasant, rather cultivated man. For about an hour they had chatted leisurely about fishing.

By comparison with the father, whose dissolute life had made him the family outcast, Haruko took a very tolerant view of her brother's revelries. The difference was that Jusaburo honoured his responsibilities. It was he who had transformed the run-down factory into a profitable concern. He supported the entire family and even paid his father an allowance, on condition that he kept his nose out of business affairs. And as for the rest, well. Haruko shrugged her shoulders. She perfectly understood the connection between those nightly parties and her brother's success as a businessman. Besides, she added, pouting her lips and glancing conquettishly at Boon, her sister-in-law could take a little more trouble to make herself attractive, couldn't she? Haruko's arguments were irresistible.

Perhaps Jusaburo had an inkling of what was going on upstairs. He was no slouch himself, and from the room where his sister was closeted with Boon under the decorous mantle of study he may occasionally have heard a tinkle of laughter which it was hard to associate with English grammar.

On the third morning of their holiday the two families set out on an excursion to a hot spring resort in the mountains. It was to be quite an outing, and they would stay overnight. They were all going, Boon and the Hiratsuka people in the Mitsubishi, Jusaburo and his family in the yellow Cadillac. But Haruko was not included in the party; she stayed at home, ostensibly to keep her mother company.

It was a beautiful drive, with lots of bends and steep ascents providing Boon with a view and Naoharu with proof of the immense superiority of the Cadillac.

"Can't touch him. Look, I've got my foot down. Second gear, and I bet you he's still in third. Just look how easily he's pulling away! No, there's no touching him on the hill. On the flat, of course, or downhill, that's a different matter . . ."

The road went all the way up the mountain, ending in a cluster of picturesque houses and large, solid, not so picturesque hotels.

Jusaburo pulled up in the deserted car park of what appeared to be the largest hotel, got out, buttoned up his chequered golfing trousers and leaned against the door of the car, peeling off his perforated driving gloves.

At the reception he was greeted with smiling ceremony. Ah, Fujiwara-*san*. He was known here. No formalities, quite unnecessary. Doubtless he and his guests were honourably tired. They were at once shown up to their rooms.

They had been allotted two rooms facing across the corridor, one for the women and children, one for the men. The rooms were furnished in a successful blend of Japanese and Western styles, *tatami* on one side where *futon* had been laid ready, a plain wooden floor on the other, with chairs, table, icebox, the usual trimmings. Four to a room seemed to be the rule, so in the men's room there was one *futon* to spare. Apparently Jusaburo had a prodigious snore. It was arranged for him and Boon to sleep in opposite corners, the spare *futon* and the hapless Naoharu constituting an intermediate no-snoring zone.

This was Boon's description, and it made Jusaburo laugh. After a couple of whiskies, laced with some grubby anecdotes and dirty jokes, the two of them were gradually beginning to thaw out. They planned the evening's entertainment. Jusaburo tapped his massive watch. Dinner, he said, would be prepared at seven in a private room. It was now five. That gave them two hours in which to take the waters.

The taking of the waters, ah, the taking of the waters! It was a legendary, almost a hallowed ritual. Perspiring they would be united in the medicinal waters, stripped to the levelling nakedness of the flesh their bared souls would mingle and converse. But first and foremost this necessitated the removal of Jusaburo's impossibly tight golfing trousers. It was no easy task.

At last they were ready. In regulation blue and white *yukata* supplied by the hotel, slippers smacking their heels, they passed along deserted corridors and descended to the basement, further still, to the very bowels of the hotel sunk deep into the mountain rock. The air was already warmer here, moist, and in Boon's imagination tinged with the fumes of sulphur. An entrance on one side was marked Men, on the other side Women. *Konyoku*, the ancient custom of mixed bathing still observed at some hot springs, had regrettably fallen into desuetude here.

Their regulation *yukata* were all the same size, tailored for a man who had never existed. For the bulky, cloth-stretching Jusaburo and Boon, barely able to hold together the seams at the front, the descent from their room to the baths had been perilous, while for Naoharu, with so much spare linen bunched at his midriff that he looked as if he were carrying a bundle of washing, it had been utterly ridiculous. Much hilarity, then, much laughter and slapping of the flesh in the chamber where they eventually disrobed, disturbing an ancient wizened bather, perched on a stool in one corner, who had fallen asleep over his hundred-year ablutions.

From a great circular pool steam rose slowly to a domed roof. On either side two lesser pools, in which the surface of the water lay as still as glass, were bedded deep in the natural rock. Cascades of water, jetting from frothy spouts four or five yards up on the wall, rebounded from the floor with bursts of spray and ceaseless overlapping echoes. Two men stood under the waterspouts, motionless, heads bowed, almost in an attitude of penitence. Others crouched facing the wall in naked rows, soaped, sluiced and pummelled the flesh with knotted towels. Bathers soaked, drifted, gently swam; and having opened the pores stretched out on slabs beside the pool, stupefied, basking, glazed with sweat. Sometimes the steam blanketed the floor as thick as wool, unravelled again and magically dispersed. Figures passed, receded and silently vanished, caught up in a scudding wraith of cloud. In this sweltering paradise Boon was reminded more of a cathedral than a bath-house, a sanctuary for the pursuit of lustral devotions.

They joined the soakers. Porous Jusaburo absorbed and shed water as copiously as a sponge, corklike Naoharu bobbed up and down, his nose no more than freckled with perspiration. After a quarter of an hour Boon felt as if his eyes were silting up and he proceeded at once to the waterspout punishment, where his two penitents, indefatigable, were beginning to show signs of erosion. The lash of hot water on his head and shoulders had a hypnotic effect, loosening the knots in his neck and back and then, less agreeably, in his brain. Boon passed on to soapers' row.

Afterwards, of course, he felt much invigorated, new-born, as if he had sloughed off a layer of skin. With shining faces they ascended to the second floor.

Jusaburo was as good as his word. Punctually at seven two women came on noiseless feet, knelt, served, bowed, withdrew. Boon's appetite had unfortunately been drained out of him downstairs and he could do no more than paddle in the feast. Pink lobster, shoals of whitebait and silver-bellied fish with blueish eyes swam on the surface of plates of ice; prawns tail by whisker in transparent ribbed corsets, octopus dismembered neatly into parts, legs of chicken, dripping skewered meat, vegetables steaming, pickled, plain, bowls of soup and pails of rice crowded the table in lavish heaps. And beer, ah, the chilled beer. Between them they drank a crate.

His smooth broad face smile-wreathed and almost beatific, Jusaburo tipped down glass after glass in long draughts that barely ruffled his throat. He did not seem to need to swallow. When the beer was finished he ordered *sake*, the small flasks first and then the large. A challenge had been laid on the table and Boon took it up, elbow to elbow and cup for cup. The two women servers wafted to and fro on the breath of their peremptory thirst. Jusaburo's eyes brightened and his face flushed, but he could hold this pace for a couple of hours and still have capacity to spare. Boon was not so sure. The level in his stomach was rising fast.

In the meantime wife and sister-in-law were growing restive. *O-niisan* had promised to take them out to "one of those places" which husbands seemed to find so attractive and where wives were never allowed to go. Yes, they were adamant, they wanted to see for themselves. Of course, why not? Jusaburo, in a fluid humour, was quite prepared to comply with this request. He knew the very place, just down the road. Oh really, his wife put in archly, how did he know that? Because he had been there many times, replied Jusaburo blandly.

At the entrance they exchanged hotel slippers for hotel clogs and clattered off in their livery of chequered blue and white. In the mountains it was a temperate summer night; a lot of people were walking out, and to Boon's surprise they were all dressed identically. They had all bathed, they had all dined, from hotels throughout the town they had all emerged to take the air, skirted and clattering and with mandatory shine.

In the open air, spread out across the streets, this impression of sameness was still diffuse, but concentrated into the auditorium of a striptease club it became quite overpowering. Boon had never sat in an audience so homogeneous. Yards, miles of that familiar blue-and-white cloth must have gone into its making, whole thermal oceans must have steamed it, bars from a very mountain of soap have given it that pervasive hygienic scent. Reflecting an artificial light which swallowed the blue and picked out the white, those shining faces in chequered ranks rose upwards from the pit of the theatre to the roof in an extraordinary luminous apotheosis.

The strip was rather smutty, the performers listless. How could they compete with such an audience? It was not a natural audience. About half of them were women, who must all have had the same idea as Jusaburo's wife; they kept their eyes on the strippers but their minds on their husbands. The husbands, of course, showed exemplary restraint; there was no craning forward in seats, no spontaneous applause. It was a disappointing evening all round, the strippers frustrated, husbands unsatisfied and wives puzzled.

Jusaburo suggested a night-cap. His wife was tired, Chieko thought it time to get back, Naoharu had not yet digested his last drink and Chieko was grasping him by the seat of his *yukata* in any case. They clattered back up the hill; Boon and Jusaburo clattered down. He knew the very place of course, just down the road.

On the second floor of a squalid establishment in the old part of the town they drank steadily for a couple of hours. Boon's focus narrowed, his world shrank, dim at the edges, to about one square yard of brilliant light where everything was experienced with heightened clarity. A lot of people could inhabit this space without it ever seeming crowded: Jusaburo, three raucous women in dishevelled gowns, a pair of hands on the table, some distance away from himself but apparently his own. He was conscious of them taking liberties. Tirelessly they replenished glasses, fondled, burrowed, squeezed. Then he became quite numb. He could hear nothing. Jusaburo's face across the table blurred into a burning copper sun.

"What's happened to her then?"

"What's happened to whom?"

"The girl you chased downstairs."

They were standing out in the street.

"I chased a girl downstairs?"

Jusaburo chuckled.

"Rascal! You gave her quite a fright, lifting her up over your head."

"I lifted someone over my head?"

"Come on, let's go home. You won't see her again tonight."

They ambled gently up the hill. Boon felt light-headed but otherwise quite sober. He couldn't remember having lifted a girl over his head. Film must have snapped. What an extraordinary thing to do.

It was past midnight when they got back to the hotel. Boon felt much fresher after the walk.

"Let's go and have a bath."

"You carry on. But I think I'll get to bed."

Boon got lost on his way down to the baths. He wandered through a maze of corridors and arrived in the kitchen. He went back to the reception and started again. This time he got it right. Everything seemed much smaller, more intimate. He heard the muffled resonance of falling water. All to himself, three pools and a dozen waterspouts. It was like a dream. He peeked into the women's baths; rather mean by comparison, one pool half the size, restricted amenities, no spouts. Probably the old theory about menstrual dirt; males the naturally cleaner animal; no point in providing floor space to spread contagion. Ichimonji had told him something like that.

He dropped his robe in the middle of the floor and strode to take possession of the baths. Three women, one standing up to her waist coiling her hair, two others squatting by a conduit sponging themselves, looked up as he entered in mute surprise. No doubt about it. He saw them with a clear and steady eye. Surely he wasn't mistaken? No longer trusting his own judgement, Boon went outside to check the sign. Mechanically his finger drew the character in the air: field above strength, the strong arm rooting in the paddy fields: *otoko*. Yes, he was within his rights. He went back.

This time they laughed and beckoned him in. All three were

safely ensconced in the water now, up to their necks, bobbing and murmuring gently on the far side of the pool. Boon slid into the water with a ripple.

From a reassuring distance he spoke courteously to the three bathers. He was agreeably surprised, he said; when taking the waters he was a traditionalist himself, and he believed that the ancient custom of *konyoku* greatly enhanced the Way of Hot Water; it was only right and proper that ladies of the charming traditionalist school should assert that principle, even if it meant flouting the management, for unless he was much mistaken this illicit midnight paddling was a breach of the house rules. One of the culprits was so startled by this emanation from the mouth of Boon that she involuntarily rose half out of the water, exposing her breasts and delicate pink nipples, which only added to her confusion. On weightless dancing feet Boon drew a little closer, taking advantage of the mermaids' laughter.

No need of stealth; the mermaids were themselves intrigued by the smooth-tongued stranger with the hairy legs. Vestiges of modesty, in the form of small white towels tucked under their chins like floating bibs, gradually swam free and drifted lazily, unregarded, out across the water. They were mermaids of the house, they said, cooks, cleaners, chambermaids, and they bathed here secretly every night when the *kyakusan* slept and undisturbed they could enjoy the male privilege. But he, who did not sleep – could they trust him with their secret? Enjoy the male privilege, said Boon, it is here, in person, to be used at your discretion. They raised their shoulders out of the water and laughed, all three of them, laughing stood up. Breasts flowered on the surface and water drained from their bellies with a rush. Come, they said, you shall have a bathing you shall never forget, and they drew him gently up the steps. Heat ran out of the soles of his feet, his skin shed water like liquid silk. Closing him in a circle, they jostled and turned him, wound him into the skein of their own white flesh, encased his legs between breasts and thighs and plied vigorous hands, soaped him all over, hair by hair and in every part, scrubbed, rinsed, towelled and padded his body and at last released him, their faces becoming less and less distinct, the sound of laughter receding into ever fainter echoes and finally utter silence.

Boon crept through corridors like a vapourised ghost, levitated and soared effortlessly up flights of stairs. He came to rest on the landing, rocking slightly as he was restored to his feet, outside the door of his room. He slid the door open and tiptoed in.

Absurd caution. The sleepers brayed like organ pipes, unleashing exhalations, whistles, squeaks, one shuddering bass snore. Boon rummaged in the drawer of the table where fortunately the lamp was on and groped for ear-plugs, ointment for his feet. The drawer was empty; perhaps he had left them by his pillow. In this way his attention was drawn to a more serious problem: somebody was sleeping in his bed.

Boon grappled with this problem, ineffectually. He made a note of it, sat down to think it over. Gradually he registered a sense of disbelief: something was not in order. But beyond this his mind refused to think, and after a promising start he again relapsed, rational disbelief gave way to stupid indignation. The cheek of it! How dare they put someone else in his bed! He cupped his eyes with his hands and scrutinised the row of sleepers. No doubt about it. All the berths were full.

He poured himself a glass of beer, lit a cigarette and settled in a chair with his back to the snores. Slumped, not sleeping, all thought processes battened down under a leaden glaze, his eyes rested drowsily on a pink suitcase. Half an hour passed. Somewhere at the back of his mind he began to feel vaguely troubled by numbers. Himself, Naoharu, Jusaburo and his brother. That made four, one berth spare. But quite apart from the puzzle of numbers, all berths full and one to spare, more urgent doubts had begun to attach to that pink suitcase. Doubts mounted to suspicion, suspicion crystallised into a portentous certainty that suddenly made him sit upright: nobody in the room had brought along that piece of luggage. He became conscious of extraordinary reasoning powers. How clear it all was, how simple! He was in the wrong room of course.

He sat there a few moments longer, relishing his freshness after long absence of mind, restored to blissful clarity. The four strange men slept on. Carefully he skirted protruding feet and padded to the door, softly opened and closed it. In the adjacent room where the same lamp burned on the same table he found ear-plugs and ointment in the drawer, two whistling sleepers, two vacant *futon*. Boon rolled out and fell fast asleep.

But when he related these events at breakfast the next morning he was no longer sure of their truth. Certainly it was a good story. Boon's dream of the hot spring in the mountains was appropriated by legend, and duly passed into the cloudy annals of the water trade.

*C*oming down to earth. Yoshida, who had first intro-duced Sugama and Boon, got married at the end of the year. The wedding reception took place at a professional catering establishment, screened off from the city in an immaculate park. Six receptions were held simultaneously in adjacent rooms. By contract the festivities began at two o'clock and ended at four, allowing the management one hour to change the bouquets and prepare the tables for bookings scheduled to start at five. Occasionally there were overlaps, but on the whole the arrangements were smooth and the caterers expressly guaranteed their clients that each reception was given a personal touch. Boon overlooked this personal touch for at least a quarter of an hour, until the entry of the bridal pair into the room established beyond doubt that unfortunately he was attending the wrong reception.

Yoshida's wedding was the first of several to which Boon was invited during the following months. It was a cramped, cheerless celebration. Boon attributed this lack of zest to the fact that the guests were mindful of the clock, of being compelled to joy under duress of time. But it was not time that was the problem. He attended other receptions, with no time limit, where he sincerely wished there had been: they were equally joyless.

236

Decorum required men to attend weddings wearing dark suits. Boon, who did not own a dark suit, was always the exception. The suits were dark, the speeches grey; the atmosphere could hardly have been other than bleak. Not Boon's idea of a wedding at all. He could only applaud the custom of giving the wedding guests presents. Bride and groom handed out sets of breakfast crockery to their departing guests, ostensibly as a souvenir, actually as a conciliatory gesture, in recognition of what they had undergone.

Two sets of wedding crockery thus made their way into Boon's and Sugama's bachelor apartment. For a month they sat heavily on the kitchen shelf, unpacked and unbreakfasted on, a silent reproach. But one Sunday morning Boon got up to find the table laid for a souvenir breakfast: cups, bowls and plates, garlanded with leaves and flowers, otherwise quite empty. Sugama was putting the finishing touches to this barren stoneware feast.

"I thought it a pity not to use them . . ."

"Use them for what?" sniffed Boon. "Man cannot live by crockery alone."

"There's a tin of tuna fish in the fridge. I'll make some tea."

Whistling he made the tea. Boon watched him suspiciously. And sure enough, later that day Sugama announced his engagement.

Sugama had been restive for the past six months, ever since Yoshida had introduced him to his fiancée. Yoshida, at thirty-five, had earned the grudging admiration of family and friends by continuing to fight a rearguard action in defence of his preference for bachelor life. One might not approve of the aim, but one had to respect the tenacity with which it was pursued. Likewise unmarried, but at thirty still a mere stripling, Sugama had looked up to his *senpai* Yoshida as a model of the Noble Bachelor, a staunch ally and a worthy precedent with which his own querulous family could be kept at bay. The news of Yoshida's forthcoming marriage struck Sugama like a bolt from the blue. A monument had been toppled, an era had drawn to a close.

By the Yoshida scale Sugama might have claimed he was entitled to five more insouciant years, but after the relapse of his friend, the Noble Bachelor, Sugama entirely lost heart; he knew the chips were down. It had come later rather than sooner, but none the less, the point was that Yoshida had succumbed: so why not sooner rather than later? What had been one of Sugama's most persuasive arguments would now inevitably be turned against him. Insouciance was no longer the mood of the day.

Quite apart from the Yoshida affair, quite apart from the increasing pressure of time and the fact that Sugama was now willing, without regard for his parents' wishes, to embark on marriage as soon as his girlfriend agreed to come on board, the last two years had brought other reasons for wanting a change in his domestic status. The problem was not Boon; the two of them had got on very well in the apartment they shared. The problem was Boon's cooking.

Boon had taken charge of the housekeeping shortly after moving in. He did so reluctantly, not because he was particularly good at it, but because Sugama would have been a great deal worse. Sugama did no cooking. He opened tins. On festive occasions he emptied the contents of the tins onto plates. He did not actually prepare meals; he presented the illusions of meals. By crowding the table with chopsticks, sauces, salt and pepper, an ashtray or two, perhaps the evening paper, he artfully sought to raise Boon's hopes that somewhere in this miscellany he would also find something to eat.

The only alternative was for Boon to take over the cooking. At first it was fun. He donned an apron, bustled with pots and pans, spiced, stirred, produced a variety of enormous meals which all disappeared inside Sugama with the same alarming speed. Appetite or lack of appetite was never the issue. Food: a job to be done. Sugama did not eat what Boon served him; he killed it. He was an assassin of meals.

Boon capitulated. The novelty of cooking had begun to wear off in any case. For well over a year he served nothing but bean-and-potato gruel.

Every evening Sugama sat at the *kotatsu* reading the newspaper and eating gruel. After a few months the strain began to tell, even on him. He was worn down by the sheer monotony of Boon's gruel. There it stood in a large pot on the gas stove, waiting for him like a punishment. Boon cooked a week's supply in advance. By the time Sugama had munched his way through a year of gruel he was heartily sick of bachelor life.

Boon and the girl's parents were the first to be informed of the engagement, as at that time they were the two parties most directly affected. The girl still lived in her parents' house. The official engagement of their daughter to Sugama made it possible for him to stay there overnight; in his double role as *bona fide* pre-marital attendant and secret refugee from gruel Sugama made use of this privilege frequently. For the rarer occasions when he brought her back to his own apartment Boon's cooperation was also needed. Sugama's parents were not informed at first. Realising that a *de jure* recognition of his marriage was not negotiable, Sugama shrewdly followed a strategy of first occupying and ploughing the land, thus establishing the right of custom and forcing his parents' consent on *de facto* grounds.

Boon's cooperation meant vacation of the premises for the night in question. Sugama hesitated to ask such a favour of his friend, but Boon fully appreciated the delicacy of his feelings; and besides, there were other reasons why he was willing to oblige. In Tokyo he resumed the acquaintance he had struck up with Haruko during the summer holidays.

At the beginning of the university term Haruko called him up and reminded him of his promise to give her English lessons. She had a test next week. The use of the subjunctive in polite forms of speech. Did he think he would be able to give her a hand? Boon thought he would. What, really? Would he really be so kind, and was he sure he didn't mind? Yes, he would and he was, or No, he didn't, which amounted to the same thing. How could Yes and No amount to the same thing? He said he would explain all on Saturday. Despite this confusing conversation Haruko arrived safely with a group of her friends and spent a decorous English afternoon at Boon's Oji seminary, where subjunctive matters were finally cleared up, and one or two others besides.

Boon's girls passed with flying colours. A celebration was held at a *yakitoriya* in Akasaka. The girls invited their boyfriends, Haruko invited Boon.

For the few months he remained in Japan she invited him into her life. It was as light as Mariko's had been dark. He did not love Haruko, but he liked her and was fond of her in a way that had somehow never been possible with Mariko. Haruko was not a dreamer. She had no expectations of Boon, and he had none of her. She wanted nothing other than to enjoy herself in his company. Somewhere in the future, she already knew him, was the man she would marry. In Tokyo, meanwhile, in the couple of years between leaving school and getting a job or getting married, there was time for the honeymoon she would never have again.

Haruko and her friends played the city like a funfair. They skipped classes and idled away window-shopping mornings on the Ginza, were bowed into the elevators of half a dozen department stores, bought knick-knacks in fashionable Harajuku boutiques ate yoghourt lunches and spent long afternoons drinking chocolate in the disco coffee-shops of Akasaka or Shinjuku, dined and danced in Roppongi. There were few parties, gatherings in private were rare. Instead they carried their social life out into the town, where restaurants, bars and discotheques hosted their shifting cliques; coffee-shops acquired the atmosphere of a private lounge, providing a temporary home to suit a temporary mood. They offered an intimate neutrality which for many of the young, either still living at their parents' home or in accommodation often not much bigger than a kennel, was in any case preferable to their own four walls.

Chie, for example, one of Haruko's closest friends, lived in a tiny rectangular box of an apartment near Shibuya for which her father had paid a hundred thousand dollars; one narrow room containing a bed, a table, a yard of kitchen and a moulded plastic shower cabin. Boon and Haruko went to pick her up there one evening and he stood in the doorway chatting for a few minutes. He asked her if she knew any of the other people living in the building. No, she didn't, said Chie, and she didn't want to; if she knew other people in the building it might occasionally lead to visits in each other's rooms; she would find that depressing; one room was indistinguishable from the next. Chie laughed.

"And then I might feel my life was not distinguishable either."

She sometimes said things that disturbed her friends. She was a melancholy girl. Chie's remark left an impression on Boon that he did not forget. This was the sort of level at which many people in Tokyo struggled to maintain a sense of their individuality.

Boon became something of a city nomad himself. When his

Ministry of Education grant ended and he started to earn his own living he spent little time at home. He took on new teaching appointments, gave weekend courses, recorded copy and wrote pamphlets for advertising agencies, translated television scripts and talked drowsily on radio programmes at seven o'clock in the morning: Boon's views on rugby, *tanka* (poems of thirty-one syllables), cabarets, autumn in Nikko . . . he had become a master of *aimai*, vague use of the Japanese language.

The distances back and forth across Tokyo were so great that between one appointment in the morning and another in the evening it was often not worth making the journey back home. Force of circumstance changed his habits: he became a coffee-shop denizen. Coffee-shops in Toranomon provided the refuge in which Boon's early work on tobacco drying barns and electric lawn mowers was brought to fruition, Edobashi ushered into the light of the world his three theses on lemon marmalade, and Kanda witnessed an unprecedented English language exposition of the ancient Japanese art of picture-card theatre known as *kamishibai*. The shops in these areas supplied him with temporary business premises which could be hired for the price of a few cups of coffee.

By this time he had learned to speak very good Japanese. He was accepted by his employers on Japanese terms; more to their own surprise than to his they treated him as one of themselves. Without conscious effort he spoke and behaved in the way that most appropriately suited the occasion. He grew accustomed to being patronised by older men and learned not to take offence. There was a kind of collegiality in these working relationships which he found he could enjoy even when he did not particularly like the person concerned. A streak of opportunism made itself evident here which was perhaps less natural to Boon than to the language through which he had come to live.

A few close friends apart, his relationships with the Japanese in general, even with some of those who claimed to have accepted him, remained a skittish balance. The temptation to attribute a different point of view or an unexpected thought to the fact that Boon was not Japanese was one to which most people eventually succumbed. The reaction was not: "this is Boon's point of view", but: "this point of view is not identifiable as Japanese". Harmless conversations which had seemed perfectly stable suddenly took this erratic plunge when the fragile self-consciousness of the Japanese chose to be offended. Any sustained argument as a matter of course, personal likes and dislikes and the customs of daily life were all susceptible to this deadly bacillus. A remark of Boon's, himself a keen smoker, about the ill effects of smoking on an empty stomach, once elicited the rejoinder that smoking before breakfast was a Japanese custom. Basta. One couldn't get much deader than that.

Boon's friends were either people who did not think in this way or people who had come to think differently as a result of their friendship with Boon. They shared and assimilated some of his attitudes just as he did theirs. Sugama, for example, had changed in ways that undoubtedly showed the influence of Boon, but perhaps Boon had merely coaxed to the surface a readiness which was latently there. After all, Sugama had originally invited him to come and live in the Oji apartment because he was curious to know what living with a foreigner would be like. Very few Japanese would have taken or considered taking a step like that.

One attitude which Sugama had acquired under Boon's tutelage was the use of irony. When Boon first arrived in Japan Sugama did not understand irony; he took everything quite literally, like a patient mule, which Boon found very distressing. By the time he left, Sugama had become a word-sharper notorious for his sleight of tongue. It was arguable that Boon had thereby not done him much of a service. Between themselves, when deployed in matters of grandfather and gruel, irony was appreciated as an art, but when broached over the heads of the uninitiated it was more likely to boomerang. Sugama's first public trial was a speech at Yoshida's wedding reception, where he deferred to custom by blandly pronouncing the formula "Let not a day pass idly till the face of a grandchild . . .", an exhortation to the bride and groom to be fruitful and bring forth children, but barbed the hallowed phrase with an unexpected dose of irony. His audience swallowed it impassively.

Although Boon and Sugama had come to share almost everything, for some reason they never shared their friends. Probably this was a wise arrangement, for if they had made demands on each other's patience outside the apartment as well as in, their friendship would not have worn so well. Sooner or later he was introduced to most of Sugama's friends, but as a rule he did not cross his circles and Sugama did not cross his. Even within his own circle, however, each of them followed this practice of compartmentalising friends, of not mixing friends. It occurred to Boon that the same thing was true of most of the people he knew.

In Japan there was no obvious forum where one's friends had an opportunity of getting to know each other. There were no parties that might have served this purpose. The only parties Boon attended were given by foreigners.

He associated many of his acquaintances with a particular area of town, even with a particular bar. He drank toasts to tobacco drying barns in Toranomon, discussed markets for lemon marmalade only within the ward precincts of Edobashi, *kamishibai* only in Kanda, and so on. Business acquaintances preferred to drink on local territory; it was quicker, cheaper, more convenient. To a lesser extent he found that private friendships were geographically restricted as well. Ichimonji's nose instinctively led him back to the watering holes of Ikebukuro, his native stamping-ground. Haruko and her friends turned just as naturally to haunts in Shinjuku and Roppongi, those urban reservations set aside for the young. When Boon made arrangements to meet someone he would bear such territorial preferences in mind.

Somehow the idea of smuggling Ichimonji across the borders of Edobashi into lemon marmalade territory struck Boon as preposterous. At a party the two sides could have been brought together and talked or not talked without any commitments. Once or twice he experimented with pairings which in theory looked compatible but in practice were a flop. Intention stifled spontaneity. Introductions that served a specific purpose opened on common ground, but when this was not the case both parties were likely to nurse the same unspoken question which doomed the meeting before it had begun: what have we been brought together for? Perhaps these failures were caused by Boon's misjudgement, and perhaps the way he compartmentalised friends reflected personal predilection rather than social reality, but he saw it as a more general issue. He saw it as another facet of the insider–outsider mentality.

His relationship with Haruko was only possible in the anonymity of Tokyo. He had already experienced what hostility could be aroused by a foreigner having an affair with a Japanese girl, even a girl from the water trade, in a provincial town like Toyama, where he was an outsider twice over, neither local nor Japanese. Haruko kept her liaison with Boon secret from her family, but in Tokyo at least they were free. It was this freedom which attracted many young people to the city, where they led lives of which their families often had not the slightest inkling.

Even on the streets of Tokyo Boon sometimes heard Haruko openly abused, by middle-aged and once or twice by younger men too. They called her *pansuke*, the slang for whore that had been current during the American occupation of Japan after the war. The use of period slang by older men who may have had unpleasant recollections at the sight of a Japanese girl walking out with a foreigner did not altogether surprise Boon, but coming from someone of his own generation it struck him almost as a betrayal.

Such instances of open prejudice were rare, at least in Boon's experience, and he found that in the smarter, cosmopolitan areas of town they did not occur at all. It was in the shabbier downtown precincts such as Oji, where the sight of foreigners was still relatively uncommon, that the *pansuke* style of prejudice survived. An acquaintance of Boon's accompanied by a Japanese girl, who turned up at his Oji apartment one night and found him out, took the first train back to Kyoto the next morning after being refused accommodation by all the cheap local hotels to which they had applied.

One English-language newspaper carried a report of increasing anti-foreigner tendencies in the restaurants and bars of Yokohama and the American base at Yokosuka where, unlike Oji, foreigners were very common. Signs refusing admittance to foreigners or Japanese girls with foreign consorts had started to appear on the doors and windows of local establishments. The real reason behind this alleged prejudice was explained to Boon some years later by a Yokohama restaurateur. The pay cheques of American soldiers stationed around Tokyo had not increased as fast as local prices. Soldiers resented the decline in their status that accompanied the decline in their dollar power; the days of cheap entertainment, liquor and local women were past, so they had started taking it out on the inventory instead, regularly demolishing bars on Saturday nights. This was expensive and discouraged custom, explained Boon's informant cautiously, which was why he and his colleagues had felt obliged to take action.

Haruko and Boon were often together during his last few months in Tokyo. Suspended in an interlude with neither a common past nor future, they lived entirely for the pleasure of the moment. Significantly, their days and much of their nights were spent between thirty and three hundred feet above the ground. The *akachochin* and the grubby bars which Boon had frequented for the first two years were all on street level, but he found that he could not take Haruko to these places except as a kind of dubious exhibit. Bars and restaurants catering for the young, in so far as they were located in the more fashionable parts of town to which the young preferred to go, could only be reached by elevator; the price of land in areas like Roppongi was too exorbitant for anything other than multi-purpose high-rise buildings.

The establishments located several storeys up were visited by clients who did not come by chance, unlike the ground-level *akachochin*, which gathered in the riff-raff off the streets, the casual drinker, the customer who dropped in on impulse. The premises were higher, and so on the whole were the prices. In the busier parts of town elevator guides marshalled their customers into different queues according to their different destinations. Two or three plexiglass elevators with their human cargo ferried up and down the surface of the building like transparent cages. The various pleasure haunts packaged in the upper storeys where these cages deposited their cargo were thus shut off from the street-level world in both a literal and a symbolic sense. For the disco freaks shuffling in carefully structured environments ten or twenty floors above the streets the effect of dissociation from the world was complete.

Haruko often took Boon to eat in the restaurant arcades at the top of a Shinjuku skyscraper. The entire floor constituted a little town where people came for no other purpose than to eat. Foreign cuisine and a dozen different types of Japanese food catered for a very broad range of tastes. The Japanese shops, in particular, designed as decorative imitations of the originals at street level, complete with *noren, chochin, tatami* and so on, suffered from the transposition to an altitude at which the sounds and smells that gave the flair of authenticity had been entirely eliminated. They were ghostly reproductions. Boon felt that this kind of despiritualisation had begun to erode Japanese culture as a whole.

For him it was essentially a low-rise culture, one or two, at most three storeys high, with no columns, cathedrals or great palaces. Buildings followed gravity and merged with the ground. Traditionally no elevation to a table was required in order to eat, or to a bed in order to sleep. Musical instruments grew out of the ground, like the bamboo *shakuhachi*, or were played on it, like the *koto*. The phlegmatic man was one whose liver sat, as the Japanese phrase had it, while the choleric man was one whose stomach stood up. The highest deference was the deepest prostration. Stunting the growth of trees so that after hundreds of years they stood no more than a foot high was considered the perfection of horticultural art. Lovers who in other parts of the world reached their mistresses vertically by way of the window were called night-crawlers in Japan, as they remained on one plane and required stealthy knees. Proverbs and sayings testified to a traditional mistrust of things that were long, tall or high. And the *tatami* on which nearly all Japanese still spent much of their lives remained astonishingly close to the natural grassy floors of thousands of years ago.

The water trade, too, could not survive the higher altitudes of modern cities. Love hotels, like the late-night bars, lay snugly at street level, unobtrusive and easy of access. A purple light, a suggestive name, gave sufficient indication for hurried clients. Service was discreet, in the form of a middle-aged woman, often wearing an apron, always with a closed face and quiet feet. Sometimes she would let the five-thousand yen note rest for a moment in her unclosed palm, subtly conveying that she received it in the spirit of a favour rather than a payment. Her own modesty, her exemplary tact, would set even the most hesitant customers at their ease. She made herself an accomplice of their feelings. This kind of service was grounded in tradition, and it was not available above the third floor. After an evening's entertainment Boon and Haruko always descended when it was time for bed.

Haruko took courses in traditional Japanese dance. Boon saw her perform in full costume once, but he was much more accustomed to watch her dance gracefully naked at the end of a bed in love hotels between Koenji and Nakano. Her body when she danced, the atmosphere in which she moved, even naked, remained chaste and supple, in some way withheld, like a sound humming to itself in a muted string; and so it was when she made love. Entire weekends passed behind closed curtains, disturbed once or twice by a soft knocking and brief transactions at the door. Haruko's dancing teacher remarked that her pupil had begun to dance like a mature woman, with a sensuousness which had not been there before.

There seemed no reason why this way of life should not have continued indefinitely. Other foreigners had made themselves a permanent home in Japan, and Boon would not have been unwilling either. Certain attitudes of the Japanese, entrenched in customs he still found alien, irritated and would probably always irritate him, but there were just as many for which he felt deep sympathy and affection. This ambiguity was never resolved. His heart remained divided.

Boon followed his instinct and went home. He did not take any decision or attempt to reason the matter out. The decision was taken for him, by the same kind of impulse that had originally brought him to the country.

In the new year he received a telephone call from one of the agencies for which he worked. At the end of the conversation he wished his invisible caller a propitious opening to the coming year and involuntarily bowed to him before replacing the receiver. Many Japanese bowed not just when visibly, but also when only audibly in the presence of another person, but this was the first time that Boon was conscious of having done so himself. Why had he bowed? Mechanically, for no other reason than that he had learned to bow. And Boon realised that imperceptibly he was beginning to lose touch with himself.

One thing remained to be done before he went home. Sugama's grandfather suddenly died at the end of January, and in February 1976 Boon made a last journey to Toyama to attend his funeral.

*G*randfather's last journey. The coffin with the old man's body had been lying in the *kyakuma* of the Sugamas' house for the past two days. It was set up on trestles in the corner of the room where grandfather himself used to say his prayers, forming a kind of memorial altar with a photograph of the deceased at the centre and propitiatory offerings, uncooked rice balls, fruit and incense, on either side. Only the flowers of the season were missing. Boon remembered the old man once saying that by choice he would die in the autumn when the chrysanthemum bloomed, for then his coffin would be covered with the flowers that were the imperial family's emblem. A hole had been cut in the white cloth draped over the coffin in order to allow the mourners to look in through a little window at the dead man's face. Boon saw nothing but a faint whiteness surrounded by shadow.

When he arrived in the early evening the friends and neighbours invited to the official wake had already gone home. Only the members of the immediate family remained to keep vigil beside the body. During the journey from Tokyo he had sought an appropriate form of words to express condolence, but in the event he said nothing. Sugama's mother met him with a smiling face. Her father-in-law, she said, placing her hand lightly on Boon's wrist, had died quickly and without pain at the age of eighty-five, leaving no dependents; death was in the course of nature, and he could not have died better. Boon answered her smile and was glad that he could agree with her from his heart. It struck him that the atmosphere in the house that evening was lighter and more festive than he had ever known it before. This was her doing, of course. In keeping with her resolute character she had made a task of joy, which at the same time must have pained her.

At a respectful distance from the coffin they ate supper. Boon found the food quite unpalatable. According to Buddhist rites no fish or meat would be eaten until the body had been buried or burned. Food obtained through the slaughter of animals remained inadmissible until the passage of the deceased into the Buddhist paradise had been safely accomplished. So for the next twenty-four hours they observed a natural diet, yams, eggplant, and something that appeared to be a kind of reed grass. Other restrictions applied to the shape of the dishes from which one was allowed to eat. The square plates they normally used were replaced by round ones. Boon would have liked to learn more about the origins of these customs, but his curiosity was restrained by feelings of tact.

On the far side of the *kyakuma* he sat and dozed. It was too cold to sleep. People came and went softly throughout the night.

The next morning they made an early start. Someone lent him a black suit, but it didn't fit; so he wore his own, the one which he otherwise only wore to weddings, with a black arm-band instead. The altar was dismantled and the coffin carried out. There had been a fresh snowfall during the night. A dozen mourners dressed in black stood at the gate shivering and stamping their feet as they waited for the funeral cars.

At the temple where the Buddhist funeral ceremony was held the Sugama family knelt to receive the formal condolences of their guests. A line of cushions had already been laid out at the entrance on a polished wooden floor. They knelt on either side of the altar that was behind them, facing the large *tatami* room where the mourners assembled. Boon settled at the back and warmed himself in a shaft of sunlight, which picked out the brilliant yellow-gold colours of the fish swimming leisurely in a tank beside him. It seemed an odd place for a fish tank. He was reminded of a film he had once seen about a temple in India that was a sanctuary for rats, and he wondered if the fish beside him had any religious significance.

Meanwhile the funeral guests had begun to arrive. At the entrance they prostrated themselves fully in front of the mourning family, palms extended and foreheads lowered to the floor. No words were spoken, or none that were audible. Boon could only see the lips of the guests moving when they got down and bowed. In the course of half an hour or so over a hundred guests arrived. They took their places in rows, starting at the front and extending back, until the large *tatami* room was almost full. They knelt upright, resting on their heels, the men in dark suits and the women in black *kimono*. It was as if the faded gold *tatami* had been slowly covered with a black cloth; everything was black except for the women's white *tabi* peeping out from under their buttocks. Some of the men took out pocket ashtrays and smoked while waiting for the ceremony to begin.

At last three priests in highly-coloured decorative costume filed into the room and knelt stiffly on the floor in front of the assembly. One of them struck a metal object which from where Boon was sitting looked very much like a kettle. He continued to strike it at intervals throughout the ceremony, perhaps as a sign that some ritual had been completed or was about to begin. The three priests at once began to drone a Buddhist liturgy in a nasal chant that was neither speech nor song, and with no variation in the pitch or speed of delivery. It seemed very fast to Boon. The monosyllables ran into one another in a monotonous unbroken hum. At first all three priests took up the chant simultaneously, but after a while they appeared to be chanting in relays; when one of them broke off to draw breath the other two continued for him, and so on, in an endless cycle.

While this dirge continued, a list of the names of those present was read out. Each person got up as his or her name was called out, again prostrated himself in front of the mourning family and went to the altar where he said a prayer and performed a brief valedictory ritual. Boon was interested to note that the practice of introducing a person first by the company for which he worked and then by his name should be observed even during the course of a funeral ceremony. And at the reception afterwards one of grandfather's sons found it appropriate to introduce himself with the words "I am employed by the prefecture bank as a dealer in sureties and bonds, and I am the second son of the deceased". Boon was introduced with reference to the university he had been attending.

His name came near the end of the list. Having closely watched the people who had been called out before him he now knew where he should go and what he was expected to do. On the question of the form of bow that would be appropriate in Boon's case there had been prior consultations with the family. He had no objection to prostrating himself in front of Sugama and his relatives; so far as his own feelings were concerned, however, he had long since felt himself to be a member of the family and had always been treated as such. As a member of the family his full prostration in front of the others was arguably not the appropriate form. Sugama's parents agreed with this view and Boon accordingly performed a standing bow, although he did not feel very comfortable.

When the last of the guests had again taken his seat the liturgy of the priests came to an abrupt close. Sugama's father, who in his capacity as *chonan* was invested with the moral authority to speak for the family, rose to his feet and delivered a short address. He described the circumstances of grandfather's death, singling out for praise the devoted nurse who had attended him during his final hours. Perhaps etiquette required the expression of thanks, but this dwelling on bedside details and the rather studied, sentimental depiction of worthy service followed by a tranquil death struck Boon as a hollow piety, a requiem for grandfather from which grandfather himself was already missing.

Outside the temple the guests relaxed, chatting for a few minutes in the sunshine. A fleet of cars stood ready to take them to the crematorium.

The crematorium was a bleak, functional building rather resembling a factory. At the entrance they were handed sticks of incense by a uniformed attendant, for a reason that became evident the moment they were inside: the pervasive odour throughout the building of charred human flesh. This, at least, was Boon's assumption, but it soon transpired that the sticks of incense were intended as the mourners' final gift to the deceased; the incense would be placed on his coffin and then accompany him into the flames. One by one they all stepped forward to take a last look at grandfather through the little window, laying a burning stick of incense on top of the coffin. It was a very dead face that Boon saw through the window. Posthumous blood emission from the nostrils had left a smear across the upper lip; stubble on the chin and cheeks. A grotesque corpse, old and ugly.

Boon had been under the impression that a further ceremony would now take place on the floor above, because they were standing in a hall outside a row of elevators. But they were not elevators:

they were furnaces. A small man in a dirty boiler suit suddenly pressed a button that opened the doors of one of these furnaces and announced in the toneless voice of one who had been doing the same work for many years "This is the moment of the final leave-taking", and at this point, for the first time, a number of women began to cry. The coffin rolled forward, the flames roared up, the doors closed. Boon was stunned.

During the cremation of the coffin and the final preparation of the ashes the mourning party sat down to a frugal meal in a gloomy hall. The director of the crematorium advised the guests that the next reception was scheduled to take place there in about three-quarters of an hour, so they did not have much time. It occurred to Boon that three-quarters of an hour would be about the time it would take for the complete incineration of coffin and corpse and the cooling of the ashes after removal from the ovens.

Unexpectedly he found himself sitting beside grandfather's younger brother and his wife, the old couple who had sought refuge from the earthquake and come to stay in the Oji apartment with their great-nephew and Boon just after his arrival in the country. The old man congratulated Boon on his remarkable progress with the language and Boon in turn told him how pleased he was to find him looking so well. Under the circumstances great-uncle seemed particularly gratified to receive this assurance, and hearing that Boon was soon to leave the country drank three different toasts to him in rapid succession. Indeed, he was looking rounder and rosier than ever, his shine undiminished.

Together they ambled back leisurely to the main hall of the crematorium and were ushered into a bare room where the remains of grandfather had been placed on a tray on a table. The heap of ash was about as much as would have filled a bucket; it was of a rusty colour and it contained larger fragments, pieces of bone clearly identifiable as joints, which had somehow survived the fire. Boon noticed a quite unexpected expression on great-uncle's face as he surveyed his brother's charred remains – an expression of keen critical interest.

Boon felt distaste at the mere sight of these bones that were still so unmistakably human, but it seemed that there was even worse to come. Beside the tray stood an urn and a large pair of chopsticks.

Each of the guests went forward in turn and used these chopsticks to transfer a piece of grandfather from the tray to the urn. Boon unwisely chose a fragile splinter of bone which crumbled and kept on slipping out of the chopsticks when he attempted to pick it up. The other guests were waiting, there was no pulling back now. So he settled for a larger fragment which he could transfer from tray to urn without risk of dropping it on the floor. When he deposited the fragment in the urn and replaced the chopsticks on the table he realised that he had been holding a section of the skull. Grandfather's ashes were still warm.

From the back of the room great-uncle watched over the guests' contributions to his brother's urn with a proprietorial eye. When the last deposition had been made and the urn was sealed, a quite substantial pile of ash still lay on the tray. Great-uncle made sure that this fact did not escape Boon's attention. "Just look at that!" he said proudly. "They'd never be able to get all that in. Biggish bones, eh? My brother always was a strong-limbed sort of fellow –"

At this moment they noticed a crematorium official standing behind them with another tray, apparently waiting for the next ceremony to begin. On this tray there were three meagre heaps of white powder. Great-uncle looked at it in astonishment, glanced back over his shoulder at his brother's tray, involuntarily making a comparison, and said to the official:

"What's happened here then? Isn't there something missing?"

"Oh no sir," replied the man respectfully, "it's just as it should be. There's nothing missing. You see, this was a child here, just a baby, only a month old."

"Ah."

Great-uncle turned away. The ceremony was over. The other guests were already pressing forward to the door and had not noticed this little episode.

Boon took his leave of the funeral party outside the gates of the crematorium and walked back into town. There was no point in returning to the Sugamas' home; he had no luggage and would make his own way to the station to catch the train to Tokyo at six o'clock.

At the Spring of Seven Waters he stopped off for half an hour to say goodbye to Mariko. She sat in her dressing gown drinking tea

253

while he told her about grandfather's funeral. He left his address on the kitchen table and she kissed him at the door.

When he left her apartment and turned into the main street he could still see the mountains clearly in the distance, but on the way to the station it began to snow and by the time he arrived there it was already dark.

Glossary

aimai	the opposite of plain speaking; ambiguous, indefinite wording
akachochin	a red-light bar; a low bar
akirame	'cutting off thoughts and feelings'; (surrendering to) resignation
amae	from the verb *amaeru*, to become familiar and fawn upon, expect to be indulged
basho-gara	the circumstances of a place; what is appropriate to the circumstances
bonsai	the cultivation of pot plants; specifically, the raising of dwarf trees in order to show off their natural elegance
bun	written with a character denoting part or division, the word means the position occupied within a whole; a person's status, social standing; that which should naturally be so, that which should be done as a matter of course
chochin	a lantern, usually collapsible, made of paper
chonan	the older (oldest) son
fusoku-shugi	aesthetic of incompleteness: perception of beauty in what has been withheld rather than in what is shown
fusuma	a (sliding) screen
futon	a bed-quilt; an eiderdown
geta	raised wooden sandals with a thong for the toes
gomen	a contraction of *gomen nasai*, "I'm sorry", or "I beg your pardon"
hai	yes
hanami	cherry blossom viewing

ittaikan	the feeling of being one body, of belonging to one kind
juku	a private school, a crammer
kakizome	the first Writing in the New Year; in earlier days congratulatory verses written on the second day of the year, the writer seated facing in an auspicious direction
kanban-musume	literally, a "shop-sign girl"; a girl standing outside business premises (formerly in place of a shop sign), whose job it is to lure customers inside
kotatsu	a latticed wooden frame, standing about thirty-five centimetres from the ground, formerly over a brazier, nowadays over an electric bulb, covered with a quilt and a loose table top, at which one can sit to warm the lower half of the body; in summer the electric flex and the quilt are removed, leaving a *kotatsu* which can be used as an ordinary table
koto	a thirteen-stringed instrument, made of paulownia wood, with a staccato sound somewhat reminiscent of a harpsichord
kyakuma	the drawing-room, parlour, where guests are entertained
mama	the owner or manageress of a water trade establishment
mibun	social rank, standing
misoshiru	bean-paste soup
mizushobai	water trade, the vulgar term for any precarious form of trade yielding an income entirely dependent on the patronage of its customers; for example entertainment provided by geisha, bars, cabarets and so on
nagashi	literally "flowing"; in the context of the water trade a person who moves from one place to another in order to entertain customers, typically with a song
nengajo	new year cards

noren	a cloth hung from the eaves as a sunshade; since the Edo period (early seventeenth to middle nineteenth century) typically a trade sign in front of a shopkeeper's house, bearing his name or trade name
o-	a prefix used in polite speech as an indicator of respect for the thing or person in question
o-kaa-san	*kaa* means mother, and is usually sandwiched between a respectful prefix and suffix
o-kyaku-san	*kyaku* means guest, and is likewise usually sandwiched between a respectful prefix and suffix
o-miyage	a souvenir; literally "local manufacture"; commonly used with the prefix
onbu	carrying on the back; depending on people; in particular, causing strangers to bear one's expenses
onnagata	an actor playing a woman's role in the theatre
oritatamu	to fold up (cf. *tatami*)
-san	a suffix used in polite speech as an indicator of respect for the person to whom it is attached
senpai	one's elder/senior, typically at school and one's place of work
sensei	a teacher; also very common as a generic title for almost any person of authority, either genuinely so, or as a form of obsequiousness
seppuku	suicide by disembowelment
shakuhachi	an oriental wind instrument, played like a recorder, conventionally made of bamboo
shamisen (*samisen*)	a three-stringed instrument with the shape and sound of a banjo; the fingerboard is made of oak or rosewood; the body is square, made of ironwood, and the sides of the body are slightly convex; the surface and underside of the body are spanned with cat or dog skin
shitamachi	loosely translated in this book as "downtown"; in the case of Tokyo, *shitamachi* is the geographically low lying, less affluent part of the city inhabited for the most part by tradespeople

shoji	a sliding screen, consisting of a latticed wooden structure covered on one side with paper
shunga	a genre of painting depicting intimate scenes from domestic life, notably sexual activities
sumo	Japanese wrestling (described in more detail on pp. 93–4)
tabi	white or (less frequently) dark blue socks, worn with sandals as part of traditional Japanese dress
tadaima	now; at present; typical as an exclamation, by way of greeting, when returning home
tanin	a person not related by blood; everyone outside oneself; persons unconcerned with the matter in hand; stranger, outsider
tatami	a floor covering; a plaited rush cover on top of a straw pallet reinforced with yarn, which is sunk into the floor
tekito	suitable, appropriate
tsumami(-*mono*)	an appetizer, either at the start of a meal or served as a snack with one's drinks
uchi	usually (and in the context of this book) the word *uchi* means one's own house, a house generally, or the surroundings to which one belongs, but it has many other unusual and interesting connotations: the imperial palace; in Buddhism, that which belongs to the Buddhist sphere of influence, as distinct from Confucianism and other doctrines which belong "outside"; that aspect of things which is not public; oneself; I, we; one's wife (or husband)
ukiyo	translated literally in this book as "floating world"; *ukiyo* derives from a combination of a Buddhist view of life, encapsulated in characters meaning "mournful world", and the Chinese word *fusei*, written with characters denoting "evanescent, floating world"; its meaning comprises both elements
ukiyoe	an art genre, depicting customs and contemporary manners, which emerged in Japan in the

second half of the seventeenth century; the term includes both paintings and woodcuts, but it was in the latter medium that the characteristic grace of the *ukiyoe* was most notably developed

wabi   oppressed thoughts and feelings; the enjoyment of peace and quiet; tranquillity of sentiment, appearance, atmosphere, as evident in the tea ceremony, for example, or in the writing of poetry

wafuku   western-style clothes

yakitori-ya   a restaurant or street stand specialising in grilled chicken and meat on spits

yukata   an unlined, broad-sleeved cotton gown, worn after taking a bath or during the summer months